Philosophy of Language

Fundamentals of Philosophy

Series editor: John Shand

This series presents an up-to-date set of engrossing, accurate, and lively introductions to all the core areas of philosophy. Each volume is written by an enthusiastic and knowledgeable teacher of the area in question. Care has been taken to produce works that while evenhanded are not mere bland expositions, and as such are original pieces of philosophy in their own right. The reader should not only be well informed by the series but also experience the intellectual excitement of being engaged in philosophical debate itself. The volumes serve as an essential basis for the undergraduate courses to which they relate, as well as being accessible and absorbing for the general reader. Together they comprise an indispensable library of living philosophy.

Published:

Piers Benn
Ethics

Colin Lyas
Aesthetics

Alexander Miller
Philosophy of Language

Forthcoming:

Alexander Bird
Philosophy of Science

Stephen Burwood, Paul Gilbert, Kathleen Lennon
Philosophy of Mind

Richard Francks
Modern Philosophy

Dudley Knowles
Political Philosophy

Harry Lesser
Ancient Philosophy

Philosophy of Language

Alexander Miller

McGill-Queen's University Press
Montreal & Kingston • London • Buffalo

© Alexander Miller 1998

ISBN 0-7735-1708-1 (bound)
ISBN 0-7735-1709-X (pbk.)

Legal deposit first quarter 1998
Bibliothèque nationale du Québec

Published simultaneously in the European Union by UCL Press
The name of University College London (UCL) is a registered
trade mark used by UCL Press with the consent of the owner.

Canadian Cataloguing in Publication Data

Miller, Alexander, 1965–
    Philosophy of language
(Fundamentals of philosophy)
Includes bibliographical references.
ISBN 0-7735-1708-1 (bound)
ISBN 0-7735-1709-X (pbk.)
    1. Language and languages—Philosophy. I. Title.
II. Series
P106.M54 1998   121'.68   C97-900743-7

OCLC #
37371287

Typeset in Century Schoolbook and Futura.
Printed and bound in Great Britain by Arrowhead Books
Limited, Reading.

For Fisun

Contents

Preface

To the student, philosophy of language can seem a bewilderingly diverse and complex subject. This is not an illusion, since philosophy of language deals with some of the most profound and difficult topics in any area of philosophy. But beneath the diversity and complexity, there is some unity. In this book I have concentrated on exhibiting this unity, in the hope that it might make some of the more profound and difficult questions a little more approachable for the student. I have adopted an approach that is broadly thematic, but also (up to a point) historical. If there are two main themes in twentieth-century philosophy of language, they could perhaps be termed *systematicity* and *scepticism*. Ordinarily, we would say that speakers of a language *understand* the expressions of that language, or *know* their *meanings*. Philosophers have been motivated by a desire to say something systematic about these notions of linguistic understanding, meaning and knowledge. One way in which this can be done is to give some *informal theory of meaning*: this is a theory that attempts to analyze and elucidate our ordinary, pre-theoretic notion of meaning. In Chapters 1 and 2 we begin with Frege's informal theory of meaning and his analysis of the intuitive notion of meaning in terms of the notions of sense, semantic value, reference, force and tone. Another way in which philosophers attempt to say something systematic about the notion of meaning is via the construction of *formal theories of meaning*. A formal theory of meaning is, roughly, a theory which generates, for each sentence of the language under consideration, a theorem that in some sense or other states the meaning of that sentence. Philosophers have attempted to get clear on the notion of meaning by asking about the nature of such a formal theory. Again, the starting point here is Frege, and in Chapters 1 and 2 we look briefly at a simple example of a Fregean formal theory of meaning. The main notion discussed in the book is that of *sense*. After an extensive discussion of Frege's notion of sense in Chapter 2, we move on in Chapter 3 to look at the logical positivists' views on sense: what constraints are there on the possession of sense? We'll look at the logical positivists' answer to this question, and show how it impacts on issues in *metaphysics*. In Chapters 4 and 5 we look at the second main theme in twentieth-century philosophy of language, that of *scepticism about sense*. Are there facts about meaning, and, if there are, how do we know them? We'll look at arguments from Quine and Kripke's Wittgenstein that attempt to argue that there are no facts about meaning, that the notion of meaning, as Kripke puts it, "vanishes into thin air". These attacks on the notion of meaning have been enormously influential, and much of contemporary philosophy of language can be viewed as an attempt to rehabilitate the notion of meaning in the face of these attacks. We look at some of these attempts to rehabilitate the notion of meaning in Chapter 6, and, *inter alia*, show that there are important and close connections between issues in the philosophy of language and issues in the *philosophy of mind*. The question of the relationship between mind and language is discussed further in Chapter 7, when we give a brief, critical account of Grice's attempt to analyze the notion of linguistic meaning in terms of the notion of intention. In Chapter 8, we return to the systematicity theme and look at Donald Davidson's views on the construction of formal theories of meaning for natural languages. We finish in Chapter 9 by returning to a theme which loomed large in Chapter 3, the relevance of questions about meaning to issues in metaphysics. I try to provide a rough map of the current debate between realism and antirealism, displaying the relevance to this debate of the issues discussed in the previous chapters.

Obviously, in a book of this length, many important topics in the philosophy of language have had to be ignored, and the discussion of chosen topics has sometimes had to be drawn to a premature close. I hope, though, that although the map provided in this book is incomplete, it is detailed enough to allow the student under-taking further study to work out where these other topics should be located, and to continue the discussion from where I have left off. Guides to further reading are provided at the end of each chapter. Likewise, it is my hope that teachers of the philosophy of language will be able to use this book in their courses, filling out the map as they go along according to their own interests in the philosophy of language.

The book has been written to be accessible to second- or third-year undergraduate students, or to anyone with a basic knowledge of the language of elementary logic, such as that taught in first-year university courses. Some knowledge of elementary general philosophy, such as that taught in first-year courses on metaphysics and epistemology, would be useful, though, I hope, not essential. Some parts of the book are more demanding than others. For readers entirely new to the philosophy of language, sections 3.3, 5.3–5.5, 6.3–6.7 and 8.5 could be left out on a first reading and returned to later. Postgraduates and more advanced under-graduates should note, though, that in many ways sections 6.3–6.7 constitute the heart of the book. It is my hope that these sections, and indeed the rest of the book, may also be of use to professional philosophers with an interest in the philosophy of language.

ALEXANDER MILLER
Birmingham March 1997

Acknowledgements

In writing this book, I have had the benefit of many comments on the preliminary draft from a number of colleagues and friends: these have resulted in many improvements and have saved me from many errors. For this, I would like to thank Michael Clark, Nick Dent, John Divers, Jim Edwards, Brian Garrett, Chris Hookway, Ian Law, Greg McCulloch, Duncan McFarland, Elizabeth Mortimore, Stephen Mumford, Philip Pettit, Jim Stuart, Mark Walker, Alan Weir and Stefan Wilson. Thanks also to the students in my honours philosophy of language classes of 1994–97 in Nottingham and Birmingham, who acted as guinea pigs for preliminary versions of much of the material. I would also like to thank my series editor, John Shand, for useful comments on the typescript and for encouragement and advice throughout. Thanks also to Mina Gera-Price at UCL for editorial assistance with the preparation of the final version. Most of all, I am grateful to Fisun Güner for her help, encouragement and tolerance of my bad temper during the completion of the book.

Notes on usage

Use and mention

When referring to linguistic expressions, I use *quotation marks.*
This also signifies that the quoted expression is being *mentioned*
rather than *used.* Thus

"Neil Armstrong" has thirteen letters

is an example of a case in which the expression is mentioned, and
in which the first expression in the sentence stands for a linguistic
expression, while

Neil Armstrong was the first man to step foot on the moon

is an example of a case in which the expression is *used,* and in
which the first expression in the sentence stands for a particular
man.

Types and tokens

In the course of the book, I sometimes make use of what is known
as the *type-token distinction.* Very roughly, this marks a distinction
between sorts (i.e. types) of things, and instances (i.e. tokens) of
sorts of things. Thus in

blue
red
Michael
blue

we have four word *tokens*, but three word *types*. "blue" and "blue" are *tokens of the same type*. Likewise, if Smith believes that Edinburgh is the capital city of Scotland and Jones believes that Edinburgh is the capital city of Scotland, we can say that Smith and Jones both token a belief of the same type.

Chapter 1

Frege: semantic value and reference[1]

We noted in the preface that contemporary philosophy of language is motivated in large part by a desire to say something *systematic* about our intuitive notion of meaning, and we distinguished two main ways in which such a systematic account can be given. The most influential figure in the history of the project of systematizing the notion of meaning (in both of these ways) is Gottlob Frege (1848–1925), a German philosopher, mathematician and logician, who spent his entire career as a professor of mathematics at the University of Jena. In addition to inventing the symbolic language of modern logic,[2] Frege introduced some distinctions and ideas that are absolutely crucial for an understanding of the philosophy of language, and the main task of this chapter and the next is to introduce these distinctions and ideas and to show how they can be used in a systematic account of meaning.

1

1.1 Frege's logical language

Frege's work in the philosophy of language builds on what is usually regarded as his greatest achievement, the invention of the language of modern symbolic logic. This is the logical language that is now standardly taught in first-year introductory courses on the subject. As noted in the preface, a basic knowledge of this logical language will be presupposed throughout this book, but we'll very quickly run over some of this familiar ground in this section.

The reader will recall that logic is the study of *argument*. A *valid argument* is one in which the premises, if true, guarantee the truth of the conclusion: that is, in which it is impossible for all of the premises to be true and yet for the conclusion to be false. An *invalid argument* is one in which the truth of the premises does not guarantee the truth of the conclusion: that is, in which there are at least some possible circumstances in which all of the premises are true and the conclusion is false.[3] One of the tasks of logic is to provide us with rigorous methods of determining whether a given argument is valid or invalid. In order to apply the logical methods, we have first to translate the arguments, as they appear in natural language, into a formal logical notation. Consider the following (intuitively valid) argument:

(1) If Jones has taken the medicine then he will get better;
(2) Jones has taken the medicine; therefore,
(3) He will get better.

This can be translated into Frege's logical notation by letting the capital letters "P" and "Q" abbreviate the whole sentences or propositions out of which the argument is composed, as follows:

P: Jones has taken the medicine
Q: Jones will get better.

As will be familiar, the conditional "If ...then ..." gets symbolized by the arrow "$... \rightarrow ...$". The argument is thus translated into logical symbolism as

$P \rightarrow Q$, P; therefore, Q.

The conditional "$\rightarrow$" is known as a *sentential connective*, since it allows us to form a complex sentence ($P \rightarrow Q$) by connecting two simpler sentences (P, Q). Other sentential connectives are "and", symbolized by "&"; "or", symbolized by "v"; "it is not the case that", symbolized by "–"; "if and only if", symbolized by "$\leftrightarrow$". The capital letters "P", "Q", etc. are known as *propositional variables*, since they are abbreviations for sentences expressing whole propositions. For instance, in the example above, "P" is an abbreviation for the sentence expressing the proposition that Jones has taken the medicine, and so on. Given this vocabulary, we can translate many natural language arguments into logical notation. Consider:

(4) If Rangers won and Celtic lost, then Fergus is unhappy;
(5) Fergus is not unhappy; therefore
(6) Either Rangers didn't win or Celtic didn't lose.

We assign propositional variables to the component sentences as follows:

P: Rangers won
Q: Celtic lost
R: Fergus is unhappy.

The argument then translates as

(P & Q) $\rightarrow R$; $-R$; therefore $-P$ v $-Q$.

Now that we have translated the argument into logical notation, we can go on to apply one of the logical methods for checking validity (e.g. the truth-table method) to determine whether the argument is valid or not (in fact this argument is valid, as readers should check for themselves).

The logical vocabulary described above belongs to *propositional logic*. The reason for this tab is obvious: the basic building blocks of the arguments are sentences expressing whole propositions, abbreviated by the propositional variables "P", "Q", "R", etc. However, there are many arguments in natural language that are intuitively valid but whose validity is not captured by translation into the language of propositional logic. For example:

(7) Socrates is a man;
(8) All men are mortal; therefore
(9) Socrates is mortal.

Since (7), (8) and (9) are different sentences expressing different propositions, this would translate into propositional logic as

P; Q; therefore, R.

The problem with this is that whereas the validity of the argument clearly depends on the *internal structure* of the constituent sentences, the formalization into propositional logic simply ignores this structure. For example, the proper name "Socrates" appears both in (7) and (9), and this is intuitively important for the validity of the argument, but is ignored by the propositional logic formalization, which simply abbreviates (7) and (9) by, respectively, "P" and "R". In order to deal with this, Frege showed us how to extend our logical notation in such a way that the internal structure of sentences can also be exhibited. We take capital letters from the middle of the alphabet "F", "G", "H", and so on as abbreviations for *predicate expressions*; and we take small case letters "m", "n", and so on as abbreviations for *proper names*. Thus, in the above example we can use the following translation scheme:

m: Socrates
F: ... is a man
G: ... is mortal.

(7) and (9) are then formalized as Fm and Gm respectively. But what about (8)? We can work towards formalizing this in a number of stages. First of all, we can rephrase it as

For any object: if it is a man, then it is mortal.

Using the translation scheme above we can rewrite this as

4

For any object: if it is F, then it is G.

Now, instead of speaking directly of objects, we can represent them by using *variables* "x", "y", and so on (in the same way that we use variables to stand for numbers in algebra). We can then rephrase (8) further as

For any x: if x is F, then x is G

and then as

For any x: $Fx \rightarrow Gx$.

The expression "For any x" (or "For all x") is called the *universal quantifier*, and it is represented symbolically as $(\forall x)$. The entire argument can now be formalized as

Fm; $(\forall x)(Fx \rightarrow Gx)$; therefore, Gm.

The type of logic which thus allows us to display the internal structure of sentences is called *predicate logic*, for obvious reasons (in the simplest case, it represents subject-predicate sentences *as* subject-predicate sentences). Note that predicate logic is not separate from propositional logic, but is rather an extension of it: predicate logic consists of the vocabulary of propositional logic *plus* the additional vocabulary of proper names, predicates and quantifiers. Note also that in addition to the universal quantifier there is another type of quantifier. Consider the argument:

(10) There is something which is both red and square; therefore
(11) There is something which is red.

Again, the validity of this intuitively depends on the internal structure of the constituent sentences. We can use the following translation scheme:

F: ... is red
G: ... is square.

We'll deal with (10) first. Following the method we used when dealing with (8) we can first rephrase (10) as

There is some x such that: it is F and G.

Or,

There is some x such that: Fx & Gx.

The expression "There is some x such that" is known as the *existential quantifier* and is symbolized as $(\exists x)$. (10) can thus be formalized as $(\exists x)(Fx$ & $Gx)$, and, similarly, (11) is formalized as $(\exists x)Fx$. The whole argument is therefore translated into logical symbolism as

$(\exists x)(Fx$ & $Gx)$; therefore $(\exists x)Fx$.

That, then, is a brief recap on the language of modern symbolic logic, which in its essentials was invented by Frege. The introduction of this new notation, especially of the universal and existential quantifiers, constituted a huge advance on the syllogistic logic that had dominated philosophy since the time of Aristotle. It allowed logicians to formalize and prove intuitively valid arguments whose form and validity could not be captured in the traditional Aristotelian logic. An example of such an argument is

(12) All horses are animals; therefore,
(13) All horses' heads are animals' heads.

It is left as an exercise for the reader to formalize this argument in Frege's logical language.[4]

1.2 Syntax

A *syntax* or *grammar* for a language consists, roughly, of two things: a specification of the vocabulary of the language, and a set of rules that determine which sequences of expressions constructed from that vocabulary are grammatical and which are ungrammatical (or alternatively, which sequences are syntactically well-formed and which are syntactically ill-formed). For example, in the case of the language of propositional logic, we can specify the vocabulary as follows:

Sentential connectives: expressions having the same shape as "→" or "–" or "&" or "v" or "↔".
Propositional variables: expressions having the same shape as "P", "Q", "R", and so on.

It is important to note that when working at the level of syntax that the only properties of expressions mentioned in the specifications of the vocabulary are *formal properties*, such as shape. This is clearly the case in the specification of the vocabulary of propositional logic just given: in principle, even someone who had no knowledge whatsoever of what the various bits of vocabulary mean could separate expressions into those that belong to the vocabulary and those that do not. In this sense, syntax is prior to semantics, the study of meaning. This is true also of the syntactical rules: these determine, in terms of purely formal properties of the expressions concerned, whether a given sequence of expressions drawn from the vocabulary counts as grammatical or not. For example, the syntactical rules for propositional logic can be stated very simply as follows:

(a) Any propositional variable is grammatical.
(b) Any grammatical expression preceded by "–" is grammatical.
(c) Any grammatical expression followed by "→" followed by any grammatical expression is grammatical.
(d) Any grammatical expression followed by "&" followed by any grammatical expression is grammatical.
(e) Any grammatical expression followed by "v" followed by any grammatical expression is grammatical.
(f) Any grammatical expression followed by "↔" followed by any grammatical expression is grammatical.
(g) Any sequence of expressions which does not count as grammatical in virtue of (a)–(f) is not grammatical.[5]

Again, someone with no knowledge of what the expressions concerned mean (e.g. that "&" means *and*, that "v" means *or*, and so on) could use these rules to determine whether an arbitrary sequence of marks counts as a grammatical expression of the language of propositional logic. To see this, consider how we could use the rules to show, for example, that "(P & Q) v R" is grammatical. First of all, on the basis of shape properties, we would identify P, Q and R as propositional variables, and that "&" and "v" count as sentential connectives. On the basis of rule (a), we would then identify "P", "Q" and "R" as grammatical. Then, on the basis of (d), we would identify "(P & Q)" as grammatical (in terms of purely formal properties, such as the shape and ordering of the constituent expressions). Finally, on the basis of (e) we would identify "(P & Q) v R" as grammatical (again, in terms of purely formal properties).

We can do the same thing for the language of predicate logic. We can specify the vocabulary of predicate logic – proper names, predicate expressions, variables, and quantifiers – in purely formal terms, and then give formal rules which determine which sequences of marks count as grammatical. The details of this needn't concern us here. What is important for present purposes is simply to note that Frege discerns the following *syntactical categories* in his logical language: proper names, predicates, declarative sentences, sentential connectives and quantifiers.

1.3 Semantics and truth

In dealing with the syntax of a language, we are dealing only with the purely formal properties of its constituent expressions. But, of course, in addition to those formal properties, the expressions can also possess *semantic* properties: they *mean* this, or *refer* to that, and so on. In semantics we move from considering the purely formal properties of linguistic expressions to considering issues concerning their meaning and significance.

Let's start by thinking a little more about arguments in propositional logic, and how we determine their validity. Consider another very simple argument:

(14) Beethoven was German and Napoleon was French; therefore
(15) Beethoven was German.

This formalizes as *P* & *Q*; therefore, *P*. Now, how do we determine whether this argument is valid or not? Recall that an argument is said to be valid if there are no possible circumstances in which all of its premises are true and its conclusion is false. One way to determine whether an argument is valid, then, is simply to enumerate the various possible distributions of truth and falsity over the premises and conclusion, and check whether there are any such that the premises all come out true and the conclusion comes out false. If there are, the argument is invalid; if there are not, the argument is valid. This, of course, is just the familiar *truth-table* method of determining validity. The truth-table for the argument above is as follows:

P	*Q*	*P* & *Q*	*P*
T	T	T	T
T	F	F	T
F	T	F	F
F	F	F	F

There are four possible distributions to the constituent sentences *P* and *Q*, and these are enumerated on the four lines on the left-hand side of the table, with T representing "true" and F representing "false". Given this, we can work out the possible distributions of truth and falsity to the premise and conclusion: this is done in the third and fourth columns. We see that there is only one circumstance in which the premise is true – when both *P* and *Q* are assigned the value true – and that in this case, the conclusion is also true. So there are no possible cases in which the premise is true and in which the conclusion is false. So the argument is valid.

What does the question about the validity of an argument have to do with semantics? Intuitively, the validity of an argument is going to depend on the meanings of the expressions which appear in it. That is to say, the validity of an argument is going to depend on the semantic properties of the expressions out of which it is constructed. In the argument above the basic expressions out of which the argument is constructed are sentences. What properties of the sentences are relevant to determining the validity of the inference? In the first instance, it seems as if it is the properties of *truth* and *falsity*. After all, the truth-table method works by determining the possible distributions of these very properties. So, truth and falsity look like good candidates for the semantic properties in question. Given assignments of truth and falsity to *P* and *Q*, we can work out the various assignments of truth and falsity to the premises and conclusion, and this allows us to say whether or not the argument is valid. So, validity is determined by the possible distributions of truth and falsity to the premises and conclusion, and this in turn is determined by the possible distributions of truth and falsity to the constituent sentences. Let's define the notion of *semantic value* as follows:

DEFINITION. *The semantic value of any expression is that feature of it that determines whether sentences in which it occurs are true or false.*

In the case we have just looked at, the constituent expressions of the argument are the sentences *P*, *Q*. Which features of *P*, *Q* are relevant to determining whether the sentences in which they occur are true or false? Well, their truth or falsity: as shown in the truth-table, the distributions of T and F to *P* and *Q* determine the truth or falsity of the complex sentence *P* & *Q* which forms the premise of the argument. Given the definition above, then, it follows that the semantic value of a sentence is its truth-value.

We have here the beginnings of a semantic theory: an assignment of a semantic property (truth or falsity) to the sentences of a language, which determines the validity of the inferences in which those sentences appear as constituents. In the next section, we develop this theory further.

1.4 Frege on semantic value: sentences and proper names

Frege's name for the semantic value of an expression, as defined in the previous section, was *Bedeutung*.[6] According to Frege, then, the semantic value of a sentence is one of the truth-values, true or false. Note that in the case above, the semantic value of the complex expression *P & Q* (its truth-value) is determined by the truth-values of the constituent sentences *P, Q*. In general, the semantic value of a complex expression is determined by the semantic values of its parts and the way they are put together. This is known as the *principle of compositionality*. Thus far, then, we can discern two theses in Frege's semantic theory:[7]

Be deutung

THESIS 1. *The semantic value of a sentence is its truth-value (true or false).*

THESIS 2. *The semantic value of a complex expression is determined by the semantic values of its parts.*   *compositionality*

From this, we can derive a third thesis. Since the semantic value of a complex expression is determined by the semantic values of its parts, substituting one part with another which has the same semantic value will leave the semantic value (truth-value) of the whole sentence unchanged.

THESIS 3. *Substitution of a constituent of a sentence with another that has the same semantic value will leave the semantic value (i.e. truth-value) of the sentence unchanged.*

So far, though, we have only considered expressions from one of the syntactic categories introduced in section 1.2, declarative sentences. Frege extends this semantic theory to cover expressions from the other syntactic categories: proper names, sentential connectives, predicates and quantifiers. The idea is to assign a type of semantic value to each type of expression: as in the case of declarative sentences, this will be the property of the type of expression that determines the contribution of instances of that type to the truth or falsity of the sentences in which they appear.

Let's begin with the case of proper names. Consider the sentence "Cicero is Roman". What feature of the proper name "Cicero" is relevant to determining whether this sentence is true or false? Intuitively, the fact that it stands for the individual *object* that is the man Cicero: if the proper name stood for some other individual (e.g. Plato) the sentence in question might have a different truth-value from the one it actually has. So, just as the semantic

11

value of a declarative sentence is a truth-value, the semantic value of a proper name is an object. This allows us to state the fourth thesis of Frege's semantic theory:

THESIS 4. *The semantic value of a proper name is the object that it refers to or stands for.*[8]

This might seem a little odd. Isn't it just a platitude that proper names refer to objects? And if it is a platitude, how can it be a thesis of a substantial semantic theory? The important thing to appreciate here is that Frege is using the notion of "semantic value" in a technical way: the notion of semantic value has its content fixed by the definition above. Given the definition, it can emerge as a *discovery* that the semantic value of a proper name is the object which it refers to. That this corresponds with our intuitive use of "reference" as applied to proper names is all to the good. However, this led Frege to some strange and unnecessary views. Just as Cicero is an object, and is the reference of the proper name "Cicero", Frege construed the semantic values of sentences, the truth-values true and false, as objects also, and this led him to construe sentences as a kind of *proper name* for these objects, which he called the True and the False: "Every assertoric sentence concerned with what its words refer to is therefore to be regarded as a proper name, and its [semantic value], if it has one, is either the True or the False."[9]

Now this seems bizarre: isn't this simply a case of an analogy being stretched past the point where it has any sensible application? Frege himself realized that his characterization of truth-values as objects is apt to evoke this sort of reaction, saying that "The designation of the truth-values as objects may appear to be an arbitrary fancy or perhaps a mere play on words." In what follows, we'll simply ignore this strange doctrine. The thing to bear in mind is that the notion of semantic value is a technical term whose content is given by our definition: sentences can be assigned semantic values in this technical sense, and so can proper names, but the fact that the semantic values of the latter are objects needn't force us into accepting that the semantic values of the former are also objects of a special and mysterious kind.

Theses 1 and 4 specify the semantic values of declarative

sentences and proper names, that is, the semantic properties of those expressions in virtue of which sentences containing them are determined as true or false, and, in turn, in terms of which arguments containing those sentences as constituents are determined as valid or invalid. But what about the expressions in the other syntactic categories discerned by Frege: connectives, predicates and quantifiers? Before answering this question, we need to prepare by considering what Frege says about mathematical functions.

1.5 Function and object

The semantics that Frege provides for the connectives, predicates and quantifiers stems from an analogy with *mathematical functions*. The idea of a functional expression will be familiar to anyone who has studied elementary mathematics. Take the functional expression "$y = 2x$". Here y is said to be a function of x: we get different values for y as we insert different numerals for x. The numbers that the variable x stands for are called the *arguments* of the function (this must not be confused with the notion of argument used in logic, as in "valid argument"). Thus, for the argument 1, we get the value 2, for the argument 2, we get the value 4, for the argument 3, we get the value 6, and so on. We can thus represent the function as a set of ordered pairs, in each of which the first member corresponds to the argument of the function and the second member corresponds to the value which the function delivers for that argument. Thus, the function $y = 2x$ can be represented as {(0, 0), (1, 2), (2, 4), (3, 6),...}.[10] Call this the *extension* of the function. Now "$y = 2x$" stands for a *function of one argument*: there is only one variable, so only one numeral can be "slotted in" to deliver a value for the function. There can also be *functions of two arguments*. For example, "$z = 2x + 5y$" stands for such a function. Here we need to slot in two numerals in order to obtain a value for the function: for example, the value of the function for $x = 1$ and $y = 1$ is 7, and for $x = 1$ and $y = 2$ its value is 12. We can represent a function of two arguments as a set of ordered triples, with the first member of the triple representing the arguments for x, the second member the arguments for y, and the third member the value delivered by the function for those arguments. Thus, the function just given has the extension $\{(0, 0, 0), (1, 0, 2), (0, 1, 5), (1, 1, 7), (1, 2, 12),...\}$.

Now, consider the process by means of which we determine the values of the function which "$y = 2x$" stands for. We slot in the arguments and calculate the values as follows: 2.0 ($= 0$), 2.1 ($= 2$), 2.2 ($= 4$), 2.3 ($= 6$), and so on. This talk of "slotting in" arguments suggests that the expression which stands for a function must have a "gap" into which expressions standing for the arguments can be slotted: so we might represent the functional expression in this case as "$y = 2(\ )$", where the brackets show that there is an empty space in the functional expression that must be filled by an expression of the appropriate sort in order for a value to be computed. In fact, representing the function as "$y = 2x$" does this just as well, since the variable "x" does not stand for a specific number, but only serves to indicate the place where a numeral may be inserted to obtain a value. Frege represents this feature of functions by saying that they are *incomplete* or *unsaturated*: "I am concerned to show that the argument does not belong with a function, but goes together with the function to make up a complete whole; for a function by itself must be called incomplete, in need of supplementation, or 'unsaturated'."[11] This contrasts with the case of proper names (including numerals, which are the proper names of numbers) and sentences, which have no such gap: in contrast to functional expressions, the objects they stand for are complete or saturated.

In the case of the functions above we have functions from numbers to numbers: both functions take numbers as arguments and yield a number as value. The insight of Frege's that led to his semantics for predicates, connectives and quantifiers was the realization that there can be functions which take things *other* than numbers as arguments and values.[12]

1.6 Frege on semantic value: predicates, connectives and quantifiers

Consider the predicate expression "... is even". Like the functional expressions discussed in the previous section, this has a gap into which a numeral can be slotted. What is the result of slotting a given numeral into the gap? It will be a *true* sentence if the number denoted by the numeral is even; it will be a *false* sentence otherwise. Thus, we can view the predicate "... is even" as standing for a function from numbers to truth-values. But there are also functions that take objects other than numbers as their arguments. Consider "... is round". This has a gap into which a proper name may be slotted, and the value delivered will be true if the object denoted by that proper name is round, false otherwise. Thus " ... is round" can be viewed as standing for a function from objects to truth-values. *In general, a predicate expression will stand for a function from objects to truth-values. Frege reserves the term "concept" for a function whose value is always a truth-value.*

This allows us to state the fifth thesis of Frege's semantic theory:

THESIS 5. *The semantic value of a predicate is a function.*

By analogy with the examples in the previous section, the extension of the function denoted by "... is even" is the set of ordered-pairs {(1, false), (2, true), (3, false), (4, true), ...}.

Intuitively, it is the extension of a predicate which determines the truth-value of sentences in which it appears. Take a subject-predicate sentence like "4 is even". That this is true is determined in sum by two things: first, that the numeral "4" stands for the number 4, and secondly, that the number 4 is paired with the value true in the extension of the function denoted by "... is even". Also, thesis 3 states that the substitution, in a complex expression, of a part with some other part having the same semantic value, leaves the semantic value (truth-value) of the whole unchanged. We can see that this condition is met if we identify the semantic value of a predicate with a function, understood in extensional terms: the substitution of a predicate having the same extension as the predicate " ... is even" will leave the truth-value of "4 is even" unchanged, since the identity in extension will ensure that the number 4 is still paired with the value true.[13] This leads us to

THESIS 6. *Functions are extensional: if function* f *and function* g *have the same extension, then* f = g.[14]

We can also include the logical connectives and the quantifiers within the scope of our semantic theory, since these too can be viewed as standing for functions. Indeed, the logical connectives introduced above are often called "truth-functions" or "truth-functional connectives". *The reason is that these can be viewed as standing for functions from truth-values to truth-values.* Take the negation operator " – ...". This can be viewed as standing for a function of one argument, which has the following extension: {(T, F), (F, T)}. For the argument true, the value false is delivered, and for the argument false, the value true is delivered. Likewise, the connective for conjunction, "... & ...", can be viewed as standing for a function of two arguments, which has the following extension: {(T, T, T), (T, F, F), (F, T, F), (F, F, F)}. As an exercise, the reader should work out the extensions of the remaining logical connectives.

Note that this allows us to respect the thesis that the semantic value of a complex expression is determined by the semantic values of its parts. Consider a complex sentence, such as "Beethoven was German and Napoleon was French". This is formalized as $P \& Q$. It is true if and only if the truth-values of P, Q are paired with T in the extension of the function denoted by "... & ...". P is T and Q is T, and (T, T, T) is included in the extension of the function. So $P \& Q$ is true.

What about the universal and existential quantifiers? Frege treats these as standing for a special sort of function: *second-level functions*. A first-level function is a function that takes objects (of whatever sort) as arguments. A second-level function is a function that takes *concepts* as arguments. Frege viewed the universal and existential quantifiers as standing for second-level functions, taking concepts as arguments and yielding truth-values as values. Let's deal with the universal quantifier first. As will be familiar, whenever we are formalizing parts of natural language by using quantifiers, we have to specify a universe of discourse: this is the group of objects our variables are taken to range over. Suppose that we select the group of humans {Quine, Boris Yeltsin, John Major, Bill Clinton} as our universe of discourse. Now consider the universally quantified sentence "Everyone is mortal". We can formalize this, taking "G" to abbreviate "... is mortal", as follows: $(\forall x)Gx$. Frege suggested that we view the quantifier as standing for a function $(\forall x)(\ )$, which takes a concept Gx as argument and yields the truth-value T if the concept G is paired with T in its extension. The concept G will be paired with T in the extension of the quantifier if every object in the universe of discourse is paired with T in the extension of G. Similarly $(\forall x)Gx$ yields the truth-value F if the concept G is paired with F in the extension of the quantifier. And the concept G is paired with F in the extension of the quantifier if at least one object in the universe of discourse is paired with the value F in the extension of G. Thus, consider "Everyone is mortal". $(\forall x)(\ )$ is a second-level function, from concepts to truth-values. If the argument is the concept Gx, then the function $(\forall x)(\ )$ yields the value T if G is paired with T in its extension. In turn, G will be paired with T in the extension of $(\forall x)(\ )$ if *every* object in the universe of discourse is paired with T in the extension of G. In the case at hand, the extension of G is {(Quine, T), (Boris Yeltsin, T), (John Major, T), (Bill Clinton, T)}. We see that every object *is* paired with T in the extension of G, so that G will be paired with T in the extension of $(\forall x)(\ )$. So, finally, "$(\forall x)Gx$" is true. Note that this shows that the semantic value (truth-value) of the sentence "$(\forall x)Gx$" is determined by the semantic values of its parts, namely, the extension of the function $(\forall x)(\ )$, and the extension of the concept G.

Likewise, consider the existentially quantified sentence "Someone is Russian", keeping the universe of discourse the same as in the example above. We can formalize this as $(\exists x)Hx$, taking "H" to abbreviate "... is Russian". We can then spell out how the semantic value of the existentially quantified sentence is determined by the semantic values of its parts as follows. $(\exists x)(\ )$ is a second-level function, from concepts to truth-values. If the argument is the concept Hx, then the function $(\exists x)(\ )$ yields the value T if H is paired with T in its extension. In turn, H will be paired with T in the extension of $(\exists x)(\ )$ if *at least one* object in the universe of discourse is paired with T in the extension of H. In the case at hand, the extension of H is {(Quine, F), (Boris Yeltsin, T), (John Major, F), (Bill Clinton, F)}. We see that at least one object is paired with T in the extension of H (Boris Yeltsin), so that H will be paired with T in the extension of $(\exists x)(\ )$. So, finally, "$(\exists x)Hx$" is true. (The reader should go through the same process to show how the truth-value of "Everyone is Russian" can be derived from the semantic values of its parts.)

It might be useful to summarize these points about predicates, connectives and quantifiers in a separate thesis:

17

THESIS 7. *The semantic value of a predicate is a first-level function from objects to truth-values; the semantic value of a sentential connective is a first-level function from truth-values to truth-values; the semantic value of a quantifier is a second-level function from concepts to truth-values.*

1.7 A semantic theory for a simple language

The above considerations provide us with one way of attaining a systematic perspective on the semantics of a given language. We identify a range of syntactic categories to which the various expressions in that language belong, and to each category we give an account of the semantic property (semantic value) in virtue of which instances of that category make an impact upon the truth of the sentences in which they appear. All this is done in such a way that the principle of compositionality is respected: the semantic values of complex expressions are determined by the semantic values of their parts.[15] Let's run through this idea in application to a very simple language. This language consists of two predicates, "*G*" and "*H*", which abbreviate "... is Greek" and "... is Scottish" respectively; four proper names, "*a*", "*b*", "*c*" and "*d*", standing for Plato, Socrates, Hume and Reid respectively. We'll suppose that the language contains just one sentential connective, negation, and, in addition, the universal quantifier and a stock of variables which range over the four objects in the quantifier's universe of discourse.

First of all, we spell out the semantic properties (semantic values) of the primitive expressions of the language in a series of *axioms*:

AXIOM 1. "a" *refers to Plato*

AXIOM 2. "b" *refers to Socrates*

AXIOM 3. "c" *refers to Hume*

AXIOM 4. "d" *refers to Reid*

AXIOM 5. *The extension of* "G" *is {(Plato, T), (Socrates, T), (Hume, F), (Reid, F)}*[16]

AXIOM 6. *The extension of* "H" *is {(Plato, F), (Socrates, F), (Hume, T), (Reid, T)}*

AXIOM 7. *The extension of "–" is {(T, F), (F, T)}*

We'll also add three *compositional axioms*:

COMPOSITIONAL AXIOM 1. *A sentence coupling a proper name with a predicate is true if and only if the object referred to by the proper name is paired with T in the extension of the predicate.*

COMPOSITIONAL AXIOM 2. *The negation of a sentence is true if and only if the truth-value of that sentence is paired with F in the extension of "–...".*

COMPOSITIONAL AXIOM 3. *A universally quantified sentence is true if and only if the predicate involved is paired with T in the extension of the quantifier; the predicate involved is paired with T in the extension of the quantifier if and only if every object in the universe of discourse is paired with T in the extension of the predicate.*

Given these compositional axioms, and the axioms 1–7, we can work out the semantic values (i.e. truth-values) of the complex *sentences* of the language. We'll look at three examples:

EXAMPLE 1. "Plato is Greek". This is translated into logical language as *Ga*.

(a) "*Ga*" is true if and only if the object referred to by the proper name "*a*" is paired with T in the extension of "*G*" (compositional axiom 1).

(b) "*a*" refers to Plato (from axiom 1).

(c) The extension of "*G*" is {(Plato, T), (Socrates, T), (Hume, F), (Reid, F)} (axiom 5).

(d) "*Ga*" is true (from (a), (b) and (c)).

EXAMPLE 2. "Everyone is Scottish". This is translated into logical language as $(\forall x)Hx$.

(a) "$(\forall x)Hx$" is true if and only if H is paired with T in the extension of the quantifier; H is paired with T in the extension of the quantifier if and only if every object in the universe of discourse is paired with T in the extension of H (from compositional axiom 3).

(b) The extension of "*H*" is {(Plato, F), (Socrates, F), (Hume, T), (Reid, T)} (axiom 6).

19

(c) Not every object in the universe of discourse is paired with T in the extension of H (e.g. Plato and Socrates are paired with F) (from (b)).

(d) H is not paired with T in the extension of $(\forall x)(\ldots x)$ (from (a)).

(e) "$(\forall x)Hx$" is false (from (a) and (d)).

EXAMPLE 3. "Not everyone is Scottish". This is translated into logical language as $-(\forall x)Hx$.

As for example 2, followed by:

(f) "$-(\forall x)Hx$" is true if and only if the truth-value of "$(\forall x)Hx$" is paired with T in the extension of "$-\ldots$" (from compositional axiom 2).

(g) The truth-value of "$(\forall x)Hx$" (F) is paired with T in the extension of "$-\ldots$" (from axiom 7).

(h) "$-(\forall x)H$" is true (from (f) and (g)).

These are examples of how we might derive, via the semantic values assigned to the primitive expressions of the language by Frege, the truth-values of the complex sentences of that language. In addition, we can also use these as examples of how the *truth-conditions* of sentences might be derived on the basis of the assignments of semantic values to their parts. The truth-condition for a sentence is not a truth-value like T, but rather the condition which must be satisfied in the world in order for the sentence to be true. What condition must be satisfied in the world in order for the sentence "Plato is Greek" to be true? Intuitively, *that Plato is Greek*. This intuition is captured by Frege's theory as follows:

(a) "Ga" is true if and only if the object referred to by the proper name "a" is paired with T in the extension of "G" (compositional axiom 1).

(b) "a" refers to Plato (from axiom 1).

(c) "Ga" is true if and only if Plato is paired with T in the extension of "G" (from (a) and (b)).

(d) Plato is paired with T in the extension of "G" if and only if Plato is Greek (from the meanings of "true" and "extension").

(e) "Ga" is true if and only if Plato is Greek (from (a) and (d)).

(f) "Plato is Greek" is true if and only if Plato is Greek (from (e) and the formalization of "Plato is Greek").

Just as we expected! (f) is called a *homophonic* statement of the truth-condition of "Plato is Greek", since the very same sentence is used on the right-hand side of the statement of the truth-condition. The notion of truth-conditions – and the idea of a semantic theory which systematically generates statements of truth-conditions for the sentences of a language on the basis of semantic properties assigned to the language's primitive expressions – will figure prominently in the rest of this book.[17]

Further reading

There are many good introductions to the modern form of symbolic logic which Frege invented. The best of these is probably E. J. Lemmon, *Beginning logic*. Other textbooks which can be recommended are W. H. Newton-Smith, *Logic*, W. Hodges, *Logic*, and R. Jeffrey, *Formal logic*. Acquaintance with at least the elementary sections of one of these textbooks is essential for following the rest of this book. For a useful discussion of the central philosophical issues surrounding logic, see S. Read, *Thinking about logic*. Further reading on Frege's notion of reference/semantic value is given in the further reading section at the end of Chapter 2.

Chapter 2

Frege and Russell: sense and definite descriptions

2.1 The introduction of sense

We have been looking at Frege's attempt to give a systematic account of meaning. We started out with the intuition that the validity of arguments depends upon the semantic properties possessed by the expressions out of which they are constructed. So, one way to find out what semantic properties a systematic treatment of meaning should employ would be to ask which properties of expressions are relevant to the validity of arguments in which they appear. We saw that a plausible answer to this question, in the case of whole sentences, was the property of truth. So we defined the semantic value of an expression as that feature of it that determines whether sentences in which it appears are true or false. This led us to identify the semantic values of proper names as their bearers, of sentences as their truth-values and of functional expressions as functions. We saw that we were able to do this in a way that respects the principle of compositionality, so that the semantic value of a complex expression is systematically determined by the semantic values of its parts. Thus far, then, we have been attempting to give a systematic account of the intuitive notion of meaning by constructing a semantic theory that trades in just *one* semantic property, semantic value (although, as noted, expressions from different syntactic categories will be assigned different sorts of semantic value). But is one semantic property a sufficiently rich basis on which to construct a philosophical account of a phenomenon as complex as that of human language? It would be odd if it were: we don't expect physics to refer to just one physical property in its explanations, or biology to refer to just one biological property in its explanations, so it would be strange if a theory of meaning could get by with just the one meaning-relevant property of semantic value. We begin this chapter by looking at Frege's reasons for thinking that we have to appeal to some other semantic property in addition to semantic value in our account of the intuitive notion of meaning: the property of having a *sense*.

2.1.1 *The problem of bearerless names*

Let's take the case of names as an example. We are trying to give a systematic account of the meanings of names, and in the theory of semantic value described in Chapter 1 we attempt to do this in terms of the assignment of the property of having a semantic value to the names, where the semantic value of a name is the object it refers to. But if having a reference were the only semantic property in terms of which we could explain the functioning of names, we would be in trouble with respect to names that simply have no bearer. Consider a sentence, such as "Odysseus was set ashore at Ithaca while sound asleep". The name "Odysseus" has no bearer, since the character is entirely fictional. Since the name has no reference, and the semantic value of a sentence is determined by the semantic values of its parts, it follows that the sentence "Odysseus was set ashore at Ithaca while sound asleep" has no semantic value either. So, if having a semantic value were the only semantic property, we would have to say that the sentence is meaningless. But we can certainly understand the sentence: it is certainly not just meaningless gibberish. So it seems that we will have to attribute some other semantic property to the name "Odysseus" in addition to its reference. We could sum this up in the slogan: *Names without a reference (semantic value) are not meaningless; so there must be some other semantic property possessed by names in addition to having a reference (semantic value).*

2.1.2 The problem of substitution into belief contexts

According to the principle of compositionality, the semantic value of a complex expression is determined by the semantic values of its parts. It followed from this that (thesis 3) substitution of a part of a sentence with another having the same semantic value will leave the truth-value of the whole sentence unchanged. This means, in particular, that substitution of one name in a sentence by another having the same reference should leave the truth-value of that sentence unchanged. But this appears to be false. Consider the following sentence, where John is a person with absolutely no knowledge about Mark Twain (except perhaps that he is the author of *Huckleberry Finn*):

(1) John believes that Mark Twain is Mark Twain.

This will be true, unless John has some very bizarre views on identity. But "Mark Twain" and "Samuel Clemens" are co-referential: they are different names for the same person. So the following, which results by substituting one of the occurrences of "Mark Twain" by "Samuel Clemens", should also be true:

(2) John believes that Mark Twain is Samuel Clemens.

But, of course, this is actually false, since John knows nothing about Mark Twain except that he is the author of *Huckleberry Finn*. This suggests that we are either going to have to give up thesis 4, that the semantic value of a name is its bearer, or thesis 3, and thereby thesis 2, the principle of compositionality. But these are both central and indispensable planks of Frege's theory of semantic value. *We shall see that Frege's attempt to solve this problem without giving up either of theses 2, 3 or 4, requires the introduction of another semantic property of names in addition to their having a reference or semantic value.*[1]

This point is perfectly general, and applies to expressions in the other syntactic categories as well. In fact, it is perhaps clearest when made with respect to sentences. Thesis 3 in that case amounts to: in a complex sentence, the substitution of a component sentence by another sentence having the same truth-value should not change the truth-value of the complex sentence. But belief contexts threaten this principle as well. Consider the following sentence, where John is a person with a working knowledge of British geography, but absolutely no knowledge of particle physics:

(3) John believes that London is south of Glasgow.

Here, the overall sentence is true, as is the "embedded" sentence "London is south of Glasgow". Now the sentence "Electrons are negatively charged sub-atomic particles" is also true, so substituting it for the embedded sentence in the above sentence should not result in a change of truth-value in the overall sentence. But it does result in such a change, since

(4) John believes that electrons are negatively charged particles

is false. Again this suggests that Frege will have to give up either thesis 1, that the semantic value of a sentence is its truth-value, or thesis 3, and thereby thesis 2. We shall see that Frege's attempt to solve this problem without giving up either of theses 1, 2 or 3 requires the introduction of another semantic property of sentences in addition to their having a semantic value (truth-value). Likewise, Frege's attempt to solve the analogous problem in the case of functional expressions, without giving up theses 2, 3, 5 or 6, requires the introduction of another semantic property of functional expressions in addition to their having a semantic value.[2]

2.1.3 The problem of informativeness

When someone understands an expression, we say that he knows its meaning: meaning is that semantic property of an expression that someone with an understanding of that expression grasps. Now suppose that the meaning of an expression, in this intuitive sense, was identified with its semantic value. What would follow? Consider Frege's famous example concerning the planet Venus. It took an empirical discovery in astronomy to discover that this planet was both the celestial object known as the Evening Star and also the celestial object known as the Morning Star. Consider the state of a competent language user before this empirical discovery (or of a competent language user after the discovery who is unaware of the discovery). Such a person understands the identity statement "The Morning Star is the Evening Star", even though they do not know its truth-value. Frege's point is that if meaning were identified with semantic value, this would be impossible. We can set out his reasoning here as follows:

(a) Suppose (for *reductio*) that meaning is to be identified with semantic value.

(b) Understanding a sentence requires understanding its constituents. In other words, knowing the meaning of a sentence requires knowing the meanings of its constituents. So,

(c) Understanding "The Morning Star is the Evening Star" requires knowing the meanings of, *inter alia*, "The Morning Star" and "The Evening Star". So,

(d) Understanding "The Morning Star is the Evening Star" requires knowing the semantic values (references) of "The Morning Star" and "The Evening Star". But,

(e) The semantic value (reference) of "The Morning Star" is the same as that of "The Evening Star": the planet Venus. So,

(f) Understanding "The Morning Star is the Evening Star" requires knowing that the semantic values (references) of "The Morning Star" and "The Evening Star" are the same: in other words, requires knowing that "The Morning Star is the Evening Star" is true. But,

(g) It is possible to understand "The Morning Star is the Evening Star" without knowing its truth-value. So,

(h) The meaning of an expression cannot be identified with its semantic value.[3]

So, in giving an account of meaning we are going to have to introduce some semantic property in addition to semantic value, the grasp of which constitutes understanding. Again, Frege introduces the property of having a sense to play the role of this semantic property. But what exactly is sense, and how exactly does the introduction of sense enable Frege to solve the three problems we have just outlined? We deal with these questions in the following section.

2.2 The nature of sense

One very important characteristic of sense is spelled out in the following thesis:

THESIS 8. *The sense of an expression is that ingredient of its meaning that determines its semantic value.*

In addition to having semantic values, expressions also have semantic properties that determine what those semantic values are. The property that determines semantic value is the property of having a certain sense. Thus, a name has a reference – stands for a particular object – and also has a sense, some means of determining which particular object this is. Take the case above, of the name "The Evening Star". The sense of this is some condition that an object has to satisfy in order to count as the reference of the name. Perhaps the simplest way of spelling out such a condition would be to specify some *descriptive condition,* such as "that object which appears in such and such a place in the sky at such and such times in the evening". If an object satisfies this condition, then it is the reference of "The Evening Star". It turns out, on empirical investigation, that Venus satisfies this condition, so it follows that the name "The Evening Star" refers to the planet Venus. Now, someone who knows which descriptive condition an object has to satisfy in order to count as the reference of "The Evening Star" understands the name; but it does not follow that he knows what the reference of the name actually is. I can know that whatever object it is that appears at such and such a place in the sky at such and such a time in the evening is referred to by "The Evening Star" without knowing which object that is: I may not have done any astronomy. Thus we also have the following thesis:

THESIS 9. *It is possible to know the sense of an expression without knowing its semantic value.*

It is this thesis that allows us to solve the problem of informativeness. We first of all set out the additional theses:

THESIS 10. *The sense of an expression is what someone who understands the expression grasps.*

THESIS 11. *The sense of a complex expression is determined by the senses of its constituents.*

Consider Frege's Evening Star–Morning Star example. Understanding a sentence requires understanding its constituents. Together with thesis 10, this entails that knowing the sense of a sentence requires knowing the senses of its constituents. So, understanding "The Morning Star is the Evening Star" requires grasping the senses of, *inter alia*, "The Morning Star" and "The Evening Star". But, from thesis 9, it is possible to grasp the senses of "The Morning Star" and "The Evening Star" without knowing their references. So, from theses 11 and 2 it is possible to grasp the sense of the sentence "The Evening Star is the Morning Star" without knowing its truth-value. So this explains how it is possible to understand a sentence without knowing its truth-value, which is just to explain how sentences can be so much as informative. The introduction of sense thus enables Frege to solve the problem of informativeness.

It might be useful to pause for a moment to see how this account also enables us to explain the *uninformativeness* of "The Evening Star is the Evening Star". In order to do so, we add a further thesis, the thesis of the *transparency of sense*:

THESIS 12. *If someone grasps the senses of two expressions, and the two expressions actually have the same sense, then she must know that the two expressions have the same sense.*

Suppose someone understands "The Evening Star is the Evening Star". Then, they must grasp the senses of the two occurrences of "The Evening Star". Since each occurrence has the same sense, it follows from thesis 12 that the speaker must know that they have the same sense. But sense determines semantic value (expressions with the same sense must have the same semantic value, from thesis 8), so since the speaker knows they have the same sense, he

29

or she must also know that they have the same semantic value. From thesis 2 it follows that he or she must know the truth-value of "The Evening Star is the Evening Star". This explains why the sentence is uninformative.

The introduction of sense also enables Frege to solve the problem of bearerless names. Consider again the example of "Odysseus". Suppose, for the sake of argument, that the sense of this is given by some descriptive condition, such as "The hero of Homer's *Odyssey* and the son of Laertes and Antikleia". Clearly, someone can grasp such a condition even if there actually is no object that satisfies it: someone can know what it would be for a person to be referred to by the name "Odysseus" even if there is in fact no such person. This is even clearer in the case of a term like "The twelve-headed student in my class". I can certainly understand this term: this in part explains why I am able to understand the sentence "The twelve-headed student in my class has more than two heads". That is, I know what would have to be the case for someone to be referred to by the term, and I can possess this knowledge even given the fact that (thankfully!) there is no twelve-headed student in my class. Thus,

THESIS 13. *An expression can have a sense even if it lacks a semantic value.*

Or as Frege puts it himself:

> The words "the celestial body most distant from the Earth" have a sense, but it is very doubtful if there is also a thing they refer to. The expression "the least rapidly convergent series" has a sense but demonstrably there is nothing it [refers to], since for every convergent series, another convergent, but less rapidly convergent, series can be found. In grasping a sense, one is certainly not assured of referring to anything.[4]

Frege thus solves the problem of bearerless names: *names with no semantic value (reference) are not necessarily meaningless, because they can nevertheless possess a sense.*

What follows about sentences containing bearerless names? For example, consider "Odysseus was set ashore at Ithaca while sound asleep". Since one of the expressions, "Odysseus", lacks a reference, and since the semantic value of a complex expression is determined by the semantic values of its parts (thesis 2), it follows that this sentence itself does not have a semantic value. In other words, it lacks a truth-value: it is neither true nor false. This gives us another of Frege's theses:

THESIS 14. *A sentence that contains an expression that lacks a semantic value is neither true nor false.*

We'll return to the question of the status of sentences containing bearerless names later in this chapter. We must now consider how Frege uses the introduction of sense to solve the problem of substitution into belief contexts.

Recall that substitution into belief contexts appeared to threaten thesis 3, that substitution of co-referential parts of a sentence should leave the truth-value of the whole sentence unchanged, plus the generalization of that thesis to the case where the parts of the complex sentence are themselves sentences, that the substitution of a component sentence by another sentence having the same truth-value should leave the truth-value of the complex sentence unchanged. For example,

(1) John believes that Mark Twain is Mark Twain

is true, whereas

(2) John believes that Mark Twain is Samuel Clemens

is false, even though the latter was obtained from the former via the substitution of apparently co-referential names.

Frege's response to this is to save the principle by denying that "Mark Twain" and "Samuel Clemens" are indeed co-referential in the relevant sort of belief context. Customarily, outside of belief contexts, they refer to the man who authored *Huckleberry Finn* and so on, as in

(5) Mark Twain was an American.

31

But within belief contexts they refer to the *senses* they ordinarily possess outwith belief contexts (as in e.g. (5)). Frege expresses this by saying that in "Mark Twain was an American", "Mark Twain" has its *customary reference* and *customary sense*. However, in belief contexts "Mark Twain" refers not to the man, but rather to the customary sense of the name. *Frege expresses this by saying that in belief contexts a name refers to its customary sense*, and he calls this its *indirect reference*. Since "Mark Twain" and "Samuel Clemens" have different customary senses and therefore different indirect references, it follows that in moving from (1) to (2) we have not actually substituted one co-referential expression for another, so that we do not after all have a counterexample to thesis 3. The identification of indirect reference with customary sense thus allows us to avoid the problem of substitution into belief contexts. We'll have more to say about Frege's solution to this problem in due course, but for the moment we can sum things up in the thesis:

THESIS 15. *In a belief context, the (indirect) reference of a proper name is its customary sense.*

It is worth noting that just as thesis 2 led to thesis 3, so thesis 11 (the compositionality of sense) leads to

THESIS 16. *Substitution of one expression in a sentence with another that has the same sense will leave the sense of the sentence unchanged.*

This can be used to give us some clue as to what the senses of sentences are. Consider again the move from

(3) John believes that London is south of Glasgow

to

(4) John believes that electrons are negatively charged particles.

Recall that since the semantic value of a sentence is a truth-value, and since the embedded sentences in (3) and (4) have the same truth-values (T), the fact that (3) is true and (4) is false appears to generate a problem for thesis 3. Again, Frege's way round this problem is to apply (an analogue of) thesis 15. In (3) and (4) the embedded sentences do not have their customary semantic values (truth-values): within belief contexts their semantic values are their *customary senses*. But what is the customary sense of a sentence? Well, what are we referring to in using "London is south of Glasgow" within a belief context such as (3)? Intuitively, we are referring to John's thought *that London is south of Glasgow*. That is to say, we are using the sentence to specify the *content* of a *thought*. Now, if we substitute the embedded sentence in (3) with one that expresses the *same thought* (as opposed to merely having the same truth-value), is it possible for (3) to change truth-value? If not, the identification of the sense of a sentence with the thought it expresses will respect thesis 16. The question as to the identity of thoughts is a thorny one (when does one sentence S1 express the same thought as another sentence, S2?), but intuitively it looks as if the substitution of "London is south of Glasgow" by another sentence expressing the same thought will leave the truth-value of (3) unchanged. For example, the sentence "London is south of Glasgow" intuitively expresses the same thought as "Glasgow is north of London", and the substitution of the latter for the former results in the true sentence

(6) John believes that Glasgow is north of London.

These considerations suggest the next of our Fregean theses:

THESIS 17. *The sense of a sentence is a thought.*

It is important to note that for Frege, a thought is not something *psychological* or *subjective*. Rather, it is *objective* in the sense that it specifies some condition in the world the obtaining of which is necessary and sufficient for the truth of the sentence that expresses it. This is a theme to which we shall return, but for the moment we note that, in the terminology introduced in section 1.6, we can re-express thesis 17 as the view that *the sense of a sentence is its truth-condition.*[5]

Before leaving this section we should pause to note one problem that will have been staring the attentive reader in the face.

According to thesis 8, the sense of an expression determines its semantic value. According to thesis 2, the semantic value (truth-value) of a sentence is determined by the semantic values of its parts. If we put these together we get the result that the sense of an expression determines the truth-values of sentences in which it appears (since the sense of an expression determines its semantic value, which in turn determines the truth-values of sentences in which it appears). This is nicely put in Michael Dummett's characterization of the notion of sense: "The sense of an expression is that part of its meaning which is relevant to the determination of the truth-value of sentences in which the expression occurs."[6] This is problematic because it is uncomfortably close to our definition of the notion of semantic value (section 1.3): the semantic value of an expression is that feature of it that determines whether sentences in which it occurs are true or false. Doesn't it follow that we have to *identify* sense and semantic value, so that there is after all no distinction to be drawn between them, so that Frege's theory of meaning, which rests on the distinction, is thrown into chaos?

Dummett points out there is actually no problem here. Recall the thesis in which we introduced the notion of sense:

THESIS 8. *The sense of an expression is that ingredient of its meaning that determines its semantic value.*

That is to say, the sense of an expression is that ingredient of its meaning relevant to the determination of the truth-values of the sentences in which it occurs. What does it mean to say that the sense of an expression is "an ingredient of its meaning"? Dummett spells this notion out as follows: "What we are going to understand as a possible ingredient in meaning will be something which it is plausible to say constitutes part of what someone who understands the word or expression implicitly grasps, and in his grasp of which his understanding in part consists."[7] In other words, the claim that sense is, in this manner of speaking, an ingredient in meaning, is more or less a restatement of

THESIS 10. *The sense of an expression is what someone who understands the expression grasps.*

34

Now the key to seeing why there is no tension here with the characterization of semantic value is to note that semantic value is not, in this manner of speaking, an ingredient in meaning. In other words

THESIS 18. *The semantic value of an expression is no part of what someone who understands the expression grasps.*

This, indeed, is the upshot of Frege's solution to the problem of informativeness. The argument is that if the semantic value of an expression was part of what was grasped by someone who understands it, there would be no possibility of, for example, understanding a sentence without knowing its truth-value. Theses 10 and 18 thus ensure that the characterization of semantic value, together with the characterization of sense given in thesis 8, do not force the identification of sense with semantic value.

It is worth noting that, although semantic value is not in the special sense introduced above an ingredient in meaning, it is still part of the intuitive notion of meaning, and something that has to be dealt with in a systematic way by a philosophical theory of meaning. Dummett writes:

> To say that reference [semantic value] is not an ingredient in meaning is not to deny that reference [semantic value] is a consequence of meaning, or that the notion of reference [semantic value] has a vital role to play in the general theory of meaning: it is only to say that the understanding which a speaker of a language has of a word in that language ... can never consist merely in his associating a certain thing with it as its referent [semantic value]; there must be some particular *means* by which this association is effected, the knowledge of which constitutes his grasp of its sense.[8]

We started out attempting to say something systematic about the intuitive notion of meaning. We have now reached the point where we have distinguished between two levels in meaning: sense, that which is grasped by someone who knows the meaning of an expression, and semantic value, that which is determined by sense. This distinction, together with theses 1–18, takes us a long way in our task of saying something systematic about the intuitive notion of meaning. We continue this task in the next section.

2.3 The objectivity of sense: Frege's critique of Locke

We noted above that the sense of a sentence is a thought, and that according to Frege thoughts are in some sense objective, as opposed to subjective or psychological. This is an extremely important part of Frege's position. Indeed, in the introduction to *The Foundations of Arithmetic*, he states the following as the first of his three "fundamental principles": "Always to separate sharply the psychological from the logical, the subjective from the objective."[9] This applies not only to the senses of sentences, but to the senses of all expressions generally. But what exactly does it mean to say that sense is objective and not subjective? One thing that it means is that grasping a sense – understanding an expression – is not a matter of associating that expression with some subjective item like a *mental image, picture,* or *idea.* Frege is quite explicit about the need to distinguish senses, which are objective, from ideas, which are subjective:

> The reference [semantic value] and sense of a sign are to be distinguished from the associated idea ... The reference of a proper name is the object itself which we designate by using it; the idea which we have in that case is wholly subjective; in between lies the sense, which is indeed no longer subjective like the idea, but is yet not the object itself.[10]

The view that understanding an expression consisted in the possession of some associated idea or image is one that has a long list of adherents in the history of philosophy. In distinguishing the sense of an expression from any associated idea, Frege was directly attacking this tradition, and setting the scene for similar attacks that were later to be mounted by Wittgenstein (see also section 5.1). The classic example of this view of sense can be found in Book III of John Locke's *An Essay Concerning Human Understanding.*

Some creatures who utter, for example, the word "cube" *understand* that word, and some don't. A parrot, for example, can say the word, but unlike a normal human speaker of English, the parrot possesses no understanding of what is said. In Fregean terminology, the human speaker grasps the sense of "cube", whereas the parrot does not. But what does this difference consist in? Locke's suggestion is that the word "cube" is, in the case of the competent human speaker, associated with an *idea of a cube* in that speaker's mind, while in the case of the parrot there is no such idea and so no such association. Locke is thus led to the view that understanding an expression consists in associating it with some idea: "Words, in their primary or immediate signification, stand for nothing but the ideas in the mind of him that uses them."[11]

Locke takes ideas to be mental images or pictures: an idea of a cube is taken to be a mental image or inner picture of a cube.[12] This is clear from the way Locke speaks throughout the *Essay*. For example, in his account of memory the talk of ideas is explicitly in terms of picturing and imagery:

> The ideas, as well as children of our youth often die before us. And our minds represent to us those tombs to which we are approaching; where though the brass and marble remain, yet the inscriptions are effaced by time, and the imagery moulders away. The pictures drawn in our minds are laid in fading colours.[13]

We could thus sum up Locke's view of sense as follows (where the sense of "cube" determines that it refers to, precisely, *cubes*):

A speaker grasps the sense of "cube" if and only if he is disposed to have a mental image of a cube whenever he hears or utters the word.

Why does Frege object to this account of sense? Locke's account leads to a tension, which the reader will probably have noticed already, between the *public* nature of meaningful language and the *private* nature of ideas and mental images. On the one hand, language is public in that different speakers can attach the *same* sense to their words, and one speaker can *know* what another speaker means by his words. Different speakers can *communicate* with each other in virtue of the common senses that they have attached to their words. On the other hand, ideas are private. As Locke himself puts it, a man's ideas are "all within his own breast, invisible, and hidden from others, nor can of themselves be made to appear". Also, my ideas, my "internal conceptions", are visible only to my consciousness, and likewise your ideas, your "internal conceptions", are visible only to your consciousness. But we are attempting to give an account of sense, an account that should help explain how we are able to *communicate with each other* via the use of language: and how can a theory which construes grasp of sense in terms of the possession of private inner items help explain our ability to use language in successful public communication?

In fact, Frege develops this rhetorical question into a powerful argument against Locke's account of sense.[14] The argument can be set out as follows:

(a) One crucial role of sense is to explain how linguistic communication is possible: the success of language in facilitating communication between two speakers is to be accounted for in terms of their grasping the same senses.

(b) Private, inner items have no role to play in explaining the practical success of language in facilitating communication between two speakers.

So,

(c) Understanding an expression – grasping a sense – cannot consist in the possession of some inner, private item.

Frege is explicit about (a): that Frege thinks sense can play this role is evident in a passage in which he again distinguishes between sense and idea, and refers to the role of sense in communication, or as he puts it, the transmission of thought:

A painter, a horseman, and a zoologist will probably connect different ideas with the name "Bucephalus". This constitutes an essential distinction between the idea and the sign's sense, which may be the common property of many people, and so is not a part or a mode of the individual mind. For one can hardly deny that mankind has a common store of thoughts which is transmitted from one generation to another.[15]

And it seems perfectly reasonable to demand that any notion of sense be able to play this role. What, though, is the argument for premise (b)? One way to argue for this is to think about a possibility which Locke himself muses on in the *Essay*, that

> The same object might produce in several men's minds different ideas at the same time; e.g. the idea that a violet produced in one man's mind by his eyes were the same that a marigold produced in another man's, and vice versa.[16]

Locke realizes that this possibility poses a problem for his account of what constitutes understanding. The possibility is one of *systematic inversion* between the ideas of the colours blue and yellow. If we consider two speakers, say Smith and Jones, the possibility is one in which the idea produced in Jones's mind by bananas, egg yolks and the skin of someone with jaundice is of the same type as the idea produced in Smith's mind by the sea on a sunny day, Glasgow Rangers shirts and city buses in Birmingham; and vice versa, the idea produced in Smith's mind by bananas, egg yolks and jaundiced skin is of the same type as the idea produced in Jones's mind by the sea, Glasgow Rangers tops and Birmingham buses.

The crucial point is this: *since the inversion is systematic in this way, if the possibility were actually to obtain, it would not manifest itself in any of the linguistic behaviour displayed by Smith and Jones.* For example: both would learn to use the word "yellow" by being shown things like bananas, egg yolks, etc., and both would learn "blue" by being shown the sea on a sunny day, Glasgow Rangers tops, etc.; other things being equal, both would call the same things blue and yellow in the same circumstances; and other things being equal, both would respond in the same way to orders framed using the words "yellow" and "blue".[17]

Now, if the possibility were to obtain, someone advancing an account of sense along the lines of Locke's would have to say that Smith and Jones were not communicating successfully: after all, they would be attaching different senses to the words "blue" and "yellow" because of the difference in the ideas that these words produce. So, one would expect Locke to provide some argument to the effect that we could always detect, somehow or other, whether the inversion possibility did or did not obtain, perhaps by showing that there is actually some way in which it eventually manifests itself in speakers' behaviour. But, surprisingly, Locke does not attempt to do this, and instead goes on to make the following comment:

> Since this [the systematic inversion] could never be known, because one man's mind could not pass into another man's body ... neither the ideas hereby, nor the names, would be at all confounded, or any falsehood be in either ... whatever [the] appearances were in his mind, he would be able regularly to distinguish things for his use by those appearances, and understand and signify those distinctions marked by the names "blue" and "yellow", as if the appearances or ideas in his mind were exactly the same with the ideas in other men's minds ... [and if the inversion hypothesis were true] it would be of little use, either for the improvement of our knowledge, or conveniency of life; and so we need not trouble to examine it.[18]

But this is an amazing thing for Locke to say, and it basically amounts to an admission that his account of sense is unable to play any role in the task of explaining linguistic communication. We can see the problems this causes by putting the admission alongside a consequence of his account of sense:

Locke's admission: *If the inversion hypothesis were true, it wouldn't really matter, because everything in our linguistic lives would be as before, we could do everything we previously did with language.*

A consequence of Locke's account of sense: *If the inversion hypothesis were true, Smith and Jones wouldn't really be communicating, because they would have different ideas annexed to their words, and so would associate different senses with those words.*

Putting the admission together with the consequence of the account of sense thus gives us:

It is possible that we could do everything we currently do with language – use language for all of the purposes for which we currently use it – and yet not really be communicating, and not really attach the same senses to our words.

But this is absurd: there is absolutely nothing in our everyday conceptions of communication and grasp of sense that allows for such a possibility. In particular, the admission of such a possibility effectively renders the notion of sense empty. The conclusion is that Locke's account of sense is unacceptable.[19] We can sum up the results of this section in a further thesis of Frege's:

THESIS 19. *Sense is objective: grasping a sense is not a matter of having ideas, mental images, or private psychological items.*

Before moving on to look at some problems surrounding the notion of sense, we should pause to spell out a further important thesis of Frege's regarding sense. This thesis will be very important in later chapters of this book. In his late essay "The Thought", Frege distinguishes between two different sorts of law: *normative* (or *prescriptive* laws) and *descriptive* laws. Scientific laws fall into the latter category: they tell us what will actually happen, given such and such initial conditions. For example, Newton's First Law of Motion tells us that a body will remain at rest or travel with constant velocity in a straight line unless it is acted upon by a net unbalanced set of forces. The law *describes* how the body will behave given these conditions. This contrasts with a moral law, such as "Do not kill". This does not describe how people will actually behave: rather, it lays down a prescription as to how they *ought* to behave. The law constitutes a norm with respect to which people ought to regulate their behaviour: for this reason it is called a *normative* law. Frege makes the distinction between normative and descriptive laws because he wants to stress the point that the laws of logic are laws of thought in the normative sense: logic lays down prescriptions on how we *ought* to reason, on what inferences it is *proper* to make. It does not describe how we *actually* reason, or describe the inferences we will *in fact* make. The important point for our purposes is that sense is also normative: this is hardly surprising, given that the laws of thought are normative and that the senses of sentences are thoughts. And it is independently plausible. Just as a normative law of conduct tells us how we ought to behave, the sense of an expression must in some sense tell us how we ought to use that expression. The sense of an expression lays down a normative constraint that determines whether a particular use of that expression is *correct* or *incorrect*:

41

someone who uses an expression in a manner that is out of accord with its sense will be deemed to have made a *mistake*. We'll return to the issue of the normativity of sense in Chapters 5 and 6. For the moment, we can sum things up thus:

THESIS 20. *The sense of an expression is normative: it constitutes a normative constraint that determines which uses of that expression are correct and which are incorrect.*[20]

2.4 Problems with Frege's notion of sense

2.4.1 Problems about objectivity

Thesis 19 really only articulates a way in which sense is not subjective: grasping a sense is not constituted by the possession of mental images, and so on. But can we say anything more positive about what the objectivity of sense consists in? Frege tries to say something more in the following passage:

> Somebody observes the Moon through a telescope. I compare the Moon itself to the reference [semantic value]; it is the object of the observation, mediated by the real image projected by the object glass in the interior of the telescope, and by the retinal image of the observer. The former I compare to the sense, the latter is like the idea or experience. The optical image in the telescope is indeed one-sided and dependent upon the standpoint of observation; but it is still objective, inasmuch as it can be used by several observers. At any rate it could be arranged for several to use it simultaneously. But each one would have his own retinal image.[21]

The objectivity of sense over images seems to consist in the fact that whereas I cannot literally have your mental image, we can nevertheless literally grasp the same sense. And recall that our grasp of a common stock of senses is supposed to help explain the occurrence of linguistic communication. So Frege needs to characterize sense in such a way that (a) two different individuals can literally grasp the same sense, and (b) their grasp of this sense helps explain how they can communicate with each other. But does he manage to do this? Let's consider the case of a proper name, such as "Aristotle". So far, the only characterization of the sense of a name that we have considered is that given by some *associated descriptive condition*. For example, we could take the sense of "Aristotle" to be given by the description "The pupil of Plato and teacher of Alexander the Great". Frege himself suggests this as one possible sense that might be attached to the name "Aristotle". But in the passage in which he makes this suggestion he makes a concession that is the exact parallel of the concession we saw Locke making in the preceding section. In fact, it turns out that, with the senses of names construed in terms of descriptions, we can aim an argument against Frege that is similar to his own argument against Locke.

Suppose that Smith and Jones associate different descriptions with the name "Aristotle". Smith, say, associates "Aristotle" with "the pupil of Plato and teacher of Alexander", while Jones associates it with "the teacher of Alexander who was born in Stagira". Frege clearly thinks that this is possible:

> In the case of an actual proper name such as "Aristotle" opinions as to the sense may differ. It might, for instance, be taken to be the following: the pupil of Plato and teacher of Alexander the Great. Anybody who does this will attach another sense to the sentence "Aristotle was born in Stagira" than will a man who takes as the sense of the name: the teacher of Alexander the Great who was born in Stagira.[22]

Now what would we expect Frege to say about such a situation, given what we know of his views on sense? Recall that the sense of a sentence is a thought (thesis 17). Since the sense of a complex expression is determined by the senses of its constituents (thesis 11), the thought expressed by "Aristotle was born in Stagira", as uttered by Smith, will differ from the thought it expresses when uttered by Jones. If the sentence is uttered in an exchange between Smith and Jones, there will be no transmission of a common thought: in short, there will be no communication. So, given his views on sense, Frege is committed to saying that in the situation envisaged Smith and Jones do not really communicate with each other. But what he actually says is somewhat different. Here is the rest of the passage quoted above:

43

> So long as the thing referred to remains the same, such
> variations of sense may be tolerated, although they are to be
> avoided in the theoretical structure of a demonstrative science
> and ought not to occur in a perfect language.[23]

Frege seems to be conceding that such variations in sense will
make no practical difference as far as the use of language in
communication is concerned. But, as with Locke's concession over
the systematic inversion possibility, this concession leaves Frege
in a somewhat precarious position. In fact, it generates the same
absurdity:

> *It is possible that we could do everything we currently do with
> language – use language for all of the purposes for which we
> currently use it – and yet not* really *be communicating, and not*
> really *attach the same senses to our words.*

Again, this really only renders the notion of sense empty. But the
problem is that it is a consequence of Frege's account of sense
together with his concession in the passage quoted above. So it
looks as though Frege, like Locke, has not succeeded in capturing a
plausible objective notion of sense. This, though, really only has
the status of a challenge to Frege at this point, since we have been
working only with a very crude conception of what the sense of a
proper name might be, namely, some associated description. The
challenge to Frege is: *explain what sense is in a way that renders it
objective and apt to play a part in explaining linguistic
communication.*

2.4.2 Problems about sense and analysis

Frege's solution to the problem of informativeness has an odd
consequence. Anglo-American philosophy in the twentieth century
has been dominated by what is known as *analytic philosophy*. One
of the main characteristics of analytic philosophy is its view of
philosophy as consisting essentially in *analysis*. Analytic
philosophers attempt to tackle the traditional problems of
philosophy via the analysis of language: a proper conception of
language will enable us either to solve or dissolve these problems.
The advances Frege made in logic greatly facilitate the task of
solving philosophical problems in this manner:[24] so much so that
Frege is often hailed as "the founder of analytic philosophy". But

what exactly is analysis? Intuitively, we would want to say that this consists in discovering relationships among *senses*: the analysis of "*X* knows that *P*" as "*X* has a justified, true belief that *P*" claims to exhibit an identity in sense between the two expressions. Alternatively, we could view identity in sense as corresponding to the intuitive notion of *synonymy*: two expressions have the same sense if and only if they are synonymous. The project of analysis would then be construed as the project of discovering philosophically interesting relations of synonymy, or identity in sense, and the employment of these in the solution or dissolution of philosophical problems.

The difficulty is that Frege's solution to the problem of informativeness appears to rule out this intuitive description of the analytic project. Recall that the problem was to account for the fact that whereas

(7) The Morning Star is the Evening Star

is potentially informative,

(8) The Evening Star is the Evening Star

is not. For Frege, (7) is potentially informative because although "The Morning Star" and "The Evening Star" both refer to the same object, they have different senses. This contrasts with (8), whose uninformativeness is explained by the fact that the two signs flanking the "is" of identity have the same sense. Thus, the informativeness of some identity statements is explained in terms of the signs on either side of the identity sign having the same reference but expressing different senses; while the uninformativeness of other identity statements is explained in terms of the signs on either side of the identity sign having the same sense as well as the same reference. *The problem with this is that given the assumption that analysis concerns relations between senses, it also entails that there can be no such thing as an informative analysis.* To see this, suppose that analytic philosophers have succeeded in showing by analysis that knowledge is justified true belief. Then consider

(9) Knowledge is justified true belief.

Suppose that analysis really is concerned with discovering relations in the realm of sense, and that (9) is a good analysis. Then consider a philosopher who understands (9). Since he grasps the sense of (9) he must also grasp the senses of its constituents. Since "Knowledge" and "Justified true belief" *ex hypothesi* have the same sense, it follows from thesis 12 that anyone who grasps (9) must know that they have the same sense. But sense determines reference (thesis 8), so since philosophers know that they have the same sense, they must also know that they have the same reference. From thesis 2, it follows that they must know the truth-value of (9). So, any philosopher who understands (9) must know its truth-value. But this is just to say that there can be no such thing as an informative and interesting analysis. And if there can be no such thing as an interesting and informative analysis, what becomes of the project of analytic philosophy?[25] The dilemma for Frege here is clear. Either he gives up his explanation of why (7) and (8) differ in their potential informativeness, or he renders himself unable to account for the possibility of informative analyses, like that encapsulated in (9). The only way of avoiding this dilemma would seem to be to reject the intuitive conception of analysis as a project concerning relations of sense. This may be possible, but it would further deepen the mystery as to what sense actually is.[26]

2.4.3 Problems about indirect reference and belief contexts

Recall that Frege's solution to the problem of substitution into belief contexts is summed up in

THESIS 15. *In a belief context, the reference of a proper name is its customary sense.*

Thus, in

(2) John believes that Mark Twain is Samuel Clemens

"Mark Twain" refers not to the celebrated American author, but rather to the sense of "Mark Twain", as it appears outside of belief contexts. As we saw, Frege expresses this point in the following way: in belief contexts expressions refer to their customary senses, or, the indirect reference of an expression is its customary sense.

Now consider the following example of a perfectly well-understood sentence:

(10) James believes that John believes that Mark Twain is Samuel Clemens.

It is natural to suppose that just as the occurrence of "Mark Twain" in an indirect context such as (2) refers to the sense it possesses in a direct context, such as (5), the occurrence of "Mark Twain" in a *doubly* indirect context such as (10) will refer to the sense which it possesses in a *singly* indirect context such as (2). So, on Frege's account, the name "Mark Twain", as it appears in (10) refers to the *sense* that it possesses in (2), what Frege calls its *indirect sense*.

But what is this indirect sense? All we know is the reference of "Mark Twain" as it appears in (2), namely, its customary sense. But this won't allow us to work out the sense of "Mark Twain" as it appears in (2), since the sense – reference relation is many – one: the same referent can be associated with indefinitely many senses (as Russell put it, "there is no route back from the reference to the sense"). The upshot of this is that we seem to be unable to say what the sense of "Mark Twain" in (2) is, and therefore unable to say what the reference of "Mark Twain" is in (10). Given that the reference of an expression is what determines the contribution it makes to the truth-values of sentences in which it appears, we should be unable to appraise sentences involving doubly indirect contexts such as (10) for truth or falsity. But, of course, we are perfectly capable of making such appraisals: so Frege's account of indirect sense and indirect reference is thrown into doubt.

Is there any way Frege can get round this problem? Why does he need to distinguish between the sense of "Mark Twain" in an indirect context such as (2) and a direct context such as (5) in the first place? In other words, why can't he just *identify* the indirect sense of "Mark Twain", the sense it possesses in (2), with its customary sense, the sense it possesses in (5)? Given that we know the sense of "Mark Twain" as it appears in (5) (or at least we are supposing that we do, for the sake of argument), this would solve the problem about the reference of "Mark Twain" as it appears in the doubly indirect sentence (10). As Dummett points out, this option is not straightforwardly available to Frege because of his adherence to thesis 8, that sense determines semantic value. It follows from thesis 8 that if an expression has a certain reference in one context, but a different reference in another, then that expression must have different senses in each of the two contexts. Now, given that "Mark Twain" as it appears in (5) refers to the celebrated American author, and as it appears in (2) refers to its customary sense, it follows that "Mark Twain" has a different reference in each of these, and hence must express a different sense in each. In other words, the sense of "Mark Twain" in (2) is different from the sense it possesses in (5). The identification of indirect sense with customary sense is frustrated, so that we are left in the dark as to what the indirect sense, and hence the doubly indirect reference of "Mark Twain", actually is.

Dummett suggests that the whole difficulty arises from interpreting thesis 8 as meaning that the semantic value of an expression must be determined by its sense *alone*. This is a mistake, based on a misleading tendency to speak about the semantic values of expressions in isolation from the sentential contexts in which they occur. Indeed, Frege explicitly counsels against this tendency in the second of the three fundamental principles set out in the introduction to *The Foundations of Arithmetic*: "Never to ask for the reference of a word in isolation, but only in the context of a proposition."[27]

Dummett interprets this as a claim that only a particular occurrence of an expression in a sentence has a semantic value, and that this semantic value is determined *jointly* by the sense of the expression *together* with the kind of *context* in which it occurs. Then, as Dummett puts it,

> The sense of a word may thus be such as to determine it to stand for one thing in one kind of context, and for a different thing in some other kind of context. We may therefore regard an expression occurring in an indirect context as having the same sense as in a direct context, though a different reference.[28]

Frege can thus after all equate the indirect and customary senses of "Mark Twain", putting the differences in reference in (2) and (5) down to the fact that the expression is appearing in different types of context in each.

How plausible is this solution to the difficulty? There are at least two points that one can make here. First, Dummett's suggestion that the difficulty can be solved by equating the indirect and customary senses of "Mark Twain" appears to be *ad hoc*. All Dummett has shown is that there is *nothing to prevent* Frege from identifying indirect and customary sense. But in order to get Frege convincingly out of trouble here, we surely require some *positive* grounds for identifying customary and indirect sense, grounds that go beyond the observation that we avoid the relevant difficulty if we make the identification. Secondly, this point is made all the more pressing by the fact that there are actually some reasons *against* making the identification. Suppose that we do equate customary and indirect sense and consider two expressions that arguably have the same customary sense, say, "chiropodist" and "foot-doctor". Then, it follows that "chiropodist" and "foot-doctor" have the same indirect sense, and therefore the same reference in doubly indirect contexts. Now it follows, from thesis 3, that the move from

(11) John believes that Frank believes that all chiropodists are chiropodists

to

(12) John believes that Frank believes that all chiropodists are foot-doctors

should not result in a change in truth-value. But of course it is easy enough to think of cases in which (11) is true yet (12) is false. So the identification of customary and indirect sense threatens a clash with one of Frege's fundamental theses about semantic value. The upshot is that Frege's solution to the problem of substitution into belief contexts is not entirely satisfactory.

2.4.4 Problems about bearerless names

We suggested in sections 1.8 and 1.9 that one of the reasons for the introduction of the notion of sense was that it gave us a way of accounting for the fact that sentences containing bearerless names are nevertheless intuitively meaningful. Names without a bearer are not meaningless, since they can nevertheless possess a sense. The key thesis is therefore

THESIS 13. *An expression can have a sense even if it lacks a semantic value.*

Some philosophers have questioned whether this thesis is so much as coherent, given the technical notion of semantic value which Frege is working with. Recall that semantic value was defined in the following way:

DEFINITION. *The semantic value of an expression is that feature of it that determines whether sentences in which it occurs are true or false.*

But can we really make anything of the idea that an expression can have sense even though no feature of it determines whether sentences in which it occurs are true or false? The difficulty is perhaps clearest when we consider the case in which the expressions dealt with in thesis 13 are whole sentences. Recall that a sentence expresses a thought as its sense and a truth-value as its semantic value. So thesis 13, in the case of sentences, amounts to the claim that a sentence can express a thought even though it has no truth-value. The intuitive implausibility of this claim is well brought out by Gareth Evans:

> What can it mean on Frege's, or on anyone's principles, for there to be a perfectly determinate thought which simply has no truth-value? ... If someone understands and accepts a sentence containing an empty name, then, according to Frege, he thereby forms a belief; not a belief about language, but a belief about the world. But what sense can be made of a belief which literally has no truth-value?[29]

Doesn't this rob the technical notion of semantic value of any importance we might have thought it possessed for an account of the meaningfulness of language? How can we introduce a technical notion like semantic value, the possession of which by expressions is supposed to contribute to an explanation of their meaningfulness, and then allow that expressions can be meaningful even if they fail to possess it? As Evans puts it:

> The semanticist seeks to account [for the fact that a certain body of discourse is significant]. Following Frege, as part of this procedure he decides to construct a theory of semantic value, the main aim of which is to help to explain how the significance of sentences depends upon the significance of their parts. But it is just not open to the semanticist to say "There is a gap in my theory; here is a group of viable sentences which might be used to express and transmit thoughts, but to which my theory does not apply".[30]

This is a problem which Frege will have to face head on, if he accepts that the semantic value of a name is the object it stands for, and that sentences containing bearerless names may nevertheless express a thought.[31]

2.4.5 Kripke's objections

In his highly important and influential book *Naming and Necessity*, Saul Kripke raised a number of objections against what he construed as Frege's views on the sense and semantic value of proper names. The issues raised by Kripke's book are deep and complicated: we can only give a brief summary of some of the main points here. Thus far, whenever we have spoken of the sense of a name, we have taken it to be some descriptive condition: an object is the referent of the name if and only if the description is true of it. Thus, we can take the sense of "Aristotle" to be given by the description "the pupil of Plato and teacher of Alexander the Great". Kripke argues that if we accept this as an account of the sense of "Aristotle", we end up saying some very implausible things about Aristotle. In order to spell out Kripke's argument we need to introduce the distinction between *necessary truth* and *contingent truth*.

Consider a true sentence such as "2 + 2 = 4". Could things have turned out in such a way that this would have been false? It seems not: there are simply no possible situations in which the sum of 2 and 2 is not 4. Likewise for "All bachelors are unmarried": there is no way there could have been a married bachelor. Philosophers attempt to capture this feature of "2 + 2 = 4" and "All bachelors are married" by saying that they are *necessary truths*. Sometimes this notion is glossed as follows: a necessary truth is one which is true not only in this, the actual world, but also in all logically possible worlds. "2 + 2 = 4" and "All bachelors are unmarried" contrast with "Major was the Prime Minister in 1995" or "Germany won the 1996 European Football Championships". Although these are actually true, we can conceive of logically possible situations in which they are false: there are logically possible worlds in which Major lost the 1992 election and so would not have been Prime Minister in 1995, and there are logically possible worlds in which some team other than Germany won the 1996 European Championships (e.g. Scotland). "Major was Prime Minister in 1995" and "Germany won the 1996 European Championships" are *contingent truths*. They are true in the actual world, but not in all possible worlds.

There is another distinction that is related to the distinction between necessary and contingent truth, but which must also be distinguished from it. An *analytically true* sentence is one which is true purely in virtue of the senses of its constituents. "All bachelors are unmarried" would be an example of an analytic truth: its truth is settled by the senses of "bachelor", "unmarried", and so on. An example of a *synthetic* truth would be "Clinton was President of the USA. in 1995". This is true, but not *purely* in virtue of the senses of the constituent expressions. The relationship between the necessary-contingent and analytic-synthetic distinctions is a matter of some controversy. Philosophers are generally agreed that all analytic truths are necessary, but not all philosophers hold that all necessary truths are analytic. Kant, for example, held that such arithmetical truths as "2 + 2 = 4" are necessary but synthetic.[32]

Kripke's objection to taking the sense of "Aristotle" to be given by a description like "the pupil of Plato and teacher of Alexander the Great" is quite simple: if we take the sense of the name to be given by this description, then certain sentences that are intuitively only contingently true turn out to be necessarily true. Suppose that the sense of "Aristotle" is given by "the pupil of Plato and teacher of Alexander the Great". Then consider the sentence

(13) Aristotle was the pupil of Plato and the teacher of Alexander the Great.

Since the sense of "Aristotle" is *given* by "the pupil of Plato and the teacher of Alexander the Great", this sentence is true, and, moreover, true purely in virtue of facts about sense. In other words, it is analytically true. But if it is analytically true, it is also necessarily true, true in all logically possible worlds. But surely it is at most a contingent truth: we have no trouble in conceiving of situations in which Aristotle was taught by someone other than Plato and did not himself teach Alexander the Great. So, if the sense of "Aristotle" is given by the description, (13) would be a necessary truth. But (13) is not a necessary truth, it is at most a contingent truth. So the sense of "Aristotle" cannot be given by the description.[33]

The above five problems give an indication of the sorts of difficulties a defender of the notion of sense must attempt to solve. It is worth noting that two of the problems (§2.4.1 and §2.4.5) turn on taking the senses of proper names to be given by descriptions. Many philosophers have pointed out, however, that although Frege sometimes speaks as if the sense of a name is given by a description, there is nothing in the notion of sense which forces him to do so. Dummett, for example, writes:

> In trying to say what the senses of different names may be, Frege is naturally driven to citing such definite descriptions: but there is nothing in what he says to warrant the conclusion that the sense of a proper name is always the sense of some complex description. All that is necessary, in order that the senses of two names which have the same referent should differ, is that we should have a different way of recognizing an object as the referent of each of the names: there is no reason to suppose that the means by which we effect such a recognition should be expressible by means of a definite description.[34]

But what *is* sense, if it is not given by definite descriptions? A clue is perhaps provided by thesis **20**, the claim that sense is normative. A norm is another term for a *rule*: rules are normative in that they lay down constraints on what counts as correct or incorrect behaviour. So perhaps we can take senses to be simply rules governing the use of expressions that determine their semantic values and that are grasped by those who understand the expression in question. We can then leave it open whether these rules, in the case of names, for example, would be spelled out in terms of definite descriptions. But what are these rules? Can they be spelled out in a way that respects all of the various theses about sense that we have attributed to Frege? And can Frege respond to the problems raised in this section? We cannot attempt to deal with all of these questions in this book: this is perhaps the starting point for further study of Frege's notion of sense. But we'll return to at least some of them in due course.[35]

2.5 A theory of sense?

In section 1.7 we gave an example of a semantic theory for a simple language: a theory that shows how the *truth-values* of complex sentences are systematically determined by the semantic values of their constituent names and predicates. We also suggested that this theory could be used to show how statements of the *truth-conditions* of complex sentences can be derived on the basis of assignments of references and extensions to their parts. Recall that thesis 17 – the sense of a sentence is a thought – can be re-expressed as the claim that the sense of a sentence is its truth-condition. What this suggests is that a semantic theory of the sort described in section 1.7 – which in the first instance shows how the semantic values of complex expressions are determined by the semantic values of their parts – might also be used as a *systematic theory of sense*. There would be no need for a separate systematic theory of sense over and above the systematic theory of semantic value. Or, alternatively, we could provide an account of how the senses of complex expressions are determined without having directly to ascribe senses to their parts. This idea has seemed attractive to a number of philosophers. For example, Gareth Evans writes:

Frege nowhere appears to have envisaged a theory which would entail, for any sentence of the language, S, a theorem of the form,

The sense of S is ...,

derived from axioms which would state the sense of the primitive words of the language. Frege had no more idea of how to complete a clause like

The sense of "and" is ...

than we do.[36]

We shall see later, when we discuss Davidson's ideas on theories of meaning (Ch. 8), that it is just as well that Frege did not envisage this type of theory of sense, since it is hopeless. The important point for present purposes is that on the basis of assignments of references and extensions to the names and predicates of our simple language, we can systematically generate statements of the truth-conditions, or senses, of the complex sentences in which they appear.[37]

2.6 Force and tone

Thus far we have been attempting to tell a story about meaning in terms of two semantic properties, reference and sense. In addition to these, Frege introduces two other semantic properties, *force* and *tone*.

We'll take tone first. Consider the two sentences

(14) Major is English and he is a good loser.
(15) Major is English but he is a good loser.

Intuitively, (14) and (15) have the same truth-value (let's take it to be T, for the sake of argument). Substituting "but" for "and" does not lead to a change in truth-value. But equally intuitively, there is also some sort of difference between (14) and (15). In order to capture this difference, Frege introduced the notion of tone (he sometimes also refers to this as "colouring" or "illumination"). Frege held that "and" and "but" have the same sense but different tones. Like sense, tone is an ingredient in meaning: the tone of an expression is part of what is grasped by someone who is competent with it. As Dummett puts it: "A mistake about the ... tone ... intended to be understood as attached to a sentence or expression would ordinarily be accounted a misunderstanding of its meaning." [38] But unlike the sense of an expression, its tone is not relevant to determining the truth-values of sentences in which it appears. This is shown by the fact that the truth-tables for (14) and (15) are identical:

P	Q	P and Q	P but Q
T	T	T	T
T	F	F	F
F	T	F	F
F	F	F	F

Other examples of expressions that have the same sense but which differ in tone are: "dog" and "cur"; "sweat" and "perspiration"; "walk" and "perambulate". [39]

The notion of sense, as developed by Frege, is a notion of *sentence-meaning*. The sense of an expression is intended to capture what a sentence strictly and literally means: in other words, the sense of an expression gives its *literal meaning* (or what it means, when stripped of its tone). Take a sentence like "Jones is an efficient administrator". The strict and literal meaning of this sentence is *that Jones is an efficient administrator*. That is, the truth-condition of this sentence is given by

(16) "Jones is an efficient administrator" is true if and only if Jones is an efficient administrator.

But what about the countless sentences of language that do not have truth-conditions, but which are nevertheless perfectly meaningful? For example, neither of "Is Jones an efficient administrator?" or "Jones, administrate efficiently!" are the sorts of sentences that *have* truth-conditions. So far, in our account of sense and semantic value, we have considered only sentences in the *indicative* grammatical mood, and we have suggested that the sense of these sentences is given by their truth-conditions. But there are other grammatical moods: the *interrogative* mood, exemplified by "Is Jones an efficient administrator?"; and the *imperatival* mood, exemplified by "Jones, administrate efficiently!" So what can we say about the literal meanings of sentences in these other moods?

Frege's idea is to represent the meaning of a sentence by an ordered pair, consisting of a sense, together with an indication of force. Since we already have a story about the senses of sentences in the indicative mood, we shall use this as a basis for giving an account of the meanings of sentences in other, non-indicative moods. This is what Frege thinks ought to be done (he never got so far as actually doing it in any detail). Consider the three sentences

(17) Jones is an efficient administrator.
(18) Is Jones an efficient administrator?
(19) Jones, administrate efficiently!

The sense of (17) is the thought *that Jones is an efficient administrator*. Now we can do a number of things with the thought that Jones is an efficient administrator. We can assert it, we can ask whether it is true, and we can command that it be made true. Each of these corresponds to a different force that might be attached to the thought: the force of an assertion, the force of a question, the force of a command. We can represent the meanings of (17) – (19) as

(Jones is an efficient administrator, force of an assertion)
(Jones is an efficient administrator, force of a question)
(Jones is an efficient administrator, force of a command).

Thus, we can give an account of the literal meanings of many types of sentences in terms of the notion of sense developed for indicative sentences together with the additional notion of force.[40] We can now enter our final Fregean thesis:

THESIS 21. *In addition to sense and semantic value, we must also introduce the notions of* force *and* tone.

Note that force and tone are invoked as part of an account of sentence-meaning.[41] It is usual to distinguish between sentence-meaning and *speaker's-meaning*. Speaker's-meaning concerns what information the utterer actually intends to convey. It is clear that the speaker's-meaning and the literal-meaning of a sentence can come apart. Consider our sentence (17). As we noted, its sentence-meaning is *that Jones is an efficient administrator*. But imagine I am having a conversation with a visitor to my department who asks of my colleague, Jones, whether he is an interesting philosopher. If I respond by uttering the sentence, what information do I intend to convey to the visitor? Roughly, I intend to convey the information that Jones is an uninteresting philosopher. Thus, I can use a sentence that literally means that Jones is an efficient administrator to assert that Jones is an uninteresting philosopher. Another way of putting this would be to say that I can utter sentence (17) to perform the *speech-act* of asserting that Jones is an uninteresting philosopher.[42] Obviously, there are many different types of speech-act: giving commands, asking questions, and so on. Note that I can even perform the speech-act of asserting that Jones is an uninteresting philosopher by uttering a sentence that is nonindicative in mood: for example, I could reply to my visitor's question with either "Are you kidding?" or "Pull the other one!"

Given that a sentence has a particular literal meaning, what determines its speaker's-meaning, or the particular speech-acts its user performs on a given occasion of utterance? Answering this question is the province of *pragmatics*. Very roughly, we can say that speaker's-meaning is determined by the *context of utterance*. Whether we can say anything more systematic than this is an extremely difficult question. For the moment, we'll sum things up by saying that pragmatics concerns the determination of speaker's-meaning, while semantics concerns the determination of sentence-meaning or literal-meaning.

We can sum up our account of Frege as follows. For Frege, whether or not a sentence is grammatically well-formed is determined by syntactical rules. These are the province of *syntax* (section 1.2). Whether or not it is true is determined by the references and extensions of its constituents (sections 1.3–1.7). The references and extensions of its constituents are determined by their senses, which in turn determine the sense (truth-condition) of the sentence (sections 2.1–2.2). In addition to sense, we must also discern force and tone as ingredients in meaning. Sense, force and tone together determine *sentence-meaning*, what a sentence literally and strictly means. All this belongs to the province of *semantics*. Given the sentence-meaning that belongs to the sentence, the context of utterance determines the speaker's-meaning, or speech-acts actually performed by the utterance of the sentence. The story as to how sentence-meaning and context of utterance jointly determine speaker's-meaning is the province of *pragmatics*.[43]

2.7 Russell on names and descriptions

Bertrand Russell, in a series of famous works, challenged some of the views of Frege's that we have been outlining. In fact, Russell raised two distinct sorts of criticism of Frege. On the one hand, he accepted, in broad outline, the account of semantic value that we outlined in Chapter 1, but argued that Frege had gone wrong on some important points of detail. On the other, he attacked Frege's introduction of the notion of sense over and above that of semantic value. We'll consider criticisms of the first sort in this section and the next, and criticisms of the second sort in section 2.9. This will allow us briefly to outline Russell's famous "theory of definite descriptions".

In section 1.4, we saw that Frege held the following thesis:

THESIS 4. *The semantic value of a proper name is the object that it stands for.*

We could also view this as a *definition* of "proper name": proper names are precisely those expressions that have objects as their semantic values. It would then be an open question whether names, as they appear in natural languages, such as English, are proper names as thus defined. Frege clearly held that ordinary names, such as "Aristotle" and "Odysseus", are proper names in this sense. He also held that *definite descriptions* are proper names in this sense. A definite description is a phrase of the form "the so and so". So examples of definite descriptions would be "the King of France", "the man in the iron mask", "the celestial body most distant from the earth" and "the least rapidly convergent series". Frege thus held that the semantic value of a definite description is the object which it stands for: the contribution a definite description makes to the truth-values of complex sentences in which it appears is determined by the fact that it stands for a certain object.

Recall that one of the problems we raised for Frege in section 2.4 was the problem of bearerless names. The easiest way into Russell's views is to see him as starting from essentially the same problem. Take a definite description, such as "the King of France". There is simply no object for which this stands, so if we view it as a proper name, it follows that it has no semantic value. But then there is no property in virtue of which it makes a contribution to the truth-values of complex sentences in which it appears. Thus, in Frege's view, the sentence

(20) The King of France is bald

has no truth-value: it expresses a thought that is neither true nor false. We saw that this notion is only dubiously coherent. One way of avoiding the problem is Meinong's: the expression "the King of France" *does* refer to an object, but a non-existent one. The King of France, even though he doesn't exist, nevertheless *subsists*. Russell attempts to avoid the problem in a way that does not involve the highly implausible postulation of non-existent, but nevertheless subsistent, objects. *Rather, Russell attempts to avoid the problem by denying that definite descriptions are proper names.* If definite descriptions are not proper names, their semantic values are not given by the objects (if any) they stand for, so the fact that there are many definite descriptions that do not stand for any object does not lead to the problem faced by Frege. But if the semantic behaviour of definite descriptions is not to be explained in terms of their standing for objects, how is it to be explained? What are definite descriptions if they are not proper names?

In order to see Russell's answer to these questions, we should think about the correct translation of (20) into Frege's logical language. (20) has the grammatical form of a subject-predicate sentence. So if we were taking grammatical form as a guide to the correct translation of (20) into logical symbolism, it would come out as

(21) *Fa.*

A property, being bald, represented by "*F*", is predicated of the King of France, represented by "*a*". Now we can say that in translating a sentence into Frege's logical symbolism we are attempting to capture its *logical form*: we exhibit the form of the sentence in such a way that the contributions its constituents make to its truth-value are thereby exhibited. Thus, in translating (20) by (21) we are suggesting that "the King of France" contributes to determining the truth-value of (20) in the manner of a proper name, and "bald" contributes in the manner of a predicate. *Russell suggests that in this instance we should not take the grammatical form of the sentence as a guide to its logical form.* In fact, the logical form of (20) is given by something quite different from (21). Russell analyzes (20) by first breaking it up into three different parts:

(i)   There is at least one King of France.
(ii) There is at most one King of France.
(iii) Anything that is a king of France is also bald.

The conjunction of (i), (ii) and (iii) amounts to the claim that the King of France is bald. Thus, the logical form of (20) can be represented by the translation of the conjunction of (i), (ii) and (iii) into Frege's logical symbolism. Taking "*F*" to abbreviate the predicate "... is a king of France"[44] and "*G*" to abbreviate the predicate "... is bald", this comes out as

(22) $(\exists x)((Fx \ \& \ Gx) \ \& \ (\forall y)(Fy \rightarrow x = y))$.

Representing the logical form of (20) by (22) does not involve representing "the King of France" as a proper name, as in (21). We can represent the logical form of sentences in which definite descriptions appear without viewing those descriptions as having objects as their semantic values. But if definite descriptions do not have objects as their semantic values, what are their semantic values? *The answer to this is that definite descriptions have second-level functions as their semantic values.* In (20), the definite description "the King of France" is translated by

(23) $(\exists x)((Fx \mathrel{\&} ...x) \mathrel{\&} (\forall y)(Fy \to x = y))$,

which stands for a function from concepts (first-level functions) to truth-values. Russell's criticism of Frege's view of definite descriptions can thus be summed up as follows. *Frege assigns definite descriptions the wrong sort of semantic values: Frege views definite descriptions as proper names, as having objects as their semantic values; but in fact definite descriptions have second-level functions as their semantic values.*[45]

Note how this solves the problem of bearerless definite descriptions. Since definite descriptions are not proper names, but rather functional expressions that do not have objects as their semantic values, the failure of a definite description to stand for an object does not imply that it has no semantic value: we still have an account of how it contributes to the truth-values of complex sentences in which it appears, an account that runs along the lines of that given for functional expressions in Chapter 1. What, then, is the truth-value of (20)? Given the analysis into (22) we can see that it is false, since $(\exists x)Fx$ is false (since there is no King of France).

In fact, Russell attempts to avoid the problem of bearerless names in exactly the same way, *by treating ordinary names as disguised definite descriptions.* That is, Russell claims that even ordinary names are not proper names in the sense defined by thesis 4. Consider the sentence

(24) Odysseus was set ashore at Ithaca while sound asleep.

Frege would analyze this as having the logical form given by

(25) *Mb*

where "*M*" translates the predicate "... was set ashore at Ithaca while sound asleep" and "*b*" translates "Odysseus". Again, Russell suggests that we should not take the grammatical form of (24) as an infallible guide to its logical form. "Odysseus" is really a disguised definite description: for simplicity, suppose that it is the definite description "the hero of Homer's *Odyssey*". (24) thus really amounts to

(26) The hero of Homer's *Odyssey* was set ashore at Ithaca while sound asleep.

We now analyze this in the same way that we analyzed (20), using "*N*" to translate the predicate "... is a hero of Homer's *Odyssey*":

(27) $(\exists x)((Nx \ \& \ Mx) \ \& \ (\forall y)(Ny \rightarrow x = y))$.

This analysis shows that "Odysseus" is not really a proper name. Rather, the semantic value of "Odysseus" is the second-level function denoted by

(28) $(\exists x)((Nx \ \& \ ...x) \ \& \ (\forall y)(Ny \rightarrow x = y))$.

So the fact that there actually is no Odysseus does not cause problems: we can still account for the contribution "Odysseus" makes to the truth-values of sentences containing it by giving a story along the lines of that we gave for functional expressions in Chapter 1. The problem of bearerless names has disappeared.

If neither definite descriptions nor ordinary names can be viewed as genuine proper names, what can? Isn't Russell committed to the view that there are *no* genuine proper names? In fact, Russell thinks that the only genuine proper names might turn out to be demonstrative expressions, such as "this" or "that":

> We may even go so far as to say that, in all such knowledge as can be expressed in words – with the exception of "this" and "that" and a few other words of which the meaning varies on different occasions – no [genuine proper] names occur, but what seem like [genuine proper] names are really descriptions.[46]

In fact, Russell's views here are even more drastic than they sound. Not only are "this" and "that" the only possible genuine proper names, but even they cannot be construed as proper names if they are taken as referring to physical objects. They can only be viewed as proper names if they are taken to refer to sense-data or "objects of sense":

> We say "This is white". If you agree that "this is white", meaning the "this" that you see, you are using "this" as a proper name. But if you try to apprehend the proposition that I am expressing when I say "This is white", you cannot do it. If you mean this piece of chalk as a physical object, then you are not using a proper name. It is only when you use "this" quite strictly, to stand for an actual object of sense, that it is really a proper name.[47]

It is easy to see the rough form of Russell's reasoning here. The only genuine proper names are those for which the problem of bearerless names cannot possibly arise. Sense-data seem like good candidates for objects whose existence cannot possibly be doubted: if it seems to me that there is a red sense-datum in my visual field, then there is. So the only genuine proper names are names of sense-data: demonstratives applied to currently existing experiences. Whether Russell's restricted conception of what count as genuine proper names is plausible is a question which we cannot enter into here, as it would take us far afield into Russell's epistemology. In section 2.9 we consider further Russell's critique of Frege.

2.8 Scope distinctions

As noted above, on Russell's analysis, the sentence

(20) The King of France is bald

comes out *false*. But what about the sentence

(29) The King of France is not bald.

Is this true or false? Russell worries that on his analysis this sentence will *also* come out as false. This would be a problem, because it would seem to lead to a counterexample to the logical law known as the law of excluded middle. This law states that for any given sentence, either it or its negation must be true. But if both (20) and (29) are false, we seem to have a case where *neither* a sentence nor its negation are true. As Russell himself puts it:

> By the law of excluded middle, either "A is B" or "A is not B" must be true. Hence either "the present King of France is bald" or "the present King of France is not bald" must be true. Yet if we enumerated the things that are bald and then the things that are not bald, we should not find the present King of France in either list. Hegelians, who love a synthesis, will probably conclude that he wears a wig.[48]

Russell responds to this worry by distinguishing between two different ways of reading (29). On one reading, it is false, but is not really the negation of (20), so that no counterexample to the law of excluded middle is generated. On the other reading, it is the negation of (20), but is actually true, so that again there is no threat to the law of excluded middle. In order to distinguish between the two readings, Russell uses the notion of *scope*.

Consider

(30) All philosophers are not stupid.

Clearly, this is not consistent with the existence of a stupid philosopher: if a stupid philosopher exists, then (30) is false. Taking "F" as "... is a philosopher" and "G" as "...is stupid", (30) formalizes as

(31) $(\forall x)(Fx \rightarrow - Gx)$.

Notice that the negation operator "$-$" occurs inside the part of (31) $(Fx \rightarrow - Gx)$ that is governed by the universal quantifier ($\forall x$). We say that the negation operator has *narrow* scope with respect to the universal quantifier (or equivalently, that the universal quantifier has *wide* scope with respect to the negation operator). Contrast this with

(32) It is not the case that all philosophers are stupid.

65

This is consistent with the existence of a stupid philosopher: so long as there is at least one other philosopher who is *not* stupid (32) still comes out true. Using the same letters as above, this formalizes as

(33) $- (\forall x)(Fx \rightarrow Gx)$.

Notice that in this case the negation operator occurs outside the part of (33) that is governed by the universal quantifier. We say that the negation operator has *wide* scope with respect to the universal quantifier (or equivalently, that the universal quantifier has *narrow* scope with respect to the negation operator).

Now just as we can distinguish between the negation operator's having wide or narrow scope with respect to a quantifier, we can also distinguish between their having wide or narrow scopes with respect to a definite description. Consider the formalization of (29), which clearly displays its falsity:

(34) $(\exists x)((Fx \ \& - Gx) \ \& \ (\forall y)(Fy \rightarrow x = y))$.

In this the negation operator has narrow scope with respect to the definite description (i.e. to the functional expression (23)). Russell points out that (34) is *not* the negation of (20): in order to get the negation of (20) we need to find something in which the negation operator has *widest* scope. The only candidate for this is

(35) $- (\exists x)((Fx \ \& \ Gx) \ \& \ (\forall y)(Fy \rightarrow x = y))$.

In this, the negation operator has wide scope with respect to the definite description. This shows that (35), and not (34) is the negation of (20). Now (35) is actually *true*, since it is the result of negating $(\exists x)((Fx \ \& \ Gx) \ \& \ (\forall y)(Fy \rightarrow x = y))$, which on Russell's analysis is false. So, the negation of (20) is true, and there is no problem for the law of excluded middle.[49] As Russell puts it "we escape the conclusion that the King of France has a wig".[50]

2.9 Russell's attack on sense

In addition to making criticisms of detail about Frege's assignments of semantic value, Russell also criticized Frege's introduction of the notion of sense. There are two main criticisms of the notion of sense. The first is that the distinction between sense and semantic value is actually *incoherent*: Russell describes Frege's attempt at drawing the distinction as leading to an "inextricable tangle" and writes that "the whole distinction of [sense] and [reference] has been wrongly conceived".[51] Russell provides the argument that the notion of sense is incoherent on pp. 48–51 of "On Denoting". But we shall not consider this argument here: it is truly one of the most mysterious passages in twentieth-century philosophy. Instead we shall concentrate on Russell's second main line of criticism of the notion of sense. This does not involve the claim that the notion of sense is incoherent: rather, Russell tries to show that the invocation of the notion of sense is simply *superfluous*. Frege introduced the notion of sense in an attempt to solve a number of puzzles. Russell argues that these puzzles can be solved in a way that does not involve any appeal to the notion of sense, so that Frege's rationale for introducing the notion is simply undercut.

Recall that Frege's introduction of sense was motivated by the desire to solve three main problems: the problem of bearerless names, the problem of substitution into belief contexts and the problem of informativeness. We have already seen how Russell attempted to solve the first of these: empty definite descriptions and ordinary names still have a semantic value because they are not actually genuine proper names, but rather have second-level functions as their semantic values. We now look at how Russell deals with the other two problems.

Recall that the problem of substitution into belief contexts was a problem because it threatened thesis 3: substituting a constituent of a sentence with another that has the same semantic value will leave the truth-value of the sentence unchanged. Consider

(36) Smith believes that the composer of *Fidelio* had cirrhosis of the liver.

Now suppose that Smith doesn't realize that the composer of Fidelio is in fact the same person as the composer of the Moonlight Sonata. That is, Smith doesn't know that

(37) The composer of *Fidelio* is the composer of the Moonlight Sonata.

Suppose that "The composer of *Fidelio*" and "The composer of the Moonlight Sonata" are proper names. Then, they have the same semantic value, since they pick out the same person, Beethoven. So we should be able to substitute "The composer of the Moonlight Sonata" for "The composer of *Fidelio*" in (36) without changing (29)'s truth-value. But in fact the substitution results in the false

(38) Smith believes that the composer of the Moonlight Sonata had cirrhosis of the liver.

So it looks as if we have a counterexample to thesis 3.

Russell wants to hold on to thesis 3, so he tries to explain away the apparent counterexample. In order to show how he attempted to do so, it will be best to first restate the problem in slightly more formal terms. On the assumption that definite descriptions are genuine proper names, we can (partially) translate (36) into logical symbolism as follows, where "a" translates "the composer of *Fidelio*" and "F" translates the predicate "... has cirrhosis of the liver":

(39) Smith believes that Fa.

Taking "b" to abbreviate "the composer of the Moonlight Sonata", (37) gets translated as

(40) $a = b$.

And (38) gets translated as

(41) Smith believes that Fb.

The counterexample is now clear: we substitute into the true (39) on the basis of the true (40) and get the false (41) as a result.

Russell's response to the problem is basically this: (39), (40), and (41) misrepresent the logical form of (36), (37), and (38), and when we see their true logical form, we'll see that there is simply no scope for the sort of substitution that takes us from (39) and (40) to (41). For Russell, "the composer of *Fidelio*" is not a proper name. Rather, it gets treated in the same way as "the King of France", so that the logical form of (36) is more accurately captured by

(42) Smith believes that $(\exists x)((Gx \,\&\, Fx) \,\&\, (\forall y)(Gy \rightarrow x = y))$,

where "G" stands for the predicate "... is a composer of *Fidelio*". The logical form of (37) is given by

(43) $(\exists x)(Gx \,\&\, Hx \,\&\, (\forall y)(Gy \rightarrow x = y) \,\&\, (\forall z)(Hz \rightarrow x = z))$,

where "H" abbreviates the predicate "... is a composer of the Moonlight Sonata".

Now whereas (40) allowed us to substitute into the true (39) to obtain the false (41), (43) simply does not allow us to substitute into (42): (42) and (43) are simply not of the right logical form to allow a substitution, so *a fortiori*, there is no possibility of a substitution that takes us from a true sentence to a falsehood. Alternatively, the logical form of (38) is given by

(44) Smith believes that $(\exists x)((Hx \,\&\, Fx) \,\&\, (\forall y)(Hy \rightarrow x = y))$.

This is false, but it cannot be reached by substituting into (42) on the basis of (43). Thesis 3 is safe. Note that since Russell views natural (i.e. ordinary) names as disguised definite descriptions, he can apply this solution of the problem to cases that involve natural names rather than explicit definite descriptions. This allows him to solve the problem as presented in section 2.1.[52]

Russell is thus able to solve the problem of substitution into belief contexts without invoking the notion of sense. But what about the problem of informativeness? Recall from section 2.1 that Frege argued for the introduction of sense on the basis of a *reductio* argument: if the only semantic property that could be ascribed to expressions was possessing a semantic value, then it would not be possible to understand a sentence and yet fail to know its truth-value. Now, a crucial step in the *reductio*, as presented in section 2.1, was premise (e): the semantic value of "The Morning Star" is the same as that of "The Evening Star", namely, the planet Venus. Russell will reply that this presupposes that "The Evening Star" and "The Morning Star" are proper names, expressions that have the objects they stand for as their semantic values. But this is false. Natural names are disguised definite descriptions, and have second-level functions, rather than the objects they pick out, as their semantic values. The fact that "The Evening Star" and "The Morning Star" both pick out the same object thus does not entail that they have the same semantic value, and Frege's argument is blocked: the assumption that the only semantic property of an expression is its possession of a semantic value does not imply that one can never understand a sentence without knowing its truth-value.

How plausible are Russell's solutions to these problems? The solution to the problem of substitution into belief contexts is supposed to save the following thesis:

THESIS 3. *Substitution of a constituent of a sentence with another that has the same semantic value will leave the semantic value (i.e. truth-value) of the sentence unchanged.*

In the case where the constituents are proper names, this amounts to: substituting one name in a sentence with another that picks out the same object should leave the truth-value of the sentence unchanged. Now Russell is quite right to say that if his theory of descriptions is accepted, the examples we considered do not constitute counterexamples to this version of thesis 3. Since the expressions which are substituted are not proper names, this version of thesis 3 simply fails to have any application. But, of course, the version involving names is just one version of thesis 3. Since expressions other than names are also taken to have semantic values, there will be other versions of thesis 3. In particular, where the expressions concerned are definite descriptions, which on Russell's theory have second-level functions as their semantic values, thesis 3 will amount to: substituting one definite description in a sentence with another that has the same second-level function as its semantic value should leave the truth-value of the sentence unchanged. Now does Russell's solution to the problem preserve this version of thesis 3? It does not, given the assumption that functions have extensional identity conditions (thesis 6). Consider the second-level function that is the semantic value of "the composer of *Fidelio*", denoted by

(45) $(\exists x)((Gx \& \ldots x) \& (\forall y)(Gy \to x = y))$.

What is the extension of this function? This is a second-level function, a function from concepts (first-level functions) to truth-values, so we can represent its extension as a set of ordered pairs of concepts and truth-values. Consider a few predicates: "*J*" for "... was an uncle of Karl Beethoven", "*K*" for "... enjoyed drinking wine", "*L*" for "... went deaf", "*M*" for "... was English". Then we can represent the extension of the function (45) as:

(46) $\{(J, \text{T}), (K, \text{T}), (L, \text{T}), (M, \text{F}),\ldots\}$.

Consider the function that is the semantic value of "the composer of the Moonlight Sonata", denoted by

(47) $(\exists x)((Hx \& \ldots x) \& (\forall y)(Hy \to x = y))$.

What is the extension of this second-level function? It can be represented as

(48) $\{(J, \text{T}), (K, \text{T}), (L, \text{T}), (M, \text{F}), \ldots\}$.

This is identical to (46), and the problem for Russell is now apparent. "The composer of *Fidelio*" and "The composer of the Moonlight Sonata" have the functions denoted by (45) and (47) as their respective semantic values. But these have the same extension, so given that functions have extensional identity conditions, "The composer of *Fidelio*" and "The composer of the Moonlight Sonata" have the same semantic value. Now go back to the sentence that led to the apparent counterexample to thesis 3:

(36) Smith believes that the composer of *Fidelio* had cirrhosis of the liver.

71

Since, *even given Russell's theory of definite descriptions*, "the composer of *Fidelio*" has the same semantic value as "the composer of the Moonlight Sonata", the following should be true given that (36) is

(38) Smith believes that the composer of the Moonlight Sonata had cirrhosis of the liver

But (38) is false. So the counterexample to thesis 3 still remains.

Note that these reflections also threaten Russell's solution to the problem of informativeness. Given that "The Morning Star" and "The Evening Star" are to be treated as disguised definite descriptions, a line of argument similar to that just given above will show that they have the same second-level functions as their semantic values. Russell's attempt to block Frege's *reductio* argument will thus fail.

Is there any way Russell can respond to these objections? I leave this question as an exercise for the reader. But if no response can be made on behalf of Russell the conclusion will be that he fails in his attempts to solve the problem of substitution into belief contexts and the problem of informativeness without invoking the notion of sense, and that accordingly some notion of sense is after all required.[53]

2.10 Russell on communication

Recall from section 2.3 that Frege invoked the notion of sense in an attempt to explain linguistic communication. Communication, or the "transmission of thought", is to be explained in virtue of the common senses speakers attach to their words. We saw in section 2.3 that Frege's attempt to use the notion of sense in an account of communication was not entirely successful, but left this worry on one side for the moment. Does Russell fare any better? That is to say, can Russell give an account of communication in a manner that does not involve the invocation of a notion of sense?

Suppose that Smith says to Jones: "Bismarck was an astute diplomat". According to Frege, a condition on Smith's successfully communicating by means of this utterance is that Smith and Jones both attach the same sense to the name "Bismarck". Russell, however, wishes to reject the idea that natural names like "Bismarck" even have a sense. So what account can he give of the conditions on successful linguistic communication? This question is all the more pressing for Russell given his view that natural names are really disguised definite descriptions and his explicit admission that different definite descriptions may be abbreviated by the same natural name for different people:

> Common words, even proper names, are usually really descriptions. That is to say, the thought in the mind of a person using a proper name correctly can generally only be expressed explicitly if we replace the proper name by a description. Moreover, the description required to express the thought will vary for different people, or for the same person at different times.[54]

So suppose that for Smith, the name "Bismarck" is an abbreviation of the description "the first Chancellor of Germany", and for Jones an abbreviation of the description "the most powerful man in Europe". Doesn't it follow from this that Smith's saying "Bismarck was an astute diplomat" to Jones will not result in a successful episode of communication? Russell suggests not: the fact that Smith and Jones abbreviate different descriptions by the name "Bismarck" need not frustrate their attempt at communication. Mark Sainsbury suggests that the key sentence in making sense of Russell's suggestion here is the following: "The only thing constant (so long as the name is rightly used) is the object to which the name applies."[55] Sainsbury fleshes this out as follows:

> Suppose I utter the words "Bismarck was an astute diplomat". As I use the name "Bismarck", the thought in my mind may be best described as that *the first Chancellor of Germany* is an astute diplomat. However, I realize that you may associate the name with a different description, perhaps "the most powerful man in Europe". So when I utter my sentence, I am not trying to get you to share my thought; rather, I am trying to get you to have a thought, concerning Bismarck (however you think of him), that he is an astute diplomat. My intentions would be

satisfied if you realized that I had tried to say, of the most powerful man in Europe, that he was an astute diplomat.[56]

Also

> It is not necessary that [Smith] and [Jones] should share a thought. All that is required is that the possibly various descriptions they associate with the name "Bismarck" should stand for the same thing; for this is what it means to say that the name "Bismarck" has a (public) reference in the language community to which [Smith] and [Jones] belong.[57]

Is this condition – that the different conditions they associate with the name "Bismarck" should stand for the same thing – really necessary for communicative success? It seems to me that it is not. Suppose that for Jones the name "Bismarck" is an abbreviation of the description "the composer of *Lohengrin*". That is to say, suppose that Jones believes that Bismarck is the composer of *Lohengrin*. Of course, Bismarck does not actually satisfy the description "the composer of *Lohengrin*". But nevertheless, on hearing Smith's utterance of the sentence "Bismarck is an astute diplomat", Jones will have a thought, concerning Bismarck, that he is an astute diplomat. So Smith will still have successfully communicated with Jones, even though the descriptions Smith and Jones associate with "Bismarck" do not stand for the same thing: one of them stands for Bismarck, while the other stands for Wagner. The condition that Sainsbury suggests is necessary is not actually so. What this suggests is that what is important in communication is not which object satisfies the relevant description, but rather what the speakers concerned *take* the descriptions to be, or the way in which the objects concerned are *presented* to the speakers. This takes us back to Frege and the requirement that the speakers associate the same senses with the relevant expressions. Of course, Frege himself faces worries about the role of sense in communication, as we saw in section 2.4. But the conclusion of the present section is that Russell's attempt to account for communication without invoking the notion of sense fares no better.[58]

Overall then, Russell runs into serious problems in his attempts to solve the problems of informativeness and substitution into belief contexts, and in his attempt to account for communication without invoking the notion of sense. What this suggests is that some notion of sense is required, even if not that invoked by Frege. But we must now leave Frege and Russell. In the next chapter we move on to look at a school of philosophers whose imposition of constraints on what can and cannot possess sense provided the central plank of their philosophical outlook, and who provide an essential backdrop for understanding the philosophy of language of the second half of the twentieth century: the logical positivists.[59]

2.11 Appendix: Frege's theses on sense and semantic value

THESIS 1. *The semantic value of a sentence is its truth-value (true or false).*

THESIS 2. *The semantic value of a complex expression is determined by the semantic values of its parts* (Compositionality of semantic value).

THESIS 3. *Substitution of a constituent of a sentence with another that has the same semantic value will leave the semantic value (i.e. truth-value) of the sentence unchanged* (Leibniz's Law).

THESIS 4. *The semantic value of a proper name is the object that it refers to or stands for.*

THESIS 5. *The semantic value of a predicate is a function.*

THESIS 6. *Functions are extensional: if function f and function g have the same extension, then* f = g.

THESIS 7. *The semantic value of a predicate is a first-level function from objects to truth-values; the semantic value of a sentential connective is a first-level function from truth-values to truth-values; the semantic value of a quantifier is a second-level function from concepts (first-level functions) to truth-values.*

THESIS 8. *The sense of an expression is that ingredient of its meaning that determines its semantic value.*

THESIS 9. *It is possible to know the sense of an expression without knowing its semantic value.*

THESIS 10. *The sense of an expression is what someone who understands the expression grasps.*

THESIS 11. *The sense of a complex expression is determined by the senses of its constituents* (<u>Compositionality of sense</u>).

THESIS 12. *If someone grasps the senses of two expressions, and the two expressions actually have the same sense, then she must know that the two expressions have the same sense* (<u>Transparency of sense</u>).

THESIS 13. *An expression can have a sense even if it lacks a semantic value.*

THESIS 14. *A sentence that contains an expression that lacks a semantic value is neither true nor false.*

THESIS 15. *In a belief context, the (indirect) reference of a proper name is its customary sense.*

THESIS 16. *Substitution of one expression in a sentence with another that has the same sense will leave the sense of the sentence unchanged.*

THESIS 17. *The sense of a sentence is a thought* (its truth-condition).

THESIS 18. *The semantic value of an expression is no part of what someone who understands the expression grasps.*

THESIS 19. *Sense is objective: grasping a sense is not a matter of having ideas, mental images, or private psychological items.*

THESIS 20. *The sense of an expression is normative: it constitutes a normative constraint that determines which uses of that expression are correct and which are incorrect.*

THESIS 21. *In addition to sense and semantic value, we must also introduce the notions of* force *and* tone.

Further reading

The student should begin by looking at the following four essays by Frege: "Function and concept" (first 13 pages), "On concept and object", "On sense and meaning" (first 10 pages), "The thought: a logical enquiry". The first three of these can be found in P. Geach and M. Black (eds) *Translations from the philosophical works of Gottlob Frege*. The last can be found in P. F. Strawson (ed.) *Philosophical logic*. After that, it would be advisable to look at some of the recent introductory textbooks, for example, A. Kenny, *Frege*; H. Noonan, *Frege*. After those, it might be useful to look at G. McCulloch *The game of the name* (especially Chs 1 and 5).

McCulloch's *The mind and its world* also contains much useful material on Frege, and is especially good on the relationship between themes in Frege's philosophy of language and current issues in philosophy of mind. Chapter III is devoted to Frege, but this book is probably best read in its entirety. The doyen of Frege scholarship is Michael Dummett. His books *Frege: philosophy of language* and *The interpretation of Frege's philosophy* are classics, and set the scene for all subsequent discussion of Frege. But they are very long and, in places, very demanding. A crash course in Dummett's Frege might consist of the Introduction, and Chapters 1, 5, 6 and 19 of *Frege: philosophy of language*, though Dummett's books require and deserve close and careful study. An alternative interpretation of Frege's views on sense – one that interprets Frege as denying thesis 13 – can be found in G. Evans, *The varieties of reference*. See also J. McDowell, "On the sense and reference of a proper name", *Mind* (1977), and the two books by McCulloch mentioned above. A spirited defence of a Lockean view of sense can be found in Chapter 7 of E. J. Lowe, *Locke on human understanding*. For a critical reply, see A. Miller, Review Article on Lowe, *The Locke Newsletter* (1995). Kripke's objections are set out in his *Naming and necessity,* one of the most important books in recent analytic philosophy. A useful discussion can be found in Chapter 4 of McCulloch's *The game of the name*. Dummett defends Frege against Kripke's objections in the appendix to Chapter 5 of *Frege: philosophy of language*. For an introduction to philosophical issues surrounding the notions of necessity and contingency, see J. Divers, *Possible worlds*.

For Russell's theory of descriptions, the relevant papers are "On denoting" and "Descriptions and incomplete symbols" (Ch.VI of "The philosophy of logical atomism"). Both of these are reprinted in R. Marsh (ed.) *Logic and knowledge*. Other relevant works are "Descriptions" (Ch. 16 of Russell's *Introduction to mathematical philosophy*), and "Knowledge by acquaintance and knowledge by description" (Ch. 5 of Russell's *The problems of philosophy*). There is a good discussion of Russell's theory, and a very useful account of how it relates to his more general epistemological doctrines, in Chapters 2 and 3 of McCulloch's *The game of the name*. Sainsbury's account of Russell on communication can be found in the section on Russell in his "Philosophical logic", in A. Grayling (ed.),

Philosophy: a guide through the subject. See also Sainsbury's entry on "Frege and Russell" in *The Blackwell companion to philosophy.* There are important discussions of Russell, which we have not been able to consider here, in P. F. Strawson's "On referring", *Mind* (1950), and K. Donnellan's "Reference and definite descriptions", *Philosophical Review* (1966). See also Chapter 9, "Reference", of S. Blackburn's *Spreading the word.*

Chapter 3

Sense and verificationism: logical positivism

3.1 Introduction

In Chapters 1 and 2 we looked at some aspects of Frege's attempt to systematize our intuitive notion of meaning. In this chapter we will look at another attempt: that carried out by the *logical positivists*. Logical positivism was a school of philosophy, centred in Vienna, that grew up in the 1920s and 1930s, and which was institutionalized in the "Vienna Circle". The leading figure in the Circle was Moritz Schlick, and it counted amongst its supporters such philosophers as Neurath, Waissman, Feigl, Gödel, Ayer, Carnap and Hahn. The main philosophical influences on the Circle stemmed from Hume, Berkeley, Frege, Russell and the Wittgenstein of the *Tractatus*. The theory of meaning was central to the Circle's concerns: the motivation was the thought that clarity about the concept of meaning would help in getting clear on the proper scope and extent of philosophical enquiry itself. This would then help remedy the fact that philosophy, unlike science, appeared to make little or no progress either in the prosecution of its central concerns, or on the question as to how those concerns are properly to be conceived. What is required, they thought, was an account of what constitutes *meaningfulness*: and the logical positivists attempted to give such an account via the provision of a *criterion of significance*. Such a criterion would give a systematic account of what counts, and what does not count, as literally meaningful or significant, or, alternatively, as possessing sense: if a sentence satisfies the criterion it counts as possessing sense, whereas if it fails to satisfy the criterion it counts as literally meaningless. The provision of such a criterion would greatly aid the progress of philosophy by ensuring that philosophers do not get embroiled in literally meaningless metaphysical speculation: if the criterion of significance entails that sentences apparently about God, the nature of moral and aesthetic facts, or about a reality that transcends the world of experience, are, appearances to the contrary, actually senseless, then we will have a clear explanation of why the metaphysical speculation about the *truth* of those sentences is utterly fruitless. If a sentence is literally meaningless, it cannot be true (or false), so speculation about its truth-value is simply misguided. As Ayer and Hahn put it

> The originality of the logical positivists lay in their making the impossibility of metaphysics depend not upon the nature of what could be known but upon the nature of what could be said. Their charge against the metaphysician was that he breaks the rules which any utterance must satisfy if it is to be literally significant.[1]

> There is no possibility of piercing through the sensible world disclosed by observation to a "world of true being": any metaphysics is impossible! Impossible, not because the task is too difficult for our human thinking, but because it is meaningless, because every attempt to do metaphysics is an attempt to speak in a way that contravenes the agreement as to how we wish to speak, comparable to the attempt to capture the queen (in a game of chess) by means of an orthogonal move of the bishop.[2]

According to the criterion suggested by the logical positivists, there are only two ways in which a sentence can be literally significant: by expressing an *a posteriori thought*, a thought which is empirically verifiable, or by expressing an *a priori* thought, a thought which is true purely in virtue of facts about meaning (sense). The first type of statement is dealt with by the positivists' *verification principle*, which attempts to spell out in detail what conditions a statement has to satisfy in order to qualify as literally meaningful or sensible in virtue of being susceptible to empirical verification.[3] The second type of statement is dealt with by the positivists' account of *a priori* truth: *a priori* truths are *analytic*, in the sense that they are true purely in virtue of meaning (sense). In sections 3.2 and 3.3 we look at A. J. Ayer's attempt to spell out the verification principle in *Language, Truth, and Logic*, his classic popularization of the logical positivist doctrine; and in section 3.4 we investigate the positivist account of the *a priori*, via a discussion of Chapter IV of that work, and see how Ayer attempts to find a place for philosophy itself as an *a priori* activity. The dichotomy between statements that are meaningful in virtue of being empirically verifiable, and statements that are true purely in virtue of meaning, receives further development in Rudolf Carnap's famous distinction between *internal and external questions*: that distinction is the subject of section 3.5. In section 3.6 we briefly consider the impact of the logical positivist theory of meaning on ethical language. Finally, in section 3.7 we look at some further aspects of Ayer's views on empirically verifiable statements: this sets the scene for Quine's assault on the logical positivist's theory of meaning, which is the subject of our next chapter.

3.2 The formulation of the verification principle

The verification principle can be summed up in Schlick's famous slogan, "The meaning of a statement consists in its method of verification." Statements that qualify as literally meaningful in virtue of being associated with a method of empirical verification are deemed to possess *factual meaning*: statements can thus be literally meaningful without possessing factual meaning if they are *a priori* and analytic (tautologies, in the terminology favoured by Ayer). This latter type of statement will be dealt with in section

3.4: our concern in this section is with statements that are literally meaningful in virtue of possessing factual meaning, in virtue of trading in matters of fact.

Ayer first introduces the criterion of factual significance in the following passage:

> The criterion which we use to test the genuineness of apparent statements of fact is the criterion of verifiability. We say that a sentence is factually significant to any given person if, and only if, he knows how to verify the proposition which it purports to express – that is, if he knows what observations would lead him, under certain conditions, to accept the proposition as being true, or reject it as being false. If, on the other hand, the putative proposition is of such a character that the assumption of its truth or falsehood, is consistent with any assumption whatsoever concerning the nature of his future experience, then, as far as he is concerned, it is, if not a tautology, a mere pseudo-proposition.[4]

Interestingly enough, almost immediately after this passage, Ayer goes on to suggest that in addition to its application to putative propositions, the verification principle can also be applied to putative questions:

> And with regard to questions, the procedure is the same. We enquire in every case what observations would lead us to answer the question, one way or the other; and, if none can be discovered, we must conclude that the sentence under consideration does not, as far as we are concerned, express a genuine question, however strongly its grammatical appearance may suggest that it does.[5]

This is interesting because it shows that Ayer's intention, in formulating the verification principle, is not just to provide a criterion for drawing a distinction within the class of *declarative* sentences, between those which possess factual meaning, with genuine factual content, apt to be true or false, and those which, grammatical appearances to the contrary, possess no such content. The verification principle can also be applied within the class of *interrogative* sentences, to distinguish those interrogatives that express genuine questions, from those which merely appear to do so. And there seems to be every reason to expect that the application of the principle can be further widened to include, for example, *imperatival* sentences, expressions of *intention*, expressions of *desire*. With respect to imperativals, the principle would distinguish between those sentences that have the grammatical appearance of commands, and that express genuine commands, and those with the same grammatical appearances that do not: a sentence in the imperatival mood would express a genuine command if there are a series of observable actions that, when carried out, would constitute obeying the command. Likewise for expressions of intention: a sentence with all the grammatical appearances of an expression of intention would express a genuine intention only if there are a series of observable actions that, when carried out, would constitute the implementation of the intention. And similarly for expressions of desire: a putative expression of desire would only count as a genuine expression of desire if there were some observable events whose occurrence constitutes satisfaction of the desire.[6] This suggests that Ayer's application of the verification principle is perhaps much wider than has been generally appreciated: the principle is intended not only to distinguish between sentences that have factual content and those that do not, but also to draw a distinction in point of genuineness within classes of sentences that are admitted to have no fact-stating function to begin with. The point of the verification principle is not so much to distinguish between sentences that possess literal significance and sentences that do not; rather it is to distinguish between sentences that possess *some sort of significance* (be it literal significance, imperatival significance, conative significance, and so on) and sentences that possess *no* sort of significance whatsoever.[7] We will return to this issue in section 3.6.

Having made the more general import of the verification principle clear, though, we shall concentrate on declarative sentences, and on what the principle has to tell us about their possession of factual significance. After the passages quoted above, Ayer proceeds to draw two distinctions: between *practical* verifiability and verifiability *in principle*, and between what he terms

the "strong" and "weak" senses of verifiability. In short, a statement is practically verifiable for me if I possess the practical means
of placing myself in a situation in which I would make observations
sufficient for verifying that statement; a statement is verifiable in
principle, if, though I do not possess the practical means of placing
myself in such a situation, I can nevertheless theoretically conceive
of what sort of position I would need to be in, and what observations I would need to make, in order to verify the statement. Thus,
the statement "I have five pennies in my pocket" is verifiable in
practice, whereas "There are horses on *Alpha Centauri*" is merely
verifiable in principle. A statement is *strongly* verifiable if its truth
could be *conclusively* established in experience, while a statement
is said to be *weakly* verifiable if it is possible for experience to
render its truth *probable*. Ayer in each case chooses the more
liberal of the two notions – i.e. verifiability in principle, and weak
verifiability – in spelling out what is involved in the verification
principle. We require only verifiability in principle, in order to
conserve the factual meaning of statements like "There are horses
on *Alpha Centauri*"; and we require only weak verifiability, in
order to avoid ruling out scientific generalizations, such as "A body
tends to expand when heated."

Given this, the question we must ask, in order to determine
whether a given indicative sentence possesses genuine factual
meaning is not: "Would any possible observations make its truth or
falsehood logically certain?" but rather: "Would any possible observations be relevant to the determination of its truth or falsehood?"
But what does it mean to say that a statement is such that there
are possible observations that are relevant to determining whether
it is true or false, or that there are observations that would count
as evidence for it? Ayer attempts to spell this out as follows:

> Let us call a proposition which records an actual or possible
> observation an experiential proposition. Then we may say that
> it is the mark of a genuine factual proposition, not that it should
> be equivalent to an experiential proposition, or any finite
> number of experiential propositions, but simply that some
> experiential propositions can be deduced from it in conjunction
> with certain other premises without being deducible from those
> other premises alone.[8]

This implies that statements about practically inaccessible parts of space and time and scientific generalizations and statements of law do have genuine factual content, as we would hope and expect. But it also implies, given the assumption that they are not analytic, that statements like "the world of sense-experience is unreal" are devoid of factual meaning: "no conceivable observation ... could have any tendency to show that the world revealed to us by sense-experience was unreal".[9] And it implies, when generalized, that a question like "Is reality ultimately composed of one substance or many?" (the traditional dispute in metaphysics between monism and pluralism) is not a genuine question: no possible observation could provide an adequate basis for answering it one way rather than the other.[10]

However, as Ayer admits in the long Introduction to the second edition of *Language, Truth, and Logic*, this formulation of the verification principle fails. Take some experiential proposition (or "observation statement", in his new terminology) "O", and any "nonsensical" statement "N". Then, since the observation statement "O" can be deduced from "N", together with "if N then O", but not from "if N then O" on its own, "N" counts as factually meaningful according to this formulation of the verification principle. Thus, if we take "N" to be "the Nothing nothings" and "O" to be "that pillar box is red", we can establish that "the Nothing nothings" is factually significant. This shows that Ayer's initial formulation of the verification principle implies that any indicative statement whatsoever possesses factual significance: in other words, that it lays down no constraints whatsoever on the ascription of factual meaning.

In response to this problem, Ayer, in the Introduction to the second edition, suggests a more sophisticated version of the principle of verification. He does this by defining verifiability in a recursive fashion: he begins with the notion of an observation statement, defines a notion of *direct verifiability* in terms of it, and then proceeds to define a notion of *indirect verifiability* in terms of direct verifiability. The verification principle is then reformulated as follows: in order for a statement to possess factual meaning, it has to be either directly or indirectly verifiable.

So how are direct and indirect verifiability defined? Ayer defines *direct verifiability* as follows: "a statement is directly verifiable if it is either itself an observation statement, or is such that in conjunction with one or more observation statements it entails at least one observation statement which is not deducible from these further premises alone".[11] Note that "N", in the counterexample raised above against the initial formulation of the principle, does not qualify as directly verifiable: it is not an observation statement, and the fact that it entails "O" when conjoined with "if N then O" does not qualify it as directly verifiable, since "if N then O" is not an observation statement, as required by the definition of direct verifiability. *Indirect verifiability* is defined as follows: "a statement is indirectly verifiable if it satisfies the following conditions: first, that in conjunction with certain other premises it entails one or more directly verifiable statements which are not deducible from these other premises alone; and secondly, that these other premises do not include any statement that is not either analytic, or directly verifiable, or capable of being independently established as indirectly verifiable".[12] On the face of it, it looks as if "N" in the original counterexample fails to qualify as indirectly verifiable too, so that it is not after all certified as factually significant by the verification principle.

Unfortunately, however, even this new and more sophisticated formulation of the verification principle turned out to be susceptible to counterexamples. Alonzo Church constructed an example to show that like the original formulation in the first edition of *Language, Truth, and Logic*, the revised formulation too admits any nonanalytic statement (and hence any arbitrary "nonsensical" statement) as factually significant.[13]

Take S = (not-$O1$ and $O2$) or (not-N and $O3$), where $O1$, $O2$, and $O3$ can be any trio of observation statements that are all logically independent of one another, and N is the "nonsensical" statement of your choice (e.g. "the Nothing nothings"). Then S qualifies as directly verifiable on Ayer's definition. To see this, note that in conjunction with $O1$, S entails $O3$ (this can be demonstrated quite easily, using elementary logic of the sort taught in first-year university courses, so this is left as an exercise for the reader). Thus S entails an observation statement ($O3$) when some other statements ($O1$) are assumed. But, by hypothesis, $O1$ is logically independent of $O3$, and so does not entail it. So S entails an observation statement ($O3$) in conjunction with some other observation statements (*O*1), though that observation statement (*O*3) does not follow from those other observation statements (*O*1) alone. *S* is thus directly verifiable.

Given that *S* is directly verifiable, it is now easy to establish that our "nonsensical" *N* is indirectly verifiable. Note that *N*, when conjoined with *S*, entails *O*2 (again, this is simple to prove, and is left as an exercise). *O*2 is an observation statement, and thus qualifies as directly verifiable. Thus, *N* entails a directly verifiable statement (*O*2) when conjoined with *S*, though *O*2 does not follow from *S* on its own. (To see why *O*2 does not follow from *S* on its own, note that there is a possible assignment of truth values to the constituents of *S* on which *S* comes out true even when *O*2 is false: take *N* false, *O*3 true, *O*1 true and *O*2 false.) *N* thus counts as indirectly verifiable on Ayer's definition, and hence as factually significant even on the revised version of the verification principle. Once again, it seems that the verification principle places no real constraints on the ascription of factual meaning.

Of course, the defender of the verification principle may now attempt to further modify the principle so that it excludes the offending counterexample, and the literature on the topic is replete with attempts at such modifications. But we shall not here enter further into questions about the precise formulation of the verification principle: details of the relevant literature are contained in the guide to further reading at the end of this chapter. Rather, we shall consider a more general question about the nature of the principle.

3.3 Foster on the nature of the verification principle[14]

John Foster has discerned two distinct versions of the principle of verification in *Language, Truth, and Logic*: the *evidence-principle* and the *content-principle*, respectively. The evidence-principle corresponds to Ayer's first-edition formulation, which attempted to demarcate the class of factually significant statements as those on which observational evidence could bear: the factually significant statements are those for which there are possible observations that would be relevant to the determination of the statements' truth or falsehood. We saw above that the evidence-principle, as formulated by Ayer in the first edition of *Language, Truth, and Logic*, allowed any statement to count as factually significant. But as Foster points out, one way in which Ayer could deal with this problem would be to return to the original formulation and then "try to impose on the notion of evidence-for-or-against whatever restrictions are needed for a suitable criterion of significance".[15] Ayer could thus attempt to provide a modified version of the evidence-principle. But, as we saw in the previous section, this is not in fact how Ayer proceeds in the Introduction to the second edition. Ayer there attempts to formulate a version of what Foster terms the *content-principle*, according to which "the factual significance of a statement lies in its observational content – that is, in its contribution to the deduction of observation-statements"[16] and "a statement has factual significance if and only if its content is purely observational, that is, if and only if the statement falls within the scope of an observational language".[17] The content-principle thus encapsulates a stronger form of verificationism than the evidence-principle. This can be seen by considering scientific hypotheses which postulate the existence of objects that are not directly observable (e.g. electrons and protons). As Foster puts it:

> "Realistically" construed, these hypotheses do not fall within the scope of an observational language, but they are still held to be subject to observational tests, according to how well or badly they explain our observational data. So under the content-principle they count as nonsensical, but under the evidence-principle they qualify as factually significant – at least they do so unless, on the lines of the radical sceptic, we reject the epistemological methods of science altogether. And quite generally, we can see that given ordinary (non-sceptical) standards of what counts as evidence, the content-principle yields a much more stringent criterion of factual significance than its rival.[18]

The content-principle actually endangers the factual significance of many everyday statements about physical objects, other minds, and so on, which we (and Ayer) would intuitively expect to be factually significant. For to count as factually significant by the lights of the content principle, such statements as *The table is square* or *Jones has toothache* will have to be shown to be translatable into statements that do have explicitly observational content. And such attempts at reductive analysis have been singularly unsuccessful, with the failure of Ayer's phenomenalistic reductionism being a case in point:

> Any attempt to translate statements about the physical world into statements about sense-contents, or statements about other minds into statements about behaviour, seems to involve a radical distortion of what the original statements mean.[19]

Given that the content-principle requires the tenability of unpromising reductionism about many of our *prima facie* factually significant statements, wouldn't it be more advisable, in attempting to reformulate the verification principle so as to avoid the various counterexamples, to go back to the more liberal evidence-principle and base the attempted reformulation on it? Foster argues, however, that this more promising line of development is closed off to Ayer: "... if there are any grounds for accepting the verification principle, they are grounds for accepting it in its content-restricting form. The less stringent evidence-principle may give more plausible results, but, by its very liberality, it becomes devoid of rationale."[20] If Foster is right in this claim, it is bad news indeed for anyone sympathetic to the logical positivist project, but sceptical about the possibility of plausible reductive analyses of our everyday talk about physical objects and other minds. But as we shall now see, the argument Foster relies on to derive the conclusion that the verification-principle must be formulated in the strong content-restricting manner is far from conclusive.

Foster argues as follows. First of all, "let us suppose that contrary to the content-principle, we take physical statements to be factually significant and construe them, 'realistically', as irreducibly about some mind-independent reality".[21] Although this view of the semantics of physical statements is contrary to the content-principle, it is allowed by the evidence-principle: even though physical objects are not directly observable, "physical statements are open to observational evidence through their explanatory role with respect to sense-experience". That is to say, certain physical statements – concerning some mind-independent reality – may be verified by the fact that they provide the best explanation of the available experiential data. They are thus secured factual significance under the evidence-principle. But now comes the crunch, according to Foster: "... given our realistic construal of physical statements, we could hardly regard their openness to this kind of observational evidence as a prerequisite of their having the significance we attach to them". Why not? Well, imagine a *radical sceptic*, someone who denies that physical statements are open to observational evidence in the way described. Then, according to Foster,

> We would not see this as a challenge to our semantic position. We would not see it as something which, if we accepted it, would oblige us to abandon the claim that physical statements are both factually significant and concerned with a mind independent reality. Rather, we would see it as raising a separate and purely epistemological issue ... We may reject the scepticism; but both we and the sceptic would accept that the epistemological issue only arises because the significance of physical statements, construed realistically, is already secure.[22]

So, we would view the radical sceptic as raising a purely epistemological worry, and even in allowing that there *is* such an epistemological issue, we would be conceding the significance of the physical object statements: more precisely, we would be granting their significance *before* the question about their openness to observational evidence has been resolved. So, "Unless we accept the content-principle, there is no rationale for making openness to observational evidence a requirement of factual significance."[23] If we are going to accept a version of the verification principle, we thus have no option but to accept it in its more stringent – and hence far more unpromising – form as the content-principle.

How plausible is this argument of Foster's? There are at least two reasons for doubting whether it does actually establish that the verification-principle can only ever be formulated as the content-principle.

First of all, Foster faces the following dilemma. The "radical sceptic" can be construed as a sceptic who questions the bearing of *a certain piece (or set of pieces) of observational evidence* on the physical statements in question. When the sceptic is thus construed, Foster's claim that we would not treat this scepticism as even posing a threat to the factual significance of the statements in question seems plausible enough. But this sort of "radical sceptic" is not the sort of sceptic we should focus on in a discussion of the evidence-principle. What we require is a much more radical sceptic, a sceptic who goes further and questions whether *there is even any possible* observational evidence that could bear on the physical statement in question. Is it so obvious that we would not treat this sort of sceptical claim as posing a threat to the significance of the relevant physical statements? The verificationist intent on defending the evidence principle will likely – and quite rightly – see this as a completely unmotivated claim. In fact, it clearly amounts only to the bald assertion that the evidence-principle is false, and as such can hardly provide any independent reasons for thinking that that principle has no rationale.

Secondly, Foster's argument appears to make the following underlying assumption: you cannot raise an epistemological doubt about a statement P without already granting that P is meaningful. On the face of it, this may seem plausible enough. But when the truly radical nature of the scepticism involved is appreciated, it begins to look less plausible. One way of seeing this is to note that certain well-known forms of constitutive scepticism can be advanced by epistemological routes. We shall look at some such versions of constitutive scepticism in the next two chapters. In Chapter 5 we shall see that Kripke's Wittgenstein attempts to argue for constitutive scepticism about meaning ("that there is no such thing as meaning") via an epistemological route. Kripke's Wittgenstein questions whether there is any fact of the matter corresponding to claims about meaning, such as "I currently mean the addition function by the '+' sign", and does so in the following way. He first of all allows us idealized epistemological access to all of the facts about our qualitative mental lives, our behavioural histories and dispositions, and so on. He then claims that even when such idealized access is granted, we could never be in a position to justify any particular claims about what we mean. The conclusion he draws is that there is, contrary to our original intuitions, no such thing as a fact about what we mean. Now, this sceptical argument, and the resulting constitutive scepticism can indeed be criticized on a number of scores, as we shall shortly see. But the important point for our present purposes is that the mere fact that such an argumentative strategy is possible – constitutive scepticism advanced via an epistemological route – shows that Foster's assumption is wrong. When the scepticism in question is sufficiently radical, we can raise an epistemological doubt about a statement without conceding its meaningfulness because we can use the radical epistemological doubt as a *route* to the conclusion that the statement is not after all factually meaningful.[24]

The conclusion to be drawn from this is as follows. Ayer's original attempts at formulating the evidence-principle and content-principle both fail, because neither sets down any genuine constraints on the ascription of factual significance. There is thus a pressing need for a revised formulation of the verification principle. But in seeking such a revised formulation, we are not constrained, in the manner argued by Foster, to seek for a version of the stronger and more improbable content-principle. For all that Foster has shown, a revised version of the evidence-principle may indeed be the best bet for the defender of the verification principle. However, we cannot discuss the verification principle further at this point. In the next section we move on to look at the logical positivist's account of the other class of literally significant statements, the *a priori*.

3.4 The *a priori*

According to logical positivism, there are only two ways in which a statement can qualify as literally possessing sense: by possessing factual significance, in the sense of factual significance defined by the verification principle, or by being *analytic*. Ayer, in Chapter IV of *Language, Truth, and Logic*, defines the notions of analytic and synthetic as follows: "a proposition is analytic when its validity depends solely on the definitions of the symbols it contains, and synthetic when its validity is determined by the facts of experience".[25] This is repeated in the Introduction to the second edition: "... a proposition is analytic if it is true solely in virtue of the meaning of its constituent symbols".[26] The class of literally significant statements is thus exhausted by, on the one hand, the class of statements that in principle admit of empirical verification, and, on the other, the class of statements that are true (or false) purely in virtue of the meanings or senses of their constituent expressions.

What, then, of the putative truths of logic and mathematics? The logical positivists wish to secure literal significance for logical and mathematical statements, such as the law of non-contradiction, the law of excluded middle, and $2 + 2 = 4$. But the necessity of these statements prevents them from qualifying as literally significant in virtue of possessing factual significance:

> As Hume conclusively showed, no general proposition whose validity is subject to the test of actual experience can ever be logically certain. No matter how often it is verified in practice, there still remains the [logical] possibility that it will be confuted on some future occasion. The fact that a law has been substantiated in $n-1$ cases affords no *logical* guarantee that it will be substantiated in the nth case also, no matter how large we take n to be. And this means that no general proposition referring to a matter of fact can ever be shown to be necessarily and universally true. It can at best be a probable hypothesis.[27]

Or, as Hans Hahn put it slightly earlier:

> Observation discloses to me only the transient, it does not reach beyond the observed; there is no bond that would lead from one observed fact to another, that would compel future observations to have the same result as those already made ... Whatever I know by observation could be otherwise.[28]

Given this, there appear to be three choices available: (1) secure factual significance for the statements of logic and mathematics by denying that they are necessarily true; (2) argue that they are analytic; or (3) reject them as literally senseless, as failing to possess literal significance.

As noted above, Ayer has no wish to embrace option (3), and finds that option (1), the option pursued by Mill, "to be discrepant with relevant logical facts".[29] If we look at cases in which, for example, a mathematical truth such as $2 \times 5 = 10$ appears to be confuted by experience, we will find that giving up the relevant mathematical statement is never a genuine option. Suppose I look into the cupboard and observe five pairs of shoes. I then count the individual shoes and find that there are only nine in total. Ayer argues that there are no possible circumstances in which we would take this sort of episode as establishing the falsity of $2 \times 5 = 10$: we would perhaps say that my initial observation of five pairs of shoes was mistaken, that one of the shoes vaporized during the process of counting, that two of the shoes had coalesced into one, or that I had made a slip while counting. But "the one explanation which would in no circumstances be adopted is that ten is not always the product of two and five".[30]

Now we might well wish to question this argument of Ayer's. The relevant consideration is surely not what explanations we would or would not *in fact* invoke in the envisioned circumstances, but rather what explanations would be *rationally optional*. Ayer needs to argue not only that giving up the mathematical statement that $2 \times 5 = 10$ is something we would never opt for *in practice*, but that it is an option we can choose only on pain of irrationality. If mathematical statements are, as he claims, analytic, then this may indeed follow: in rejecting the statement we would be violating one of the conventions that governs our use of language, and in that sense, we would be violating a norm of rationality. But he cannot *assume* that mathematical statements are analytic at this stage without simply begging the question against Mill and the defenders of option (1). Be that as it may, Mill's view that the statements of logic and mathematics are *a posteriori* and contingent is widely rejected, so we will not discuss it any further here. Instead, we shall concentrate on assessing the plausibility of Ayer's defence of option (2), the claim that the statements of logic and mathematics are analytic.

Ayer's defence of the claim that mathematics and logic are analytic takes the following form. He argues that it enables us to explain the central – and historically problematic – features of both of those disciplines. The first feature has already been mentioned: the *necessity* of mathematics and logic. How can the claim that mathematics and logic cannot possibly be confuted in experience be squared with the widespread belief that we possess knowledge of mathematical and logic truths? Kant, in order to answer this question, claimed that in the case of geometry, for example, that "space is the form of intuition of our outer sense, a form imposed on us by the matter of sensation".[31] Likewise, in order to account for the necessity of arithmetic, Kant postulated that it was "concerned with our pure intuition of time, the form of our inner sense".[32] Ayer's thought is that we can explain the necessity of geometry, arithmetic and logic, without getting embroiled in the metaphysical and epistemological extravagances of Kant's transcendental idealism. The truths of mathematics are analytic in the sense that they "simply record our determination to use words in a certain fashion".[33] Given this, it is easy to see why they are necessary and logically certain:

> We cannot deny them without infringing the conventions which are presupposed by our very denial, and so falling into self-contradiction. And this is the sole ground of their necessity ... There is nothing mysterious about the apodeictic certainty of logic and mathematics. Our knowledge that no observation can ever confute the proposition "7 + 5 = 12" depends simply on the fact that the symbolic expression "7 + 5" is synonymous with "12", just as our knowledge that every oculist is an eye-doctor depends on the fact that the symbol "eye-doctor" is synonymous with "oculist". And the same explanation holds good for every other *a priori* truth.[34]

Mathematical and logical truths arise from conventional connections between the symbolic expressions of our language. In denying such truths, then, we deny the very conventions that make the meaningful use of language possible. The denial of an analytic truth is in this sense "self-stultifying", and this accounts for the necessity which analytic statements possess. As Hahn puts it:

> Logic does not by any means treat of the totality of things, it does not treat of objects at all but only of our way of speaking about objects: logic is generated by language. The certainty and universal validity, or better, the irrefutability of a proposition of logic derives just from the fact that it says nothing about objects of any kind.[35]

The fact that it is impossible to find an object which is both red all over and not-red all over, for example, stems not from the way in which the mind and the noumenal world co-operate in the transcendental constitution of the world of experience, but from the conventions underlying our use of language. The law of noncontradiction is not a deep truth about reality, but just a prescription of a method of speaking about things: it expresses our conventional stipulation that "the designation 'red' is to be applied to some objects and the designation 'not-red' to all other objects".[36]

If Ayer is right, the necessity of logical and mathematical statements can thus be explained. We now move on to the second feature that has troubled philosophers of logic and mathematics: their *utility*. If mathematics and logic "say nothing about objects of any kind", or have no factual significance, does it follow that it is a mistake to think that there can be genuine *discoveries* in mathematics and logic? And what of the usefulness of these *a priori* disciplines? If mathematical statements merely illustrate the way in which we use certain symbols, how could we ever make any interesting discoveries in mathematics, and how could such "discoveries" have any utility? Ayer and Hahn answer this worry as follows:

> The power of logic and mathematics to surprise us depends, like their usefulness, on the limitations of our reason. A being whose intellect was infinitely powerful would take no interest in logic and mathematics. For he would be able to see at a glance everything that his definitions implied, and, accordingly, could never learn anything from logical inference which he was not fully conscious of already.[37]

> Logical propositions, though being purely tautologous, and logical deductions, though being nothing but tautological transformations, have significance for us because we are not omniscient. Our language is so constituted that in asserting such and such propositions we implicitly assert such and such other propositions – but we do not see immediately all that we have implicitly asserted in this manner. It is only deduction that makes us conscious of it.[38]

To take the simplest sort of case: if I know that Jones is not wearing a rose in his buttonhole, and that either Jones is wearing a rose in his buttonhole or is wearing a carnation in his buttonhole, I may not be consciously aware that it follows from these pieces of knowledge that Jones is wearing a carnation in his buttonhole. I may fail to pick up one of the implications of the factual knowledge I currently possess. But my knowledge of the logical truth "if (not-P and (P v Q)) then Q" allows me to work out the *consequences* of what I already know: in this case, that Jones is wearing a carnation in his buttonhole. In this way logic allows me – as a mortal, finite being, not aware of all of the logical implications of my current factual knowledge – to work out those implications. It thus extends my knowledge, and can serve as an instrument of discovery: and such discoveries can be genuinely interesting and surprising when the process of deriving those consequences is very intricate and complicated, as it often is in logical and mathematical practice. That said, however, it should be noted that there is a restriction on the way in which logic and mathematics can extend our knowledge. As Ayer puts it, "there is a sense in which they may be said to add nothing to our knowledge. For they tell us only what we may be said to know already."[39] Thus, in the simple case above, if I know that Jones is not wearing a rose in his buttonhole, and that Jones is wearing either a rose or a carnation in his buttonhole, I know *already*, or know *implicitly*, that Jones is wearing a carnation in his buttonhole. What logical deduction does is enable me to make this implicit knowledge *explicit*. Logic thus never widens the extent of my factual knowledge: it serves merely to make explicit that factual knowledge that previously I possessed only implicitly. But this process of rendering implicit knowledge explicit, Ayer and Hahn will claim, is enough to secure the utility of mathematics for finite beings like ourselves, and enough to show how there can be a sort of discovery in those disciplines.

The logical positivist account of the *a priori* thus seems attractive: it accounts for the necessity and utility of logic and mathematics without incurring the metaphysical and episte-mological debts of rival conceptions, such as Kant's. But is it plausible? We shall see in a moment that there are strong reasons for thinking that, though attractive, the logical positivist account of *a priori* truth is deeply flawed. Before that, however, it might be worthwhile to pause for a second to reflect on the implications of the discussion so far for the nature and practice of philosophy itself. Philosophy itself is an *a priori* activity, so it follows from the logical positivist account of the *a priori* that the propositions of philosophy are themselves analytic. Philosophy is not a body of factual knowledge, but rather an activity of *analysis*, as the following two quotes from Russell and Carnap make clear:

> "Logical Positivism" is a name for a method, not for a certain kind of result. A philosopher is a logical positivist if he holds that there is no special way of knowing that is peculiar to philosophy, but that questions of fact can only be decided by the empirical methods of science, while questions that can be decided without appeal to experience are either mathematical or linguistic.[40]

> There is no such thing as a speculative philosophy, a system of sentences with a special subject matter on a par with those of the sciences. To pursue philosophy can only be to clarify the concepts and sentences of science by logical analysis.[41]

Just as the analytic nature of logic and mathematics is consistent with their utility and interest, so too is that of philosophy itself. Ayer cites Russell's theory of definite descriptions as a good example of the utility of philosophical analysis: the correct analysis of statements involving descriptive phrases ensures that we do not get lost in the undergrowth of Meinong's Jungle (see section 2.7). There is much that can be said about this extremely influential conception of the nature of philosophy, but we must now move on to assess the plausibility of the logical positivist account of the *a priori* itself.

The main objection to the idea that *a priori* truths are true in virtue of the conventions governing our use of language is due to Quine, in a paper first published in 1936:

> In the adoption of the very conventions whereby logic itself is set up, however, a general difficulty remains to be faced. Each of these conventions is general, announcing the truth of every one of an infinity of statements conforming to a certain description;

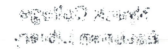

derivation of the truth of any specific statement from the general convention thus requires a logical inference, and this involves us in an infinite regress.[42]

This is somewhat cryptic, but Quine's idea can be quite easily unpacked. Take a logical truth, such as

(1) If (Jones is English and (If Jones is English then Jones is British)) then Jones is British.

According to logical positivism, this is true in virtue of convention. But which convention? Do we have a separate convention for (1), stipulating that (1) is to be held true come what may? This will obviously not do, since there are an infinite number of logical truths (for example, we can generate an infinite number of substitution instances of (1), "If (Jacques is French and (If Jacques is French then Jacques is European)) then Jacques is European), and so on, *ad infinitum*), and we can hardly be credited with setting up an infinite number of conventions, one for each individual truth of logic. So the convention that governs (1) must be a *general* convention, from which the convention governing (1) is derivable. What might that convention be? Consider

(2) If (*P* and (If *P* then *Q*)) then *Q*.

Then we might state the convention which covers (1) as follows:

(3) If (1) results from (2) by uniform substitution of *P* and *Q*, then that statement is to be held true come what may.

Given this, and

(A) (1) results from (2) by uniform substitution of *P* and *Q*,

we can now derive the convention specifically governing (1):

(4) (1) is to be held true come what may.

Thus we have generated, on the basis of a general convention, a convention specifically governing (1). But in deriving (4) from this more general convention we have relied on logic itself! In deriving (4) from (3) and (A) we have relied on

(5) If ((1) results from (2) by uniform substitution of P and Q and (If (1) results from (2) by uniform substitution of P and Q then (1) is to be held true come what may)) then (1) is to be held true come what may.

But (5) is of the same logical form as (1)! In order to secure its status as true in virtue of convention we would need

(6) If (5) results from (2) by uniform substitution of P and Q, then (5) is to be held true come what may.

Given

(B) (5) results from (2) by uniform substitution of P and Q,

we could then derive

(7) (5) is to be held true come what may.

However, in deriving (7) from (6) and (B) we have relied on logic again! In this derivation we rely upon

(8) If ((5) results from (2) by uniform substitution of P and Q and (If (5) results from (2) by uniform substitution of P and Q then (5) is to be held true come what may)) then (5) is to be held true come what may.

But, again, this is of the same logical form as (1), so in order to secure its status as true in virtue of convention we would need

(9) If (8) results from (2) by uniform substitution of P and Q, then (8) is to be held true come what may.

And now we are off on an infinite regress: deriving the conclusion that (9) is to be held true come what may will in its turn presuppose a logical truth, and so on *ad infinitum*.

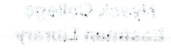

The dilemma faced is thus as follows. We either suppose that (5) is true in virtue of convention, in which case our account leads us off on an infinite regress, because we have to presuppose logic itself in order to derive the relevant convention. Or, on the other hand, we suppose that (5) is not true in virtue of convention, in which case we have conceded that the logical positivist account fails with respect to (5) (and by implication, with respect to (1) as well). Either way, the account grinds to a halt. As Quine himself sums matters up "the difficulty is that if logic is to proceed mediately from the conventions, logic is needed for inferring logic from the conventions".[43]

The logical positivist account of the *a priori* thus looks at the very best an inherently unstable position.[44] The notion of convention has resurfaced somewhat in more recent philosophy of language in the work of David Lewis, but we cannot discuss Lewis's account of convention here. In the next section, we move briefly away from Ayer's conception of the distinction between empirically verifiable and analytic statements and take up another historically influential angle on that distinction, Carnap's famous distinction between "internal" and "external" questions.

3.5 Carnap on internal and external questions

Rudolf Carnap was one of the most influential members of the Vienna Circle, which we mentioned briefly in section 3.1. An appreciation of his work is extremely important, not just for getting to grips with logical positivism, but for understanding many of the subsequent developments in analytic philosophy. In this section, however, we will look only at one strand in Carnap's philosophy, the distinction between what he termed "internal" and "external" questions.

In his "Empiricism, Semantics, and Ontology", Carnap reflects on some of the metaphysical disputes that have traditionally exercised philosophers. For example, there is the dispute between nominalists and Platonists concerning the ontological status of abstract entities, such as numbers, sets and propositions. Traditionally, Platonists about, for example, arithmetic take the truth of statements such as "5 is a prime number" to imply the existence of a range of abstract objects, numbers, not existing in space and time, and completely disconnected from the causal order of concrete entities. Nominalists, thinking Platonism to be ontologically profligate and epistemologically far-fetched, take a different tack: they attempt to analyze statements like "5 is a prime number" in such a way that their truth does not imply the existence of abstract entities. Carnap introduces a distinction that is intended to pull the rug out from under the feet of both sides in this traditional debate. In order to explain this distinction, we need first to explain Carnap's notion of a linguistic framework.

Very roughly, a linguistic framework consists of a vocabulary, together with a set of rules and conventions governing the use of that vocabulary. Consider the case of arithmetic. In arithmetic, a linguistic framework would consist of vocabulary, such as numerals ("3", "4", "5", and so on), variables ("x", "y", "z"), general terms ("is a prime number", "is an integer"), and various conventions ("... is a number" is true, where any numeral may stand in place of the dots; "... is a prime number" is true when and only when the numeral replacing the dots stands for a number divisible only by itself and unity; and so on). This is an example of what Carnap calls a "logical framework" (we'll see why in just a moment). But it is also possible to have a "factual framework". For example, we could have a framework consisting of mass terms ("sugar", "salt", "beer"), general terms ("sweet", "spicy", "hoppy"), and linguistic conventions ("... is soluble" is false if the mass term replacing the dots stands for a substance which does not dissolve in water at normal temperature and pressure).

Using this notion of a linguistic framework, Carnap distinguishes between *internal* and *external* questions:

It is above all necessary to recognize a fundamental distinction between two kinds of questions concerning the existence or reality of entities. If someone wishes to speak in his language about a new kind of entities, he has to introduce a system of new ways of speaking, subject to new rules; we shall call this procedure the construction of a linguistic *framework* for the new entities in question. And now we must distinguish two kinds of questions of existence: first, questions of the existence of certain entities of the new kind *within the framework*; we call them internal questions; and second, questions concerning the existence or reality *of the system of entities as a whole*, called *external questions*.[45]

So, for instance, in the arithmetical example, "Is there a prime number between 5 and 9?" is an internal question. Given the linguistic framework consisting of numerals and so on, we can answer it by applying the logical methods of arithmetic. For example, calculation reveals that the only divisors of 7 are itself and 1, so by the convention governing "prime", 7 is a prime number, so that there is a prime number between 5 and 9. We can see now why Carnap called this framework a logical framework: it is because answering the internal questions that are formulable given that framework requires only *a priori* calculation in addition to the application of the relevant conventions. In other words, the framework is a logical framework because the answers to the relevant internal questions are analytic. Matters stand differently in the case of the second linguistic framework we introduced. Consider an internal question such as "Is lead soluble?" In this case, answering the question requires, in addition to an application of the relevant convention, an appeal to empirical evidence and observation. We need to make the relevant observations to check whether lead dissolves in water at normal temperature and pressure. Some of the internal questions that can be answered given this framework therefore depend on *a posteriori* matters, and this explains why Carnap would call this framework a factual one.

Very roughly, then, a linguistic framework is a *logical* framework if all of the internal questions formulable within it admit of analytic answers, but a *factual* framework if at least some of the internal questions formulable within it admit of nonanalytic answers.

We can thus see, using the terminology of the previous sections, that the answers to internal questions are literally significant, since they are either analytic or resolvable by empirical means. What, though, of *external* questions? An example of an external question in the arithmetical case would be "Are there numbers?" or "Do numbers exist?" This is the sort of question that Platonists and nominalists argue over: the Platonist claims that numbers, construed as abstract objects lying outside of space and time, do actually exist, whereas the nominalist denies this. Carnap develops an ingenious dilemma that cuts against both sides in the dispute. Both sides in the dispute take themselves to be disagreeing over a substantial matter of fact: the existence of abstract entities. But the question they are debating can be interpreted either as an internal or an external question. If it is an internal question, the debate is not a substantial one, for the existence of numbers follows trivially and analytically from the linguistic framework. "5 is a number" is true by the first convention stated when introducing the framework, and "there exists an x such that: x is a number" immediately follows from this by a step of elementary logic. *This*, clearly, is not what the Platonists and nominalists have been arguing about:

> If we were to ask them: "Do you mean the question as to whether the framework of numbers, if we were to accept it, would be found to be empty or not?", they would probably reply: "Not at all, we mean a question *prior* to the acceptance of the new framework."[46]

So the question must be an *external* one. And this takes us on to the second horn of Carnap's dilemma. For according to Carnap, external questions are not literally significant. External questions concern decisions we have to make about the adoption of the linguistic frameworks themselves, and these decisions are made purely on the basis of pragmatic considerations regarding the capacity of the framework to help us organize our thinking or predict and explain the course of future experience:

> The acceptance [of a linguistic framework] cannot be judged as being either true or false because it is not an assertion. It can only be judged as being more or less expedient, fruitful, conducive to the aim for which the language is intended ... The acceptance or rejection of abstract linguistic forms, just as the acceptance or rejection of any other linguistic forms in any branch of science, will finally be decided by their efficiency as instruments, the ratio of the results achieved to the amount and complexity of the efforts required.[47]

There may be a substantial question as to which framework best satisfies the relevant pragmatic criteria. But the external questions themselves do not concern any issue of truth or falsity, only decisions based on purely pragmatic considerations of the type mentioned. The traditional metaphysical debate is really only a psuedo-debate, and the questions it raises are pseudo-questions. There are, says Carnap, no substantial, metaphysical questions about matters of ontological commitment: we are only fooled into thinking that there are such questions by confusing external questions for internal questions.

Carnap thus attempts to dissolve traditional metaphysical dispute about the existence of abstract entities, and he suggests that other traditional disputes can be dissolved in the same way (for example, the debate between realists and subjective idealists about physical objects). The affinities of this position with that of Ayer's are clear. Before returning to Ayer, however, a few remarks about Christopher Hookway's recent discussion of Carnap's distinction are in order.

Hookway, in summing up the epistemological implications of Carnap's position, writes:

When we attempt to reconstruct any body of knowledge, we can expect to find two things: (1) A framework of analytic principles, whose adoption reflects a practical decision based upon pragmatic considerations. Shared frameworks reflect adoption of conventions to the effect that these principles should be used. (2) A body of internal knowledge, which is justified by reference to the rules and principles that make up that framework.[48]

In summing matters up thus, though, Hookway is in danger of misleading the reader. By framing the contrast in terms of the distinction between analytic principles and internal knowledge, he seems to be suggesting that the distinction between external and internal matters mirrors the distinction between the analytic and synthetic. But this is not so. As we saw in our exposition of Carnap, *both* of the categories of the analytic and the synthetic fall within the province of internal questions: analytic truths are those that follow from the framework's conventions alone, synthetic truths are those that follow from the framework's conventions in the presence of empirical evidence. *The conventions in the framework themselves are neither true nor false, since their adoption reflects a response to an external question.* That is to say, in referring to the conventions as "analytic principles", Hookway's presentation confuses the conventions that appear in the linguistic framework, the statements of which are neither true not false, with the analytic truths that are answers to internal questions. The conventions themselves are not analytic truths, because they are not truths at all.[49]

We shall return to Carnap in the discussion of Quine in the chapter which follows. Before that, however, we briefly return to Ayer.

3.6 Logical positivism and ethical language

In Chapter VI of *Language, Truth, and Logic*, Ayer presents the emotivist theory of ethics. What can a logical positivist say about an ethical sentence like "Stealing is wrong"? The criterion of literal significance discussed in section 3.2 appears to entail that sentences such as this are not literally significant: they are not analytic, and they do not admit of empirical confirmation or disconfirmation either – there are no possible observations we could make that would verify or disconfirm the sentence. Thus, "Stealing is wrong" is not the sort of thing that can be assessed for truth and falsity: it is not *truth-apt*. So "Stealing is wrong" does not even purport to represent some fact about the world: its semantic function is not to state facts. But what then is its semantic function? According to Ayer's emotivist theory the function of ethical statements is to express feelings or emotions:

> If I say to someone, "You acted wrongly in stealing that money", I am not stating anything more than if I had simply said, "You stole that money". In adding that this action is wrong, *I am not making any further statement about it. I am simply evincing my moral disapproval about it.* It is as if I had said, "You stole that money", in a peculiar tone of horror, or written it with the addition of some special exclamation marks. The tone, or the exclamation marks, adds nothing to the literal meaning of the

sentence. *It merely serves to show that the expression of it is attended by certain feelings in the speaker.*[50]

It is important to be clear about the status of Ayer's conclusion that moral statements are not literally significant. He sometimes describes this conclusion as the claim that "ethical concepts are mere pseudo-concepts".[51] This might suggest that he was claiming that ethics is *nonsense*. This is further suggested by his remarks on metaphysical statements (such as "We have an enduring self" or "Reality is one substance and not many"): he concludes from the fact that these are neither analytic nor empirically verifiable that they are "nonsensical", and that metaphysics ought to be eliminated (the title of Chapter I of *Language, Truth, and Logic* is "The Elimination of Metaphysics"). So why isn't Chapter VI similarly entitled "The Elimination of Ethics"? Why doesn't Ayer simply conclude from the fact that moral judgements are neither analytic nor empirically verifiable that they are *verbiage*? Ayer realizes that this might be taken to be an implication of the emotive theory, and in the Introduction to the second edition he writes:

In putting forward the principle of verification as a criterion of meaning, I do not overlook the fact that the word "meaning" is commonly used in a variety of senses, and I do not wish to deny that in some of these senses a statement may properly be said to be meaningful even though it is neither analytic nor empirically verifiable.[52]

The idea seems to be this. Although moral judgements are not literally significant, they are not nonsensical, because they possess some other sort of significance: *emotive significance.* Two questions now suggest themselves: (1) By what criterion does Ayer distinguish between judgements that possess emotive significance and those which are nonsensical (and which therefore ought to be eliminated)?; (2) Can that criterion be stated in such a way that it grants emotive significance to ethical judgements, but refuses it to the putative judgements of the metaphysicians?

We can answer the first question by reflecting further on the generalized version of the verification principle that we mentioned briefly in section 3.2. Recall that we could use the verification principle to demarcate not only the class of sentences that were literally significant, but also the classes of sentences that possessed imperatival significance or conative significance. It is not difficult to generalize the verification principle further so that it can be used to distinguish those sentences that possess genuine emotive significance from those that only appear to do so: *a sentence that appears to evince feeling will only be counted as possessing genuine emotive significance if there is some observable behaviour the occurrence of which constitutes the expression of the feeling.*

The problem with this is that when we attend to the sort of feeling that Ayer takes ethical judgements to express, it seems to follow that ethical judgements violate the generalized version of the verification principle. Ayer quite clearly takes the utterance of an ethical sentence to express a special sort of *ethical* feeling: note the reference to moral disapproval and special exclamation marks in the quote from *Language, Truth, and Logic,* p. 107, given above. Also,

a special sort of moral disapproval is the feeling which is being expressed.[53]

Ethical symbols ... occur in sentences which simply express ethical feeling about a certain type of action or situation.[54]

But is there observable behaviour the occurrence of which would constitute the expression of this special sort of moral or ethical emotion? It is difficult to see how Ayer could answer this in the affirmative: we can perhaps imagine patterns of observable behaviour that would express disapproval,[55] but what observable behaviour could possibly manifest the presence of a distinctively *moral* sort of disapproval?[56]

This suggests that the second of our two questions above has to be answered in the negative: ethical sentences then get relegated to the category of nonsense along with the sentences of metaphysics. If this is so, then it is bad news for logical positivism: it shows that *even by its own lights*, logical positivism cannot find room for the idea that ethical sentences possess *any* sort of significance. It is one thing to suggest that ethical sentences do not have the semantic function their surface form suggests, another thing altogether to suggest that they have no semantic function whatsoever. Ayer, then, is perhaps closer to having to embrace moral nihilism than he was willing to admit.

3.7 Moderate holism

What can we say about the process of verification of sentences that do possess genuine factual significance, that are in fact genuine empirical hypotheses? Ayer is a moderate *holist* with respect to such sentences: he thinks that empirical hypotheses are never *individually* subject to the test of experience, but rather face experience *en bloc*. As he puts it, "When one speaks of hypotheses being verified in experience, it is important to bear in mind that it is never just a single hypothesis which an observation confirms or discredits, but always a system of hypotheses."[57] Ayer uses the example of an experiment devised to test a particular scientific generalization. Suppose that the generalization states that "In conditions C, all As are Bs". Suppose also that we observe, in what appear to be circumstances C, an A that is not B. Then, Ayer argues, we are not compelled to give up on our scientific generalization: we could also give up the claim that our observation of an A which is not B is veridical; we could give up the claim that the circumstances were actually of type C; and so on. Each of these options will require compensating adjustments in our overall theory, but "so long as we take suitable steps to keep our system of hypotheses free from contradiction, we may adopt any explanation we choose".[58] In practice, we will choose the explanation that best helps us to anticipate the course of our sensations, and though "these considerations have the effect of limiting our freedom in the matter of preserving and rejecting hypotheses", it is still the case that "logically our freedom is unlimited". Ayer sums the point up thus:

> The "facts of experience" can never compel us to abandon a hypothesis. A man can always sustain his convictions in the face of apparently hostile evidence if he is prepared to make the necessary ad hoc assumptions. But though any particular

instance in which a cherished hypothesis appears to be refuted can always be explained away, there must still remain the possibility that the hypothesis will ultimately be abandoned. Otherwise it is not a genuine hypothesis."[59]

But Ayer's holism is only moderate: it applies only to the subset of literally significant sentences which qualify as such in virtue of possessing factual significance. The other sort of literally significant sentence, the analytic sentences, are exempt from the holistic picture: "A proposition whose validity we are resolved to maintain in the face of any experience is not a hypothesis at all, but a definition. In other words, it is not a synthetic but an analytic proposition."[60]

In the next chapter we will look at Quine's attempt to generalize Ayer's moderate holism to include even those sentences that have traditionally been regarded as analytic. As we shall see, this thoroughgoing holism has drastic consequences, not only for the logical positivist conception of meaning, but for the notions of meaning and analyticity in general.

Further reading

The interested student should begin by reading through Ayer's *Language, truth, and logic*: this is a concise, and brilliantly written exposition of logical positivism. Ayer's editorial introduction to *Logical positivism* provides a useful summary of the main themes of logical positivism, and a useful short history of the movement. This volume contains many of the classic papers of logical positivism: especially good are "The elimination of metaphysics through the logical analysis of language" and "The old and the new logic", both by Rudolf Carnap; "Positivism and realism" and "The turning point in philosophy", by Moritz Schlick; and "Logic, mathematics, and knowledge of nature", by Hans Hahn. A thorough summary of the various objections to the verification principle can be found in section VII of Crispin Wright, "Scientific realism, observation, and the verification principle", in *Fact, science, and morality,* C. Wright and G. MacDonald (eds). In this paper Wright attempts to formulate a version of the verification principle immune to these objections. Wright's own proposal is discussed in David Lewis, "Statements partly about observation", *Philosophical Papers* (1988) and Crispin Wright, "The verification principle: another puncture, another patch", *Mind* (1989). A useful full-length study of Ayer's work is John Foster's *Ayer*. Quine's main objections to conventionalism can be found in "Carnap on logical truth" and "Truth by convention", both reprinted in P. Benacerraf and H. Putnam (eds) *The philosophy of mathematics*. For a more recent discussion of convention, see D. Lewis, *Convention*. In addition to the collection edited by Wright and MacDonald, mentioned above, the following also contain many articles of interest: L. Hahn (ed.), *The philosophy of A. J. Ayer*; A. Phillips-Griffiths (ed.), *A. J. Ayer: memorial essays*; B. Gower (ed.), *Logical positivism in perspective*. Finally, the two volumes of Ayer's autobiography, *Part of my life* and *More of my life*, provide well-written and entertaining background reading.

Chapter 4

Scepticism about sense (I): Quine on analyticity and translation

In the previous chapters we have concentrated on the various ways in which Frege, Russell, and the logical positivists attempted to systematize our intuitive notion of meaning. In this chapter we move on to look at a much more negative outlook on meaning: *scepticism*. We will look at three main lines of philosophical scepticism about the notion of meaning. In sections 4.1–4.5 we discuss Quine's attack on the analytic/synthetic distinction; in sections 4.6–4.10 we discuss Quine's thesis of the indeterminacy of translation; and in the next chapter, Kripke's Wittgenstein's attack on the idea that the expressions of our language possess such a thing as a determinate meaning. These discussions will set the scene for Chapter 6, where we look at a number of attempts to respond to these sceptical challenges.

4.1 Quine's attack on the analytic/synthetic distinction: introduction

The distinction between analytic and synthetic truth loomed large in Chapter 3. Recall that Ayer defined an analytically true sentence as one that was true purely in virtue of the senses of its constituent expressions, and he attempted to use this definition of analyticity to develop an account of *a priori* truth. Synthetic truths are those whose truth does not consist solely in facts about sense, and in the logical positivist picture these are factually significant, in virtue of being in principle susceptible to empirical verification. Likewise, the distinction between the analytic and the synthetic played a large part in Carnap's distinction between logical frameworks and factual frameworks: a logical framework is a linguistic framework which is such that all of the internal questions formulable within it are analytic; a factual framework is a framework such that at least some of the internal questions formulable within it are synthetic. In this section we introduce Quine's attack on the analytic/synthetic distinction in his 1951 paper "Two Dogmas of Empiricism", one of the most influential papers in twentieth-century philosophy. Quine's main target in this attack was the logical positivist theory of meaning and Carnap's distinction between external and internal questions. But as we will see, Quine's attack extends further than logical positivism and threatens our intuitive notion of meaning itself.

4.2 The argument of "Two Dogmas" (part I)

Quine's article falls into two main parts. In the first four sections he claims that no philosopher has ever succeeded in giving an acceptable explanation of the notion of analyticity. In the final two sections he explicitly concerns himself with the logical positivist theory of meaning, the verification theory. He argues that to the extent that the logical positivist conception of analyticity can be made sense of, the concept of analyticity simply fails to have any application: there are no analytic truths. We shall introduce the arguments of Quine's final two sections in section 4.4. In this section we outline the shape of Quine's argument in the first four sections of "Two Dogmas" by looking at his rejection of two distinct attempts philosophers have made to explicate the notion of analyticity.

Quine first considers Kant's attempted explication of analyticity in the *Critique of Pure Reason*. According to Kant, "Analytic statements are those which attribute to the subject no more than is already conceptually contained in the subject concept."[1] There are two main problems with the Kantian characterization. First of all, the notion of "conceptual containment" is no more than a *metaphor*, and stands in as much need of explication as the notion of analyticity itself. What exactly does it mean to say that the concept bachelor "contains" the concept unmarried male of marriageable age? Secondly, the Kantian characterization limits itself to sentences of the subject-predicate form. The Kantian definition has no application to sentences that are not of this form. For example, consider "Mary drinks with those with whom she herself tipples", or "John eats those he himself devours". Intuitively, these are in some sense true purely in virtue of meaning: we do not need to observe the behaviour of Mary or John to know that they are true.

Kant's attempt to define an analytic truth "as one whose denial results in contradiction" fares no better. Quine writes: "This definition has small explanatory value; for the notion of self-contradictoriness, in the quite broad sense needed for this definition of analyticity, stands in exactly the same need of clarification as does the notion of analyticity itself. The two notions are the sides of a single dubious coin."[2] A little explanation is perhaps in order here. Take a putative analytic truth, such as "If Jones is a bachelor then he is unmarried". Kant's thought is that the analyticity of this statement consists in the fact that its denial results in a self-contradiction. But what is a self-contradiction? One way to characterize self-contradiction would be *syntactically*: a self-contradiction is simply any statement of the syntactic *form P &−P*. Call this the *narrow syntactic notion of self-contradiction*. This notion may be well-understood, but it is of no help to us in explaining analyticity, since "Jones is a married bachelor" is not of the syntactic form $P \& -P$. So we need a notion of self-contradiction *broader* than the narrow syntactic notion. But, Quine claims, outlining a broad notion of self-contradiction which includes "Jones is a married bachelor" is no easier a task than explaining the notion of analyticity itself.

Both of Kant's attempts at explaining analyticity are thus inadequate. Quine then moves on to consider a more modern account of analyticity, an account due in its essentials to Frege. Very roughly, analytic truths are characterized as those that can be demonstrated or proved using only logical laws and definitions as premises. Logical laws are those statements that are true, and remain true, under all interpretations of their component parts, excluding the logical vocabulary. The logical vocabulary consists of words like "not", "and", "or", "If ... then ...", and so on. "No unmarried men are married" thus counts as a logical law, since it is true, and remains true under all reinterpretations of its nonlogical vocabulary (e.g. "No unwashed Englishmen are washed", "No ungodly Scotsmen are godly", and so on). Given this notion of a logical law, we can say that *an analytic truth is any statement which is either (a) a logical law, or (b) derivable from logical laws using only definitions as premises.* Thus "No unmarried men are married" counts as analytic under (a). But what about "No bachelors are married", which is not a logical law (since e.g. "No Welshmen are married" is false)? This counts as analytic under the Fregean characterization because it is derivable from a logical law using only definitions as premises. The derivation could be set out informally as follows:

(1) No unmarried men are married (logical law)
(2) Bachelors are unmarried men (definition of "bachelor")
(3) No bachelors are married (from (1) and (2)).

The fact that "No bachelors are married" is derivable in this way shows that it counts as analytic under (b).

Quine spends quite some time arguing that this Fregean characterization of analyticity is not satisfactory as it stands. The main problem is that analytic statements of type (b) have to be characterized as those that are derivable from logical truths by means of *correct* definitions. Without this proviso about correctness, Frege's account of analyticity would allow us to prove that, for example, "No philosophers are married" is an analytic truth! Witness

(1) No unmarried men are married (logical law)
(2) Philosophers are unmarried men (definition of "philosopher")
(3) No philosophers are married (from (1) and (2)).

The problem here is clearly that the definition of "philosopher" is incorrect. But what does it mean to say that a definition is correct or incorrect? Quine's strategy at this point is to argue that answering this question presupposes an answer to our original and as yet unanswered question about analyticity.

One way of answering the question about definition is as follows: a definition is correct if and only if the defined and defining terms are *synonymous*. But now we must give an account of synonymy. What does it mean to say that two expressions are synonymous? Quine considers the suggestion that two expressions "F" and G" are synonymous whenever they are *intersubstitutable salva veritate*. To say that "F" and "G" are intersubstitutable *salva veritate* is just to say that whenever we have a sentence which contains "F", we can always substitute "G" for "F" without changing the truth-value of the overall sentence (and vice-versa, whenever we have a sentence which contains "G", we can always substitute "F" for "G" without changing the truth-value of the overall sentence).

How plausible is this attempt at explicating synonymy? If it works, we can use it to explain the notion of a correct definition, and we can then use that notion to characterize analyticity along Fregean lines. But, according to Quine, this attempt at explicating synonymy is hopeless. Whether the account of synonymy in terms of intersubstitutability is plausible will depend on the richness of the language within which we are working. So suppose, first, that our language is an *extensional* language: a language whose sentences are formalizable using only the standard vocabulary of first-order predicate calculus with identity. Then it is easy to see that intersubsitutability *salva veritate* is not a sufficient condition for synonymy. "Renate" and "Cordate" are co-extensional, and thus intersubstitutable *salva veritate* in such a language, but they are plainly not synonymous by any intuitive criterion, since the first means "Creature with kidneys" while the second means "Creature with a heart".[3]

The problem here is that it is a mere *accident of nature* that

117

"Renate" and "Cordate" are co-extensional and hence intersubstitutable *salva veritate*. In order to rule out this sort of case we need to have the resources within our language to express the thought that two predicates, for example, are more than merely accidently co-extensional. In other words, we will need to work within a language which includes something like the modal adverb "necessarily", and which is thus richer than standard first-order predicate calculus with identity. This will allow us to say that two expressions are synonymous if and only if they are *necessarily* intersubstitutable *salva veritate*. This would ensure that cases like "Renate" and "Cordate" do not count as synonymous by our account of synonymy: although they are co-extensional, they are not necessarily co-extensional, since we can quite easily imagine possible worlds in which there are creatures with kidneys but no heart, and so on. Thus, "Renate" and "Cordate" are not necessarily intersubstitutable *salva veritate*, and hence do not count as synonymous by our account of synonymy.

But now we face the new problem of making sense of "necessarily". What does it mean to say that "Necessarily *P*" is true? Quine says that this can mean nothing more than that *P* is analytic: "But can we condone a language which contains ['necessarily']? Does the adverb really make sense? To suppose that it does is to suppose that we have already made satisfactory sense of 'analytic'. Then what are we so hard at work on right now?"[4] So we are back where we started. In order to explain analyticity along Fregean lines we had to explain the notion of a correct definition, in order to explain the notion of a correct definition we had to explain the notion of synonymy, and in order to explain synonymy we had to explain the meaning of "necessarily", which in turn requires an explanation of analyticity!

The Kantian and Fregean attempts at explaining analyticity thus fail, since they presuppose the notion of analyticity or notions just as unclear as analyticity at some point in their attempted explanations. In the remainder of the first four sections of "Two Dogmas", Quine looks at several other attempts at explaining analyticity, and makes essentially the same objection. He concludes that to the extent that no intelligible characterization of the distinction has been forthcoming, we have evidence that there is simply no coherent distinction between the analytic and the synthetic.

How plausible is the attack against analyticity which Quine mounts in the first four sections? Before answering this question, we must pause to make three comments about the nature of Quine's attack.

Comment 1. Note that although Quine takes the Kantian and Fregean attempts at explaining analyticity as his stalking horses, his real target is the logical positivist characterization of analytic truth as "truth purely in virtue of meaning". We can view the Kantian and Fregean explanations as attempts to explain what it is for a statement to be true purely in virtue of meaning. To the extent that they fail, we have not been given an explanation of the logical positivist's characterization of analyticity.

Comment 2. We can perhaps make an *ad hominem* point against Quine here. Recall Quine's comment that "a logical truth is a statement which is true and which remains true under all reinterpretations of its components other than the logical particles". Now Quine is quite happy to countenance a class of logical truths: his concern is to question whether there is any coherent way in which that notion can be used to characterize a class of analytic truths. But Quine doesn't seem to realize that his arguments against analyticity militate against his own characterization of logical truth. Consider "$(\forall x)((Fx \mathbin{\&} Gx) \to Gx)$". Clearly, if anything counts as a logical truth, this does. But "All green banks are banks" is an instance of this, and it is false if the token occurrences of "bank" have different meanings (for example, if the first token refers to a river bank and the second token refers to a financial institution). Quine thus needs to include in his definition of logical truth some stipulation to the effect that the substituted expressions are *synonymous*. For example, in the example above, the stipulation requires that the tokens of "bank" that are substituted for the tokens of "F" are synonymous. This shows that if Quine's attack on the notion of synonymy is successful, his own definition of logical truth will be jeopardized.

Comment 3. Quine's attack on the notion of analyticity is, *inter alia*, an attack on the idea that sentences have such a thing as meaning. This is brought out very clearly in a passage from "In Defense of a Dogma", an early reply to "Two Dogmas", by Paul Grice and Peter Strawson:

If talk of sentence-synonymy is meaningless, then it seems that talk of sentences having a meaning at all must be meaningless too. For if it made sense to talk of a sentence having a meaning, or meaning something, then presumably it would make sense to ask "What does it mean?" And if it made sense to ask "What does it mean?" of a sentence, then sentence-synonymy could be roughly defined as follows: Two sentences are synonymous if and only if any true answer to the question "What does it mean?" asked of one of them, is a true answer to the same question, asked of the other ... If we are to give up the notion of sentence-synonymy as senseless, we must give up the notion of sentence-significance (of a sentence having meaning) as senseless too. But then perhaps we might as well give up the notion of sense.[5]

This shows that Quine's attack is far more radical than might initially appear. It is one thing to give up a philosophical distinction, another thing entirely to give up the intuitive notion that there is such a thing as sentence-meaning. Quine is thus arguing for a fully fledged version of meaning-scepticism: there is no fact of the matter as to what any given sentence or linguistic expression means.

4.3 Criticism of "Two Dogmas" (part I)

The main objection which Quine raises against the Kantian and Fregean attempts to explain analyticity is that they are *circular*: at some point in the explanation they need to presuppose the notion of analyticity itself, or some other cognate notion – such as correct definition, synonymy, or necessity – which is just as problematic. This objection appears to rest on the assumption that a putative concept is not fully intelligible unless it admits of an explicit noncircular definition. An explicit definition of a concept P, say, is a statement of a set of conditions necessary and sufficient for the instantiation of P:

x is P if and only if Fx.

An explicit definition is noncircular when the concept P (or any concept whose definition itself presupposes P) does not appear on the right-hand side in the specification of F. That this assumption underlies Quine's argument here is clear from the fact that almost all of the attempts at developing, for example, the Fregean definition of analyticity are ruled out because analyticity or one of its cognates appears, or is presupposed, on the right-hand side of the proffered definition. For example, where s is a sentence, the definition

s is analytic if and only if s is derivable from logical laws and definitions

is ruled out because the explanation of definition on the right-hand side makes sense only if we eventually presuppose the notion of analyticity itself.

Call this assumption *Quine's Socratic Assumption*.[6] Is it justified? On the face of it, it appears to impose much too strong a condition on a concept's being intelligible. Aren't there many concepts that we perfectly well understand but which fail to satisfy this condition? Take colour concepts for example. We can perfectly well understand sentences containing colour concepts (or at least it would be to ascend to another level of philosophical implausibility to deny that we do), but no one has ever succeeded in giving a noncircular set of necessary and sufficient conditions for, for example, the correct application of "red" or "blue" or "green".

Another consideration which suggests that Quine's Socratic Assumption is unjustified is that in order for a language to contain resources sufficient for an explicit noncircular definition of each of its expressions, it would need to contain infinitely many semantic primitives. Given this, a semantic theory (see section 1.7) for the language in question would need to contain infinitely many axioms. But as we shall see when we come to discuss Davidson in Chapter 8, a language is learnable only if a finitely axiomatizable semantic theory for that language is possible. So a language all of whose expressions satisfy Quine's Socratic Assumption would turn out to be in principle unlearnable.

These considerations suggest that Quine's Socratic Assumption can at best constitute only a *local* requirement, a requirement imposed on *some but not all* expressions of the language concerned. Given the local nature of the requirement, then, the onus is on Quine to explain why "analytic" is one of the expressions that have to meet it. What sort of explanation could Quine give here? It would have to rest on some claim to the effect that there were *independent* reasons for thinking "analytic" to be problematic, perhaps that in practice we always find ourselves hesitating over its application. He comes close to offering such a reason in the following passage: "I do not know whether the statement 'Everything is green is extended' is analytic. Now does my indecision over this example really betray an incomplete understanding, an incomplete grasp of the 'meanings' of 'green' and 'extended'? I think not. The trouble is not with 'green' or 'extended', but with 'analytic'."[7] Granted, we do feel some hesitancy here. But in order for Quine to meet our challenge here he would have to show not just that we occasionally hesitate over the application of the concepts, but that such hesitancy was *widespread*. Grice and Strawson argue convincingly (pp. 149–53) that this is not the case, since (a) mastery of the concepts *analytic* and *synthetic* can quite easily be imparted to novices, and (b) those with even a very modest philosophical training tend, non-collusively, to agree over the application of the concepts to new cases (think about your own reaction to the examples involving Mary and John in section 4.2). And even in the isolated case in which there does appear to be some hesitancy, the hesitancy is not conclusively traceable to the presence of "analytic":

> If, as Quine says, the trouble is with "analytic", then the trouble should doubtless disappear when "analytic" is removed. So let us remove it, and replace it with a word which Quine himself has contrasted favourably with "analytic" in respect of perspicuity – the word "true". Does the indecision at once disappear? We think not. The indecision over "analytic" (and equally, in this case, the indecision over "true") arises, of course, from a further indecision: viz., that which we should feel when confronted with such questions as "Should we count a point of green light as extended or not?" As is frequent enough in such cases, the hesitation arises from the fact that the boundaries of application of words are not determined by usage in all possible

directions. But the example Quine has chosen is particularly unfortunate for his thesis, in that it is only too evident that our hesitations are not here attributable to obscurities in "analytic".[8]

Our conclusion is thus that Quine's Socratic requirement on the legitimacy of concepts appears to be unreasonable and unmotivated. The fact that "analytic" does not meet that requirement does not establish that it is unintelligible, no more than the failure of "red", "green", and so on, to meet it establishes the unintelligibility of our colour concepts. Quine's general line of argument in the first four sections of "Two Dogmas" fails to show that analyticity and its cognate concepts are unintelligible.

4.4 The argument of "Two Dogmas" (part II)

In the final two sections of "Two Dogmas", Quine invites us to consider whether the verificationist theory of meaning propounded by the logical positivists can provide us with a satisfactory elucidation of analyticity. Recall that the verificationist theory of meaning was the doctrine that the meaning of a statement consists in the method whereby it can be empirically confirmed or disconfirmed. This seems to furnish us with an appropriate definition of synonymy: two sentences are synonymous if they have the same method of empirical verification. Given this definition of synonymy, we could go on to frame a definition of analyticity: analytic statements are those that are synonymous with logical truths (see above), or, in other words, analytic statements are those that would be confirmed by experience *come what may*.

We can put this thought another way. The truth of a sentence is a function of two things: of its meaning, on the one hand, and of the way the world is, on the other. For example, "grass is green" is true, and this is a function of the fact that it means that grass is green, and that grass is, in fact, green. If the sentence had meant that Newcastle is in Scotland it would have been false. So we can view sentences as having both a factual component and a linguistic component. Analytic sentences can now be characterized as those whose factual components are vacuous or empty.

Quine attacks the story that we have just outlined: he denies that the verificationist theory of meaning can provide us with a plausible characterization of analyticity. It cannot do this because it rests upon a faulty assumption: the assumption that individual statements, considered in isolation, can admit of confirmation or disconfirmation. This assumption is shown to be faulty by Quine's doctrine of *epistemological holism*, according to which all significant statements face the tribunal of experience not *individually*, but *en masse*: "our statements about the external world face the tribunal of sense experience not individually, but only as a corporate body".[9] When faced with a *recalcitrant* experience – an experience that conflicts with our currently held theory of the world – we have to revise that theory. But in principle any part of the theory can be dropped, subject to this being accommodated by changes in other areas of the theory: which part of the theory should actually be dropped will be determined by purely pragmatic standards, such as the preservation of simplicity and the minimization of future recalcitrance. Unlike the holism espoused by Ayer (see section 3.7), Quine's holism is not modest but *thoroughgoing*: even the statements that would be held by the positivists to be analytic, such as the statements of logic and mathematics, are, in principle, rationally revisable:

Total science is like a field of force whose boundary conditions are experience. A conflict with experience at the periphery occasions readjustments in the interior of the field. Truth values have to be redistributed over some of our statements. Reevaluation of some statements entails reevaluation of others, because of their logical interconnections – the logical laws being in turn simply certain further statements of the system, certain further elements of the field. Having reevaluated one statement we must reevaluate some others, which may be statements logically connected with the first or may be the statements of logical connections themselves. But the total field is so underdetermined by its boundary conditions, experience, that there is much latitude of choice as to what statements to reevaluate in the light of any single contrary experience.[10]

The holistic picture implies that there are no statements of theory that are in principle immune to rational revision. It follows from this that the notion of analyticity, as characterized by the verificationist theory of meaning, simply fails to have any application. In the verificationist picture, analytic truths are those statements that are confirmed come what may (that are immune to rational revision in the light of experience) because their factual components are vacuous; synthetic statements are those that hold contingently on experience since their factual components are nonempty. Quine's holism appears to destroy this distinction:

> It is misleading to think of the empirical content of an individual statement – especially if it is a statement at all remote from the experiential periphery of the field. Furthermore it becomes folly to seek a boundary between synthetic statements, which hold contingently on experience, and analytic statements, which hold come what may. Any statement can be held true come what may, if we make drastic enough adjustments elsewhere in the system. Even a statement very close to the periphery can be held true in the face of recalcitrant experience by pleading hallucination or by amending certain statements of the kind called logical laws. Conversely, by the same token, no statement is immune to revision. Revision even of the law of excluded middle has been proposed as a means of simplifying quantum mechanics; and what difference is there in principle between such a shift and the shift whereby Kepler superseded Ptolemy, or Einstein Newton, or Darwin Aristotle?[11]

In other words, the distinction between the linguistic and factual components of an individual sentence, upon which the verificationist account of the analytic/synthetic distinction depends, is blurred beyond recognition by holism.[12] Again, Quine's conclusion is that we have not been given an intelligible distinction between the analytic and the synthetic.

4.5 Criticism of "Two Dogmas" (part II)

Crispin Wright has argued that Quine's holism is implausible because it is actually *incoherent*: he claims that Quine's holism cannot provide us with a coherent account of scientific methodology. In this section we attempt to reconstruct this objection.

Wright asks us to consider the following example. Suppose we have a theory of the world T together with an underlying logic L. Suppose that, together, they generate the conditional $I \to P$, "whose antecedent describes certain initial conditions and whose consequent formulates a prediction relative to those conditions".[13] Suppose also that we suffer a recalcitrant experience E, that inclines us to believe, contra T and L, both I and $-P$. Quine's holism implies that the following are all in principle candidates for revision:

$I \& -P$
T
L
$T \vdash_L I \to P$

Given that all of these are in principle revisable, which of them ought we to revise? For Quine, this question has to be answered on pragmatic grounds, and on pragmatic grounds alone. So the question we are facing is: how do pragmatic considerations determine whether or not, for example, the rejection of $T \vdash_L I \to P$ is "a good move"? According to Quine, we answer this by considering whether the rejection of $T \vdash_L I \to P$ best minimizes future recalcitrance (a "good move" is one that best minimizes the possibility of future recalcitrance). If it does, we reject it, if it doesn't we keep it, and reject some other part of our overall body of beliefs. However, and this is the crucial point in Wright's objection, *verdicts about recalcitrance are in the same boat as all our other judgements*. That is to say, judgements about recalcitrance are themselves in principle up for revision.

Now suppose that pragmatic considerations do tell us that

(a) The rejection of $T \vdash_L I \to P$ best minimizes future recalcitrance.

Then holism, together with the fact that judgements about recalcitrance are in the same boat as all the rest, forces us to ask: do pragmatic considerations determine whether the rejection or acceptance of (a) itself is a good move? Suppose we get the answer

(b) The rejection of (a) is a good (bad) move (that is, best minimizes the possibility of future recalcitrance).

Once again, holism, together with the fact that judgements about recalcitrance are in the same boat as all the rest, forces us to ask: Do pragmatic considerations determine whether the rejection or acceptance of (b) is a good move? Suppose we get the answer

(c) The rejection of (b) is a good (bad) move.

Then holism forces us to ask ... And so on, *ad infinitum.* Because judgements about recalcitrance are in the same boat as all the rest, we get an *infinite regress* of such questions: and because of the regress, the Quinean methodology can never actually get off the ground. Wright's conclusion is that Quine has failed to provide a coherent account of the methodology we use in revising our theory of the world in the light of the deliverances of experience.

According to Wright, what this shows is that in order to stop the regress, we have to exempt some judgements (for example, $T \vdash_L I \rightarrow P$, since exempting this would be to refuse to view the recalcitrance of the experience E as a mere hypothesis, something in the same boat as all the rest of our empirical judgements) from pragmatic appraisal. These judgements are the analytic judgements. So we are left with a distinction between the analytic and the synthetic after all.

Wright's objection to Quine's holism is subtle and difficult to appraise, and we cannot attempt an evaluation of it here. In the next section we move on to look at the second source of Quine's scepticism about the notion of meaning, his arguments for the indeterminacy of translation.

4.6 Quine on the indeterminacy of translation: introduction

In the previous sections we looked at Quine's arguments against the analytic/synthetic distinction, and we saw that these arguments were, *inter alia*, arguments against the very notion of meaning. They were arguments for *meaning scepticism*: there is simply no fact of the matter as to whether a given sentence is analytic or synthetic, no fact of the matter as to what it means; and for any given pair of sentences, there is no fact of the matter as to whether they are synonymous or not. We now move on to look at a different set of arguments for meaning-scepticism: Quine's arguments for the indeterminacy of translation.

Suppose that you are a speaker of a language $L1$, and that you are setting out to translate the sentences of some other language, $L2$, into your own language. Your aim in this task would be to construct a *translation manual* that correlated each sentence of the language $L2$ with a sentence of your own language $L1$. Now intuitively, we would say that there is an objective fact of the matter as to whether the translation manual that you come up with is *correct*. Thus, if $L1$ is English and $L2$ is German, a translation manual that correlates "Schnee ist weiss" with "Snow is white" is correct, whereas a translation manual that correlates it with "Instantiations of snow-hood are cold" is surely incorrect. Quine claims that this is an illusion: actually, there is no fact of the matter as to which of these two translation manuals is correct. In general, there is no fact of the matter as to whether a given translation manual for a given language is correct. When we are faced with a choice between two different translation manuals, there is no fact of the matter we can "get right" in our choice: some translation manuals may be more useful, more elegant, more natural, more simple, and so on, but these are purely pragmatic considerations.

This, in essence, is the indeterminacy of translation. Quine clearly thinks that the importance of this result lies in the consequences it has for the notion of meaning. The conclusion that it is not an objective factual matter whether a given translation manual for a language is correct or not is supposed to point to the conclusion that there is no objective fact of the matter as to what the sentences of that language mean. This connection between translation and meaning initially seems clear enough: a translation manual has the job of pairing the sentences of one language with the sentences of another, and the manual will be correct if it pairs the sentences of the first language with sentences of the second language that *have the same meaning*. Thus if there is no fact of the matter about the correctness of the translation manual, there will be no fact of the matter about sameness of meaning, and, as we saw when discussing analyticity, this entails that there are no facts about meaning at all.

We can now state the doctrine of the indeterminacy of translation in more detail. Given a language L, it is possible, at least in principle, to construct two translation manuals, $T1$ and $T2$, both of which fit all of the possible evidence that is relevant to translation, but which are nevertheless incompatible with each other. In fact, Quine would claim that for any language L there will be an infinitely large number of translation manuals which equally fit all of the possible evidence relevant to translation, but which are pairwise incompatible (that is, if you pick any two of these manuals, they will be incompatible with each other). Quine concludes that there is no fact of the matter as to which manual is correct: if one manual translates "Schnee" as "snow" and another translates "Schnee" as "instantiation of snow-hood", there may be nothing to choose between them, other than the sorts of purely pragmatic considerations mentioned above. Now this seems shocking: surely there is a fact of the matter as to which translation manual best captures the nature of the language under consideration? Quine claims not, so we must now examine his arguments for this intuitively shocking claim.

4.7 The argument from below

In fact, there are at least two general lines of argument for the thesis: the "argument from below", which comes from Chapter 2 of Quine's most important book, *Word and Object*; and the "argument from above", based on general considerations concerning the underdetermination of scientific theory by all possible observational evidence, which comes from Quine's short paper "On the Reasons for the Indeterminacy of Translation". In this and the following section we concentrate on the argument from below; the argument from above is discussed in section 4.9.

A crucial figure in Quine's argument is the *radical translator*. This is a translator who is engaged upon the project of translating the language of the natives who belong to some hitherto completely unknown tribe. The only evidence the radical translator has at his disposal is that which he can obtain from his *observation of the natives' behaviour*: he has no help in his task from dictionaries, or existing partial translation manuals that translate some native sentences into his own language, or from translations of the native language into some other language for which the translator already has a translation manual. The radical translator does not even have access to things like historical studies of the natives' language and culture – he has nothing at all to go on, except what he can observe in the behaviour of the speakers of the native language.

What is the motivation for looking at the process of translation in this very artificial setting? An assumption underlying Quine's entire argument here seems to be this: if there are facts that could determine whether a given translation manual is correct, that is, if there are facts about meaning, then those facts must be determined by facts about the behaviour of the speakers of the language under consideration. What else could constitute a fact about the meaning of an expression? Intuitively, the meaning of any given expression is something settled by *convention*: "grass" only means grass because of the existence of a certain convention among speakers of English. But conventions do not just come magically into being: they are brought into being by the *behaviour* of the various parties to the convention. So, the fact that "grass" means grass and not snow must in some sense be determined by our behaviour with the word. *Quine's strategy will be to argue that the facts about behaviour are not sufficient to determine whether a given translation manual is correct: the facts about behaviour will be consistent with the adoption of an altogether different translation manual.* So there is no fact of the matter as to which translation manual is correct.

Now given that Quine's interest is in the relationship between the behavioural facts and the facts about meaning, using the device of the radical translator allows him to focus on the relationship between the putative facts about meaning and the behavioural facts in their purest form: the radical translator's angle on the facts about behaviour at his disposal is in no danger of being tainted by collateral information, which might already have some implicit semantic import. This is the motivation for looking at translation in this radical context. The task facing the radical translator is thus as follows: *given all of the observable facts about the behaviour of the natives (and only those facts), construct a translation manual that yields a translation in your own language of each of the sentences of the natives' language.*

But what counts as a fact about the natives' behaviour? What counts as a behavioural fact? Speaking a language is a form of behaviour, so could we count the fact that someone *said that it was raining* as a behavioural fact? Quine would not count this as a behavioural fact, since it already invokes a semantic notion, the notion of a speaker *uttering a sentence with a certain content.* The whole point of the enterprise is to try to get some handle on what facts about content and meaning could be, so Quine will want to work with a notion of behaviour constrained by the requirement that that behaviour be described in completely nonsemantic and nonintentional terms. In fact, Quine works with a very thin notion of the behavioural facts that can legitimately be invoked in the process of radical translation. For Quine, the only facts about native behaviour that can legitimately be counted as evidence for or against the correctness of a given translation manual are facts about what he terms *stimulus meaning.* The stimulus meaning of an expression is defined to be an ordered pair consisting, on the one hand, of those sensory stimulations that prompt assent to the sentence (the *affirmative stimulus meaning*) and, on the other hand, those sensory stimulations that typically prompt dissent from the sentence (the *negative stimulus meaning*). Thus, another way of describing the task the radical translator faces is: *given all of the facts about the stimulus meanings of the sentences of the native language, construct a translation manual that provides an acceptable translation of those sentences into your own language.* And of course, the indeterminacy thesis is the claim that this task cannot be discharged:

> Manuals for translating one language into another can be set up in divergent ways, all compatible with the totality of speech dispositions, yet incompatible with one another. In countless places they will diverge in giving, as their respective translations of the sentences of the one language, sentences of the other language which stand to each other in no plausible sort of equivalence however loose.[14]

One thing to note at this point is the *restricted* nature of the evidence which Quine allows as relevant to the process of radical translation: all of the evidence the translator is allowed by Quine concerns the dispositions the natives have to assent to (and dissent from) sentences in response to various stimulations of their sensory receptors. No other kind of evidence is allowed.

Note also that the meaning-scepticism that is the intended upshot of Quine's argument is *constitutive scepticism* (scepticism about the *existence of a certain sort of fact*), as opposed to traditional *epistemological scepticism* (which concedes that the sort of fact in question exists, and then questions our right to claim *knowledge* of that sort of fact). It is important to bear this distinction in mind, because it would be easy to make the mistake of seeing Quine as propounding only epistemological scepticism about meaning. Easy, because his argument has a distinctively epistemological flavour: given all of the facts about stimulus meanings, you are still not in a position to *know* which of the competing translation manuals is the correct one. But note that although Quine's argument has this epistemological flavour, it questions whether we could know which manual was correct, even given *idealized epistemological access* to all of the *possible* facts about stimulus meanings and the natives' behavioural dispositions. Even if we imagine our knowledge acquiring powers with respect to stimulus meanings idealized, we *still* would not be in a position to justify our choice of one of the competing translation manuals over its rivals. It is this idealization that allows Quine to argue for a constitutive scepticism *via* an epistemological argument.

So, all the evidence the radical translator has to go on in constructing his translation manual are facts about stimulus meanings, although as noted above he has idealized access to all such facts. Let's now think about how he fares in his task of constructing the manual. The translator first of all identifies the native signs for *assent* and *dissent*. He can do this by repeating his own volunteered pronouncements and then taking note of the natives' reaction:

> How is he to recognize native assent and dissent when he sees or hears them? Gestures are not to be taken at face value; the Turks' are nearly the reverse of our own. What he must do is guess from observation and then see how well his guesses work. Thus suppose in asking "Gavagai?" and the like, in the conspicuous presence of rabbits and the like, he has elicited the responses "Evet" and "Yok" often enough to surmise that they may correspond to "Yes" and "No", but has no notion which is which. Then he tries the experiment of echoing the native's own volunteered pronouncements. If thereby he pretty regularly elicits "Evet" rather than "Yok" he is encouraged to take "Evet" as "Yes". Also he tries responding with "Evet" and "Yok" to the natives' remarks; the one that is the more serene in its effect is the better candidate for "Yes". However inconclusive these methods, they generate a working hypothesis. If extraordinary difficulties attend all his subsequent steps, the linguist may decide to discard that hypothesis and start again.[15]

Suppose, then, that the translator notices that the natives are generally prepared to assent to the expression "Yo, gavagai" whenever there is a rabbit somewhere close nearby, and that they are generally prepared to dissent from "Yo, gavagai" when there are no rabbits present. In other words, the translator discovers that "Yo, gavagai" and our expression "there is a rabbit" have the same stimulus meaning: the natives assent to and dissent from "Yo, gavagai" in exactly the same circumstances (under the same conditions of sensory stimulation) as we would assent to and dissent from "there is a rabbit". On this basis, the radical translator (let's suppose for the sake of argument that he is English) tentatively proposes to translate "Yo, gavagai" into English as "there is a rabbit".

Now the trouble starts. What if we choose to translate "Yo, gavagai" not as "there is a rabbit", but rather as "there is an undetached rabbit part"? Intuitively, we want to say that this alternative translation is inaccurate: but facts about stimulus meaning – remember, the only facts that we are allowed to appeal to – will be of no help to us in choosing between these two candidate translations. Each of the translations is consistent with all of the relevant evidence about the natives' behavioural dispositions: "there is a rabbit" and "there is an undetached rabbit part" have exactly the same stimulus meanings (since whenever there is a rabbit present there is also an undetached rabbit part present, and vice versa), so that so far as the relevant evidence goes, the translation of "Yo, gavagai" as "there is an undetached rabbit part" is just as good as the translation of "Yo, gavagai" as "there is a rabbit". Since stimulus meanings constitute the only relevant evidence, the only facts relevant to translation, there is no fact of the matter as to which of the translation manuals is the correct one. By the same reasoning, there is no fact of the matter as to whether "Yo, gavagai" should be translated as "there is a rabbit", or "there is an undetached rabbit part", or "there is a time slice of a four-dimensional rabbit-whole", or "there is an instantiation of rabbit-hood". No doubt, Quine is prepared to admit, in practice we will choose one of these translations over the others, but in so doing we will not thereby be faithful or unfaithful to some *fact* about the meaning of "Yo, gavagai". Our choice will merely be a reflection of pragmatic standards: each of the translations is equally justified by the facts about stimulus meanings, so that as far as the facts of the matter are concerned, all of the translations are equally acceptable.

Quine considers and quickly rejects the following response to the above argument: perhaps it is possible, on the basis of facts about stimulus meaning alone, to tell whether or not "Yo, gavagai" is better translated as "there is a rabbit" or "there is an undetached rabbit part". We can find out which translation is really the correct one by putting certain *questions* to the native. Suppose that we have identified the expression the natives use for *numerical identity* (such as "is the same as"), and also some of the expressions they use as *demonstratives* (such as "that", or "this"). Then surely all we need to do to see which translation is correct is to point to one part of the rabbit (e.g. its tail) and ask, after pointing to its nose, "Si hit gavagai emas sa hat gavagai?" (in other words, "Is this gavagai the same as that gavagai?"). If the native responds with

"Evet", which we have already identified as his sign for assent, then this would be genuine behavioural evidence in favour of the translation of "gavagai" as "rabbit" and against the translation of "gavagai" as "undetached rabbit part". And vice versa if he responded with "Yok" to the same query.

Quine points out that this reply assumes that the correct translation of the native expression "emas" is "same rabbit", so that when we put the query above we were asking "Is this rabbit the same rabbit as this rabbit?". The answer "Evet" then spoke in favour of the straightforward "rabbit" translation. But if we take the correct translation of "emas" to be "is an undetached part of the same rabbit as" the answer "Evet" to our query will actually be consistent with the less straightforward "undetached rabbit part" translation. "Si hit emas gavagai sa hat gavagai?" will come out as "Is this undetached rabbit part an undetached part of the same rabbit as that undetached rabbit part?", and if the natives mean "undetached rabbit part" by "gavagai" the answer "Evet" is precisely what we would expect. So there are ways of rendering even this new source of behavioural evidence compatible with each of the competing translation manuals. Gareth Evans sums up this reply of Quine's very nicely:

An expression may sensibly be regarded as a predicate only if it interacts with the "apparatus of individuation", and the stimulus conditions that trigger assent to the sentences in which such interaction occurs provide the only empirical evidence that bears upon what extension the expression, as a predicate, should be regarded as possessing. But the identification of the apparatus of individuation in a foreign language is empirically quite underdetermined; the expression that one theory regards as the identity predicate, may, with suitable adjustments be treated by another as an expression for some distinct equivalence relation – both theories assigning to whole sentences a significance completely in accordance with the behavioural data. Consequently, whether an expression is a predicate at all, and if a predicate, what extension it has, are matters underdetermined by all actual and possible observations.[16]

That, then, is the essence of the argument from below. In the next section we examine Evans's own response to this argument.

4.8 Evans and Hookway on the argument from below

Recall that the conclusion of the argument from below was as follows. For any language L, there will be indefinitely many translation manuals $T1, \ldots, Tn, \ldots$ each of which accommodates the facts about the speakers' behavioural dispositions, but which offer what are intuitively incompatible translations of the sentences of L. Since the facts about speaker's behavioural dispositions (the facts about stimulus meaning) are the only facts relevant to translations, it cannot be a factual matter which of the candidate translation manuals is the correct one. And since a translation manual is supposed to tell us what the speakers mean, it is not a factual matter as to what the speakers mean either.

We shall now look at the response to Quine's argument from below developed by Gareth Evans in his paper "Identity and Predication". Evans's response is complex, so we shall simplify it somewhat in order to get across the general line of thought behind it.

Evans's strategy is to deny that it follows from the claim that there is an indeterminacy afflicting the construction of translation manuals that a similar degree of indeterminacy afflicts the notion of meaning. He denies that indeterminacy in the construction of translation manuals for a language implies indeterminacy in the construction of *theories of meaning* (or semantic theories) for that language. Quine clearly thinks that it follows from the indeterminacy of translation that "different theories of meaning could be constructed each of which entails semantical properties for the totality of jungle sentences adequate to the data but which make quite different assignments of semantical properties to those sentences' parts".[17] Evans denies this: according to him the project of constructing a translation manual and the project of constructing a theory of meaning are quite separate enterprises, governed by different sorts of constraints.

But what is a theory of meaning? As explained in section 1.7, a semantic theory is a theory relating to a single language that attempts to *state the meaning* of every sentence in that language. Such a theory delivers, for each well-formed declarative sentence of the language under consideration, a *theorem* that in some sense states the meaning of that sentence. We saw in Chapter 1 that, according to Frege, the sense of a sentence is its *truth-conditions*, and we will follow Frege on this point here. Thus, a theorem specifying the meaning of the sentence "snow is white" would be a theorem that stated the truth-conditions of that sentence, namely:

"Snow is white" is true if and only if snow is white.

Thus, we can say that a semantic theory for a language, if correct, should issue a theorem that states the truth-conditions of each well-formed declarative sentence in the language. So what is the *difference* between a translation manual and a semantic theory? Evans writes:

> A translation is one thing, a theory of meaning another. A manual for translation aims to provide, for each sentence of the language under study, a way of arriving at a quoted sentence of another language which has the same meaning. A theory of meaning, on the other hand, entails, for each sentence of the language under study, a statement of what it means. A translator states no semantical truths at all, nor has he any need of the concepts of truth, denotation, and satisfaction. Semantical truths relate expressions to the world, and can be stated only by using, not mentioning, expressions of some language or other.[18]

More importantly, Evans claims that there are constraints on the construction of theories of meaning that rule out the indeterminacy Quine claims to have found in translation manuals. The constraint that rules out the indeterminacy in theories of meaning concerns *structure*. A theory of meaning has to be structured in a way in which a translation manual does not, and it is the presence of this structure in the theory of meaning that rules out indeterminacy. The translator can divide a sentence or phrase into parts in any way that is convenient for the practical task of setting up a mapping between expressions. Quine realizes that finding structure in sentences (constructing *analytical hypotheses*, as he calls them) is in fact how the practical business of constructing a translation manual will have to proceed: "[The translator] segments heard utterances into conveniently short recurrent parts, and thus compiles a list of native 'words'. Various of these he hypothetically equates to English words and phrases, in such a way [as to respect the facts about stimulus meanings]. Such are his analytical hypotheses."[19] Evans's point is that the only constraint the translator has to respect on the choice of analytic hypotheses is that they generate the right answers about stimulus meanings of the whole sentences in which the relevant expressions occur. The theorist of meaning, however, is not so unconstrained in projecting structure into his theory: the semantic theory must be so structured that (a) the truth-conditions of the sentences of the language are shown to be dependent upon the semantic properties of the *parts* of those sentences, and (b) the structure of the theory *mirrors* the structure of the linguistic *abilities* of the actual speakers of the language.

Let's try to get clearer on this. The theorist of meaning aims to give a systematic account of the truth-conditions of the sentences of the language under study: he must show how those truth-conditions depend functionally on the semantic properties of those sentences' parts. Thus, for example, he will want to construct a theory of meaning that shows how the truth-condition of, for example, "Lightning is a white cat" is a function of the semantic properties of "Lightning", "white", "cat", and so on. But the semantic theorist is not free to assign semantic properties to those parts in any way that he or she chooses. Semantic properties must be assigned to those parts in such a way that the following additional constraint is respected:

The mirror constraint: A theorem specifying the truth-condition of a sentence S should be derivable from a specification of the semantic properties of the subsentential expressions $s1, \ldots, sn$ if and only if actual speakers of the language are able to move to an understanding of S on the basis of training with and exposure to $s1, \ldots, sn$ as they appear in sentences other than S.

Suppose that speakers of English who understand "Lightning is a white dog" and "Archie is a black cat" are able, without further training and exposure, to understand "Lightning is a white cat":

given this, the mirror constraint says that the theory of meaning must show how the truth-condition of "Lightning is a white cat" is dependent upon the semantic properties of "white", "cat", etc. In other words, the theory of meaning must have axioms for "white", "cat", etc. from which the theorem spelling out the truth-condition for "Lightning is a white cat" is derivable. The structure thus projected into the theory of meaning mirrors the structure of the speakers' linguistic abilities: just as, on the basis of their prior understanding of the subsentential expressions "Lightning", "white" and "cat", and so on, they are able to understand the sentence "Lightning is a white cat", the theory of meaning shows us how the truth-condition of "Lightning is a white cat" is derivable from the semantic axioms for "Lightning", "white", "cat", and so on.

What is the relevance of all this to the indeterminacy of translation? In other words, how does the imposition of the mirror constraint on theories of meaning ensure that they are not prey to indeterminacy? Suppose that we set out to construct a theory of meaning (as opposed to a translation manual) for the native language, and decide, on the basis of facts about stimulus meaning, to interpret "blap" and "gavagai" as meaning *white* and *rabbit* respectively. That is, we decide to include the following as axioms in our theory of meaning:

(1) $(\forall x)(x$ satisfies "gavagai" iff x is a rabbit).
(2) $(\forall x)(x$ satisfies "blap" iff x is white).[20]

Now Quine, wishing to claim indeterminacy in the theory of meaning, will claim that there will be an alternative theory of meaning for the native language, adequate to all of the behavioural data, incorporating not (1), but rather an axiom along the following lines:

(3) $(\forall x)(x$ satisfies "gavagai" iff x is an undetached part of a rabbit).

How can Evans rule out this alternative theory of meaning? Evans claims that, because of the imposition of the mirror constraint, the alternative theory of meaning incorporating (3) will give us an incorrect account of the truth-conditions of some complex sentences in which "gavagai" features. Suppose the theorist of meaning discovers that after exposure to or training with sentences containing "gavagai" and sentences containing "blap", speakers of the native language are able to use and understand "blap gavagai". Then the mirror constraint requires that the theorist of meaning give an account of the truth-conditions of "**a** is a blap gavagai" which shows how this condition is systematically dependent upon the satisfaction conditions of "blap" and "gavagai". That is, we must be able to generate a truth-condition for "**a** is a blap gavagai" on the basis of the axioms that deal with "blap" and "gavagai". Now, on the basis of our axioms (1) and (2), we will get the following truth-condition for "**a** is a blap gavagai"[21]:

(4) "**a** is a blap gavagai" is true iff **a** is a white rabbit.

But what kind of truth-condition for "**a** is a blap gavagai" will a theory of meaning containing axiom (3) generate? If we want to hold on to axiom (2) it will have to be something like

(5) "**a** is a blap gavagai" is true iff **a** is a white undetached rabbit part.

But this won't do! It gets the native stimulus meaning for "**a** is a blap gavagai" entirely wrong. We notice that the natives are prepared to assent to "**a** is a blap gavagai" only when **a** is a wholly white rabbit; whereas if (5) accurately captured its truth-condition, we would expect to find the natives assenting to "**a** is a blap gavagai" in the presence of an otherwise brown rabbit with a white foot. But they don't: in fact they dissent from "**a** is a blap gavagai" in the presence of such a rabbit.

Is there a way out of this for Quine? Perhaps the trouble arose only because we also attempted to hold on to axiom (2) for "blap", treating "blap" as meaning white. Maybe Quine can hold on to (3), and yet respect the facts about stimulus meaning, by dropping (2) and switching instead to

(6) $(\forall x)(x$ satisfies "blap" iff x is a part of a white animal).

This, together with (3), would give us the following truth-condition for "**a** is a blap gavagai":

(7) "**a** is a blap gavagai" is true iff **a** is an undetached rabbit part that is a part of a white animal.

Given these adjustments we can account for the conditions under which "**a** is a blap gavagai" is assented to: the native assents to this when a wholly white rabbit is around because there is an undetached rabbit part around which is a part of a white animal; but he dissents from it when there is a brown rabbit with a white foot around because, although we have an undetached rabbit part around, it is not a part of a white animal.

Is this enough to give Quine his desired alternative but incompatible translation scheme? As Evans points out, it is not. The reading of "blap" encapsulated in (6) now precludes any account of the functioning of "blap" as it appears conjoined with terms other than "gavagai": it cannot account, for example, for the natives' applications of blap to white huts or white pieces of paper.

This, then, is the crux of Evans's argument against Quine. The theorist of meaning has to assign semantic properties to the parts of sentences in such a way that the observed assent conditions of those sentences can be accommodated, and in such a way that the assignment is consistent with the occurrence of those parts in all of the contexts in which they appear. But given this, we can see that the interpretation of "gavagai" as "undetached rabbit part" faces the following dilemma. *If we leave the satisfaction conditions of the expressions with which "gavagai" couples unchanged then we get an account of the truth-conditions of the complex sentences that contain "gavagai" that is out of step with their observed assent conditions; but if we change the satisfaction conditions of some of the other expressions in such a way as to accommodate these assent conditions, then we get an account of the truth-conditions of other sentences containing "blap" that is out of step with their assent conditions.*

Evans thus sees the extra constraints on theories of meaning concerning the systematic relation of sentences' truth-conditions to the semantic properties of their parts as ensuring that a theory of meaning cannot include an axiom to the effect that "gavagai" means *undetached rabbit part*. If we construe "gavagai" as ranging over undetached rabbit parts we do not get a workable account of how the truth-conditions of complex sentences containing "gavagai" depend systematically on the semantic properties of their parts. So the indeterminacy which Quine claimed to find in translation does not vitiate theories of meaning.

Christopher Hookway has suggested that there may be a response available to Quine that would allow him to say that there is still an indeterminacy even in the case of theories of meaning. Contrary to what Evans claims, there is a way of amending the axiom for "blap" that (a) allows us to interpret "gavagai" as meaning *undetached rabbit part*, and (b) is faithful to the stimulus meaning of the sentence "**a** is a blap gavagai", and (c) does not preclude the possibility of "blap" meaningfully occurring with terms other than "gavagai". Hookway's suggested Quinean axiom for "blap" is:

(8) ($\forall x$)(x satisfies "blap" if and only if either (a) "blap" occurs together with "gavagai" and x is part of a white animal, or (b) "blap" occurs in some other context and x is white).

Having a "disjunctive" axiom like (8) allows us to keep axiom (3) for "gavagai", while remaining faithful to the stimulus meaning of "**a** is a blap gavagai", and yet, through clause (b), allows "blap" to occur with terms other than "gavagai". Quine will of course admit that we will prefer a simpler axiom for "blap", such as (2), but again he will say that this preference merely reflects our pragmatic inclinations, rather than our faithfulness to any fact of the matter.

How might Evans respond to this? He might respond that there is a way of distinguishing, on empirical grounds, between a theory of meaning containing axiom (2) and a theory of meaning containing axiom (8) (this response is suggested by Hookway himself). The mirror constraint is designed to ensure that a theory of meaning for a language mirrors the structure of the linguistic abilities of speakers of that language. At the level of the semantic axioms, what this means is that each axiom will attribute to a speaker a disposition corresponding to the relevant primitive expression.[22] Thus, a theory containing axiom (2) will attribute a *single* dispositional state underlying the speaker's uses of "blap". And a theory containing axiom (8) will attribute two dispositional states underlying the speakers uses of "blap": a state underlying the use of "blap" as it occurs together with "gavagai", and another state underlying the use of "blap" as it appears together with expressions other than "gavagai". So which theory should we accept? It looks as if it is going to be the theory that contains axiom (2), since we find, by empirical observation, that the initial training the natives get with "blap" is sufficient to equip them to use it in all contexts, and that there is no need for separate training with it as it appears conjoined with "gavagai". This suggests that there is only a single dispositional state underlying the speaker's uses of "blap", so that there are good empirical reasons to opt for the theory of meaning containing (2) rather than that containing (8).[23]

4.9 The argument from above

In this section we move on to look at Quine's other main line of argument for the indeterminacy of translation, the "argument from above". This is presented in Quine's short paper "On the Reasons for the Indeterminacy of Translation", which appeared ten years after the publication of *Word and Object*. Quine writes:

> My gavagai example has figured too centrally in discussions of the indeterminacy of translation. Readers see the example as the ground of the doctrine, and hope by resolving the example to cast doubt on the doctrine. The real ground of the doctrine is very different, broader and deeper.[24]

The argument from above is thus conceived by Quine to be independent of and more fundamental than the argument from below. It depends on the idea that physical theory is underdetermined by all possible observational evidence. As Quine puts it:

> Theory can still vary though all possible observations be fixed. Physical theories can be at odds with each other and yet compatible with all possible data even in the broadest sense. In a word they can be logically incompatible and empirically equivalent. This is a point on which I expect wide agreement, if only because the observational criteria of theoretical terms are commonly so flexible and so fragmentary.[25]

Now there is no doubt quite a lot to be said about this idea, but here we can only accept it as given and see how far it takes Quine towards the indeterminacy of translation. Quine notes that although most people will agree that physical theory, at some level or other, will be underdetermined by all possible observational evidence, there will be disagreement about the precise level at which the underdetermination kicks in:

> Some will acknowledge such slack only in the highest and most speculative reaches of physical theory, while others see it as extending even to common-sense traits of macroscopic bodies.[26]

Quine does not have to enter into this debate at this point, since his aim in the argument from above is to convince us that the indeterminacy of translation extends as far as the underdetermination of physical theory by possible observations, however far the latter underdetermination is thought to extend:

> What degree of indeterminacy of translation you must then recognize ... will depend on the amount of empirical slack that you are willing to acknowledge in physics. If you were one of those who saw physics as underdetermined only in its highest theoretical reaches, then ... I can claim your concurrence in the indeterminacy of translation only of highly theoretical physics. For my own part, I think the empirical slack in physics extends to ordinary traits of ordinary bodies and hence that the indeterminacy of translation likewise affects that level of discourse.[27]

How, then, does Quine intend to get from the premise that physical theory is underdetermined by all possible observations, to the conclusion that translation is indeterminate? The whole of the argument is contained in one paragraph (pp. 179–80) of "On the Reasons ...". This time we are attempting radical translation of some foreign physicist's theory. Following Robert Kirk's excellent presentation in *Translation Determined*, the argument is best broken down as follows:

[1] The starting point of the process of radical translation is the equating of observation sentences of our language with observation sentences of the foreigner's language, via an inductive equating of stimulus meanings.

[2] In order afterward to construe the foreigner's theoretical sentences we have to project analytical hypotheses.

[3] The ultimate justification for the analytical hypotheses is just that the implied observation sentences match up.

[4] Insofar as the truth of a physical theory is underdetermined by observables, the translation of the foreigner's physical theory is underdetermined by translation of his observation sentences.

Therefore:

[T] Translation of physical theories is indeterminate at least to the extent that physical theories are underdetermined by all possible observations.

Some comments are in order here. First of all, Quine is adamant that the indeterminacy of translation the argument purports to establish is not just another example of the underdetermination of theory by observational evidence, as applied to the special case of translation manuals:

> The indeterminacy of translation is not just an instance of the empirically underdetermined character of physics. The point is not just that linguistics, being a part of behavioral science and hence ultimately of physics, shares the empirically undetermined character of physics. On the contrary, the indeterminacy of translation is additional.[28]

Quine obviously has to say this, since the fact that translation is indeterminate is supposed to establish *that there are no facts of the matter* about the correctness or otherwise of translation manuals. But he certainly does not want to conclude from the fact that physics is observationally underdetermined that there are no facts of the matter about physics. As Hookway points out, Quine endorses J. J. C. Smart's claim that "the physicist's language gives us a *truer* picture of the world than the picture of common sense".[29] Now physics can only give us a truer picture of the world if it is possible to have a *true* picture of the world, and to say that it can give us a true picture of the world is to say that there are *facts* about physics. So Quine must say that the indeterminacy of translation is "additional". But how can he say this? Chomsky has expressed well the thought that the "indeterminacy" Quine claims to find in translation is just *another* instance of the undetermination of theory by observational data:

> It is quite certain that Quine has failed to show that serious hypotheses concerning a native speaker's knowledge of English ... will "go beyond the evidence". Since they go beyond mere summary of data, it will be the case that there are competing assumptions consistent with the data. But why should all of this occasion any surprise or concern?[30]

Chomsky thus attempts to argue that no invidious distinction can be drawn between linguistics (or translation) and physics. However, Kirk spells out well why the indeterminacy of translation is indeed additional, and thus how Quine gets the better of Chomsky here. The point to appeciate is that Quine's claim is that

> Theories of translation are not only underdetermined *as* physics is underdetermined, but underdetermined even *by* the totality of truths expressible in terms of physics.[31]

Likewise, Hookway says that

> Quine has several times stressed that, while theory choice in physics is not determined by all possible evidence, his point now is that, once we have made a choice of physical theory, our choice of translation manual is still open.[32]

Given Quine's physicalism, the claim that incompatible translation manuals are consistent with the totality of *physical facts* does entail that there is no fact of the matter as to which translation manual is correct. This contrasts with, for example, chemical theory: although this too is underdetermined by all possible observational evidence, once we have made a choice of physical theory, our choice of chemical theory would *not* remain open.

Now for some comments on individual premises. [1] seems plausible enough. I begin the process of radical translation by trying to match my observation sentences (see *Word and Object*, section 10) with the observation sentences of the foreigner on the basis of facts about sameness of stimulus meaning. And as Kirk puts it, "In general the sentences of physical theory, regardless of the extent to which they are supposed to be underdetermined by observables, are not observation sentences. So there will not be much – if any – equating of theoretical sentences in the early stages."[33] Likewise, [2] seems plausible enough. As Kirk says, "There seems no way to construct a useful translation manual at all without devising analytical hypotheses."[34] Kirk notes that on one way of reading [3], it is simply a *restatement* of the *argument from below*. All it says is that the choice of analytical hypotheses is underdetermined by all of the possible facts about stimulus meanings: in other words, there will be incompatible analytical hypotheses which are each compatible with all of the facts about stimulus meanings. But, as Kirk stresses, it is very important to note that [3] cannot be allowed to have this significance in the argument from above: if we read [3] in this way, the indeterminacy of translation is *already* derived at [3] and the rest of the argument becomes redundant. But the argument from above is explicitly constructed by Quine with the aim of convincing those who find the argument from below *unconvincing*. And the argument from above is supposed to be the real ground of the indeterminacy doctrine, not the argument from below. So we must not read [3] as a restatement of the argument from below.

How plausible is the argument from above? It is difficult to assess, since it is unclear precisely how Quine sees the move from the premises to the conclusion being effected, and he gives us little in the way of elucidation. In any event, we shall now see that Kirk has a powerful objection against the argument from above. *The objection is that given that [3] is not to be read as a restatement of the argument from below, there is a* non sequitur *in the move from [4] to [T].*

This *non sequitur* can be brought to light by considering the example of Fred the Physicist. Fred is trying to translate Chinese physics. He believes (a) that physics is underdetermined by observational evidence only at the level of quark theory and above, and (b) that physics is not underdetermined by observational evidence below this (for example, at the level of protons, electrons and positrons, etc.). Quine's argument from above has the aim of convincing him that his translation of the Chinese physics *at the level of quarks and above* is indeterminate. Also, Quine must grant Fred, for the sake of argument, that his translation of Chinese physics below the level of quark theory is not indeterminate. Kirk claims that Fred can now maintain that he can determinately translate Chinese quark theory on the basis of his determinate translation of Chinese physics at all of the levels lower than quark theory:

> Fred maintains that there is a large class C of theoretical sentences of Chinese physics [those dealing with levels lower than quark theory] which (a) are not observation sentences, yet (b) are determinately translatable; and that his supposedly determinate translations of all members of C supply him with a sufficiently solid basis to ensure that his translations of Chinese high-level particle physics [quark theory and beyond] are determinate too.[35]

Kirk's point is that unless Quine takes [3] to already establish the indeterminacy of translation, he has nothing to say in response to this suggestion about how Fred can determinately translate Chinese quark theory. In order to see this, note that the conclusion [T] can actually be spelled out as

> [T*] To the extent that the truth of a physical theory is underdetermined by observables, the translation of the foreigner's physical theory is underdetermined by the totality of facts.

But [T*] would follow from [4] only given the assumptions that *the only facts relevant to translation are facts about the translations of observation statements and that those facts do not serve to determine a uniquely correct translation*. But those assumptions amount to the argument from below. If Quine does not make those assumptions, as he must not if the argument from above is not to *assume* the argument from below as one of its premises, he has nothing to say in response to the question, "Why should the determinacy of translation of higher-level theoretical sentences not be guaranteed by behavioural dispositions relating to lower-level theoretical sentences?"[36]

Thus, the argument from above is either invalid (if [3] is not read as a statement of the argument from below); or valid only at the cost of presupposing the argument from below (if [3] is read as a statement of the argument from below). Either way, it seems that Quine has no compelling argument for the indeterminacy doctrine which is "broader and deeper" than the argument from below.

4.10 Conclusion

We have now examined both the argument from below and the argument from above for the indeterminacy thesis, and we have found that there are serious objections that either argument must face. Deciding whether these objections are ultimately compelling is outwith the scope of the present work. Instead, we should end by noting an inherent weakness in Quine's arguments. The only facts that are allowed as possible candidates for constituting the correctness of a translation manual are observable facts about the behavioural dispositions of the speakers, where the notion of "behaviour" involved is a very austere one (see section 4.7). As Kripke has put it: "Quine bases his argument on the outset on behaviouristic premises ... Since Quine sees the philosophy of language within a hypothetical framework of behaviouristic psychology, he thinks of problems about meaning as problems of disposition to behaviour."[37] So even if Quine's arguments can get over the hurdles we have considered, they will even then fail to convince those who fail to find this restriction to thin behavioural facts, and the associated behaviouristic psychology, compelling. It would be much more interesting if we could find arguments that have the same conclusions as Quine's – that there are no facts that render ascriptions of meaning true or false – which do not depend on such behaviouristic assumptions.[38] We consider one such argument – that developed by Kripke's Wittgenstein – in the next two chapters.[39]

Further reading

On analyticity, the reader should certainly start with a careful reading of Quine's "Two dogmas of empiricism", reprinted in his *From a logical point of view*, since we have only been able to give a flavour of his arguments from this classic paper. After that, the thing to read is Grice and Strawson's "In defense of a dogma", *Philosophical Review* (1956), which contains much interesting and useful argument in addition to that mentioned in the text. Grice and Strawson are criticized by G. Harman in his "Quine on meaning and existence (I)", *Review of Metaphysics* (1967). Another useful paper is H. Putnam's "The analytic and the synthetic", in his *Mind, language, and reality*. Chapters 2 and 3 of Christopher Hookway's *Quine* contain much useful background material on Quine's relationship to the logical positivist tradition. A detailed and comprehensive survey of the issues surrounding the notion of analyticity can be found in Paul Boghossian's "Analyticity", in *The Blackwell companion to the philosophy of language*. This also contains an extensive bibliography on the topic.

It is worth noting here that the arguments of the final two sections of "Two dogmas" have received more acceptance than the arguments of the first four sections, which are now generally acknowledged to be unsuccessful. So suppose, for the sake of argument, that Wright's criticisms of holism are unsuccessful. Is there any way a defender of Quine can hive off the arguments in the final two sections from the arguments of the first four sections – in other words, can Quine concede that the arguments in the first four sections are unconvincing without thereby giving the game away to Carnap and the logical positivists? See Hookway, *Quine*, pp. 37–47, and Wright, *Truth and objectivity*, pp. 154–5, for arguments to the effect that Quine may indeed be able to do this.

On indeterminacy of translation, the classic texts are Chapter 2 of Quine's *Word and object*, and his paper "On the reasons for the indeterminacy of translation", *Journal of Philosophy* (1970). The most important papers in the secondary literature are G. Evans's

"Identity and predication", *Journal of Philosophy* (1975), and Noam Chomsky's "Quine's empirical assumptions", in D. Davidson and J. Hintikka (eds), *Words and Objections*. Some of these papers can make very heavy reading: Christopher Hookway's *Quine*, Chapters 8–10, contains much superlatively clear exposition and valuable discussion of the main issues (the influence of Hookway's presentation on my own should be clear enough). Robert Kirk's *Translation determined* is a very detailed discussion of the issues: Chapter 6 is extremely good on the "argument from above". An overview of the issue can be found in Crispin Wright's "Indeterminacy of translation", in *The Blackwell companion to the philosophy of language,* which also contains a list of further reading.

Chapter 5

Scepticism about sense (II): Kripke's Wittgenstein's sceptical paradox

In this chapter we move on to look at another form of scepticism about sense, that developed by Kripke's Wittgenstein (KW) in Kripke's *Wittgenstein on Rules and Private Language.*[1] Let Jones be a typical or representative speaker of English, and consider such sentences as "Jones means *addition* by '+'", "Jones understands the '+' sign to mean *addition*", "The sense that Jones associates with the '+' sign is such that it stands for the *addition* function". KW argues for a form of constitutive scepticism about such claims: there is no fact of the matter that constitutes Jones's meaning one thing rather than another by the "+" sign, no fact of the matter that constitutes his attaching one sense rather than another to the "+" sign. Another way of putting the conclusion would be: ascriptions of meaning or sense do not themselves possess sense, they do not have truth-conditions, and are neither true nor false. This is KW's "sceptical paradox". After arguing for this, KW goes on to try to neutralize its impact: even though there are no facts in virtue of which ascriptions of sense and meaning are true or false, we can still find a place for them by viewing them as possessing *some non fact-stating* role. This is KW's "sceptical solution". In this chapter we'll outline KW's arguments for the sceptical paradox, and his own sceptical solution to that paradox. We'll see that the sceptical solution fails, so that some more direct response to the sceptical paradox is called for. In the next chapter, we'll look at a number of such responses that have been developed by contemporary philosophers of language.

5.1 The sceptical paradox

The conclusion of KW's sceptical argument is that there is no fact of the matter in virtue of which such sentences as "Jones means *addition* by '+'" or "Smith means *green* by 'green'" are either true or false. The general strategy that KW adopts in arguing for this conclusion is as follows. First, it is argued that if the species of fact under suspicion is to be found, then it must be found within some set of particular areas. Once this has been done, our knowledge acquiring powers are imagined to be idealized with respect to those areas: we are given *unlimited epistemic access* to the areas in question. Given this, and the ensuing conclusion that even under *these* conditions the sought-after facts still elude our grasp, that any particular claim about the character of these facts still cannot be justified by us, it follows that there simply were *no* such facts there in the first place. For if there were any such facts, given unlimited epistemic access we would surely have found them, and would surely have been able to justify at least some claims concerning their character. But we cannot do this, so, the argument goes, there cannot be any such facts.[2]

KW outlines his argument with an example from simple arithmetic, and asks, "In virtue of what fact did I mean, in the past, the addition function by my use of the '+' sign?"[3] In order to make the question vivid, he imagines the following example. Suppose that "68 + 57" is a computation that I have never performed before. Since I've performed at most only finitely many computations in the past, we can be sure that such an example exists (even if you have performed this computation before, just suppose, for the sake of argument, that you haven't: the argument would work just as well for any other computation you haven't actually performed). Also, the finitude of my previous computations ensures that there is an example where both of the arguments (in this case 68, 57) are larger than any other numbers I've previously dealt with (again, even if this is not the case in the present example, we can easily enough imagine one for which it is the case, and nothing turns on this).

Now suppose that I perform the computation and obtain "125" as my answer. After checking my working out, I can be confident that "125" is the correct answer. It is the correct answer in two senses: first, it is correct in the arithmetical sense, since 125 is indeed, as a matter of arithmetical fact, the sum of 68 and 57; and it is correct in the metalinguistic sense, since the "+" sign really does mean the addition function. (You can imagine how these two senses of correctness might come apart: if the "+" sign really stood for the subtraction function, 125 would still be the sum of 68 and 57, but the correct answer to the question "68 + 57 = ?" would now be "11"). But is my confidence that I have given the correct answer justified? KW imagines a "bizarre sceptic" arguing that it is not:

Now suppose I encounter a bizarre sceptic. This sceptic questions my certainty about my answer, in what I just called the "metalinguistic" sense. Perhaps, he suggests, as I used the term "plus" in the past, the answer I intended for "68 + 57" should have been "5"! Of course the sceptic's suggestion is obviously insane. My initial response to such a suggestion might be that the challenger should go back to school and learn to add. Let the challenger, however, continue. After all, he says, if I am now so confident that, as I used the symbol "+", my intention was that "68 + 57" should turn out to denote 125, this cannot be because I explicitly gave myself instructions that 125 is the result of performing the addition in this particular instance. By hypothesis, I did no such thing. But of course the idea is that, in this new instance, I should apply the very same function or rule that I applied so many times in the past. But who is to say what function this was? In the past I gave myself only a finite number of examples instantiating this function. All, we have supposed, involved numbers smaller than 57. So perhaps in the past I used "plus" and "+" to denote a function which I will call "quus" and symbolize by " $\oplus$ ". It is defined by

$x \oplus y = x + y$, if $x, y < 57$
$\qquad = 5$ otherwise.

Who is to say that this is not the function I previously meant by "+"?[4]

KW's challenge is thus: cite some fact about yourself that constitutes your meaning *addition* rather than *quaddition* by the "+" sign. Any response to this challenge has to satisfy two conditions. First, it has to provide us with an account of the type of fact that is constitutive of the meaning of "+". Secondly, it has to be possible to *read off* from this fact what constitutes *correct* and *incorrect* use of the "+" sign – it must show why the answer to the problem "68 + 57 = ?" is *justified*.

KW is thus challenging us to provide an acceptable answer to the question: In virtue of what fact are you now justified in answering "125" to the query "What is 68 + 57?"? In accordance with the general strategy outlined above, KW begins his argument that this challenge cannot be met by allowing us unlimited epistemic access to two areas, and inviting us to find a suitable meaning-constituting fact from within either of those two areas. The areas in question are *(a) our previous behaviour, linguistic and non-linguistic; and (b) the entire contents of our previous mental histories.*[5]

Nothing from the finite pool of my previous behaviour will do, since *ex hypothesi* I have never dealt with numbers larger than 57 and "+" and "$\oplus$" have the same extensions for numbers smaller than 57. Anything that is a "correct" answer to "$x + y = ?$" will also be a "correct" answer to "$x \oplus y = ?$" so long as $x, y < 57$. Enlarging the pool of previous behaviour won't make a difference, since no matter how it is enlarged, a "deviant" interpretation of "+", such as that which takes it as standing for the quaddition function, will always be possible: even if we enlarge the pool of previous behaviour so that we have encountered numbers larger than 57, there will always be some number that is larger than those we have previously encountered, and the sceptic can use this to construct an analogue of the quaddition interpretation.

At this point, KW imagines the following protest:

[O]ur problem arises only because of a ridiculous model of the instruction I gave myself regarding "addition". Surely I did not merely give myself some finite number of examples from which I am supposed to extrapolate the whole [function] ... Rather I learned – and internalized instructions for – a *rule* which determines how addition is to be continued. What was the rule? Well, say, to take it in its most primitive form: suppose we wish to add x and y. First count out x marbles in one heap. Then count out y marbles in another. Put the two heaps together and count out the number of marbles in the union thus formed.[6]

Isn't it this fact about what I had previously learnt and internalized that constitutes the fact that I meant *addition* and not *quaddition*? Alas, the sceptic has a response to this suggestion:

True, if "count", as I used the word in the past, referred to the act of counting (and my other past words are correctly interpreted in the standard way), then "plus" must have stood for *addition*. But I applied "count", like "plus", to only finitely many past cases. Thus the sceptic can question my present interpretation of my past usage of "count" as he did with "plus". In particular, he can claim that by "count" I formerly meant Quount, where to "quount" a heap is to count it in the ordinary sense, unless the heap was formed as the union of two heaps, one of which has 57 or more items, in which case one must automatically give the answer "5".[7]

Thus, if I follow the "counting" rule properly, I really ought to answer "5" when asked "68 + 57 = ?" We are back to where we started: citing something like a *general thought or instruction* in response to the sceptical challenge won't work, because the sceptic can always respond by giving a deviant interpretation of the symbols of the general thought or instruction itself. And the point can be generalized: any set of instructions that come before the mind requires interpretation as much as the linguistic expression whose understanding they are supposed to facilitate, and are thus as susceptible to deviant interpretation as that original expression. Clearly, invoking instructions for interpreting the instructions will send us off on a fruitless infinite regress. Kripke takes himself here to be expounding Wittgenstein's remarks in the *Philosophical Investigations* on "a rule for interpreting a rule": "… any interpretation still hangs in the air along with what it interprets, and cannot give it any support. Interpretations by themselves do not determine meaning."[8] We'll return to this in due course.

It thus looks as if no fact about my previous behaviour will do the trick. Does the search within our *mental histories* fare any better? Does the possession of some *mental image*, or some other specific mental item possessed of its own distinctive qualitative character provide what we are after? KW argues that it does not.

First, it is not a *necessary* condition for understanding that some particular item come before one's mind when one hears or uses a given expression. As a matter of empirical fact, it seems to be the case that no one "mental entity" comes before one's mind when one correctly understands a linguistic expression. And even in cases where there does seem to be an empirical regularity between a particular expression and a particular such item we can still perfectly well *conceive* of someone understanding the expression in the absence of that item (indeed, we can conceive of someone understanding the expression even when *no* such item is present at all). KW's conclusion is that it is no more necessary for understanding an expression that I have an inner mental picture before my mind than it is that I have a concrete physical picture ready to hand – just as I can perfectly well understand "cube" without having a drawing of a cube in front of me on the table, so I can understand it without having to call up a mental image.

Secondly, neither is it a *sufficient* condition for meaning a sign in a particular way that some item, be it a picture or otherwise, come before one's mind. *The essential point is that the picture does not by itself determine the correct use of the associated word, because the picture thus associated is really just another sign whose meaning also requires to be fixed.* There is no logical route from the properties of an image or picture to the meaning of an associated word, because of the possibility of deviant applications of the word consistent with some interpretation of the picture; the relation of any picture or image to the associated word can be construed in such a way that any future pattern of use of the expression can count as correct. Whatever comes before the mind can be made to accord with a deviant application of the expression. Thus, mental images set no standards for the correct use of an expression: one cannot "read off" from a mental image what counts as the correct use of an associated expression. In order to drive this point home, we can imagine someone at the hands of an omnipotent but curious experimenter, conditioned by the experimenter to have the image of a cube every time he hears the word "cube"; but again, this will not be sufficient to determine what he understands by the word in question. We might of course admit that images *naturally suggest* certain applications, but the important point is rather that they do not logically determine them. It is possible that two people might understand a word differently – they might go on to use it differently – even though the same images occurred to them on hearing it.[9]

KW considers a further reply, which, drawing on the subject's past mental life, might be adduced in response to the sceptical argument. This is that in the paragraphs above we have concentrated too exclusively on what might be called "quotidian" states of the mind – such as mental images, sensations, headaches and other introspectible mental states with their own distinctive phenomenological character. Perhaps meaning addition is not a state of these kinds, but rather an irreducible state, "a primitive state ... a state of a unique kind of its own".[10] This response, however, is castigated by KW on the grounds that it is "desperate" and leaves "completely mysterious" the character of the primitive state thought to constitute understanding. For one thing, it is not an introspectible state, and yet its possessor is thought to be aware of it with some fair degree of certainty whenever they have it. How could this be possible? It is also completely mysterious, moreover, how "a finite object contained in our finite minds" could be such as to reach out to a number of future uses of an expression and determine whether or not they are correct in the light of that expression's meaning. It is a mystery what the relationship is between these future uses and the putative primitive state; the response as it stands gives no clue as to what the nature of this relationship is, or how it is forged.

KW now considers a suggestion that at first seems to issue in a plausible refutation of his sceptical argument. The suggestion is that in limiting us to facts concerning our *past* actual behaviour and our previous *occurrent* mental states, KW has already guaranteed himself success: rather, we should consider *dispositional* facts about language users. These will enable us to distinguish between the hypothesis that I meant *addition* in the past and the hypothesis that I meant *quaddition* in the past. The claim that I meant *addition* would be true if I was disposed in the past, when asked to compute "$x + y$", to produce the *sum* of the two numbers. Similarly, the claim that I meant *quaddition* would be true if I was disposed, when faced with the same query, to respond with the result of *quadding* the two numbers. Thus, were my knowledge acquiring powers concerning my dispositional properties sufficiently idealized, I would no doubt see that I was disposed to give the answer "125" to the query, even though in fact I never did, because I was never asked to. KW's claim that I meant some function other than addition would thus be refuted.

KW, however, has two powerful objections to the dispositionalist account. The first objection is that the dispositionalist account completely fails to take account of the *normativity* of meaning – in effect, it fails to satisfy the second of the two conditions laid down earlier in this section on any candidate fact for meaning addition. We say that a competent language speaker *ought*, given their previous meanings and their intention to remain faithful to them, to respond to arithmetical questions, for example, in certain determinate ways, and we believe that the response they ought to give is logically independent of the response they *did* give, or *would have given*, had they actually been faced with the query. But the dispositionalist account leaves no room for such a distinction between the answer they ought to have given and the answer they would have given, for, according to the dispositional account, the answer they ought to have given simply collapses into the answer that they would have given. In a nutshell, the dispositionalist response appears to involve the intuitively unacceptable equation of *competence* and *performance*. Kripke sums the problem up as follows:

> Suppose I do mean addition by "+". What is the relation of this supposition to the question how I will respond to the problem "68 + 57"? The dispositionalist gives a *descriptive* account of this relation: if "+" meant addition, then I will answer "125". But this is not the proper account of the relation, which is *normative*, not

descriptive. The point is *not* that, if I meant addition by "+", I *will* answer "125", but rather that, if I intend to accord with my past meaning of "+", I *should* answer "125". Computational error, finiteness of my capacity, and other disturbing factors may lead me not to be *disposed* to respond as I *should*, but if so, I have not acted in accordance with my intentions. The relation of meaning and intention to future action is *normative*, not *descriptive*.[11]

This problem shows up further in the fact that intuitively we want to be able to leave room for the possibility that someone is *systematically mistaken*, in the sense that they are disposed to make mistakes. For example, someone might be disposed to miscarry systematically when carrying out addition problems, and we want to leave room for the possibility that such a person means addition but is giving answers out of line with those that they ought to give: we do not want to be committed to the conclusion that they in fact mean are some different arithmetical function and are after all counting correctly.

The second problem for dispositions is that they are, like the totality of our previous linguistic behaviour, finite. For example, it simply is not true that I am disposed in such a way that I will always give the sum of two numbers when faced with "What is $x + y$?": some numerals will simply be too long for me to handle and some will be so long that I will die before having an opportunity to respond to the query. Given this, it is easy for KW to construct unwelcome interpretations that are nevertheless compatible with all of the dispositional facts concerning me – for example, perhaps I meant skaddition, where this is defined as

$x * y = x + y$, if x, y are small enough for me to handle,
$\quad = 5$, otherwise.

I would then be unable to cite any fact about my dispositions that could constitute my meaning addition and that would be incompatible with the hypothesis that I meant skaddition. Dispositions are thus unable to fix the meaning of the "+" sign.

So none of the facts we have considered – facts about our previous behaviour, facts about our behavioural dispositions, facts about general thoughts or instructions, facts about "quotidian" mental states like mental images, facts about *sui generis* and irreducible states of meaning and understanding – appear to be plausible candidates for constituting the fact that we mean *addition* rather than *quaddition* by "+". We appear to be facing the conclusion that there is no fact of the matter as to what we meant in the past by "+", and since our present understanding of "+" will be up for retrospective viewing in the future, it follows that there is no fact of the matter as to what we mean at present by "+" either. And, since the sceptical argument could, without any loss, be rerun against anyone else and any other linguistic expression, it follows that there are no facts of the matter as to what anyone means by any expression.[12] The notion of meaning apparently has, as Kripke puts it, "vanished into thin air".[13]

Before continuing, it is perhaps worthwhile to pause to note how KW's argument relates to some of the Fregean theses about sense that we outlined in Chapter 2. Recall that, according to thesis 8, the sense of an expression determines its semantic value. In the case of an incomplete sign such as "...+...", this means that its sense has to determine which function it stands for (or, alternatively, its extension). KW's argument in effect proceeds as follows: no fact could constitute Jones's attaching a particular sense to "+" because all of the possible facts that we could cite as constituting Jones's grasping a sense are themselves compatible with "+" standing for different functions (or having incompatible extensions). For example, facts about Jones's dispositions are compatible with "+", as he understands it, standing for either the addition function or the quaddition function. So, no facts about Jones's dispositions – nor any of the other sorts of fact considered – determine the extension of "+" as he understands it. So since the sense of "+" determines its extension, none of these facts can constitute Jones's grasping its sense. So, given the assumption about idealized epistemic access, there is no fact of the matter as to the sense of "+". Note also that some of the other Fregean theses play a role in the argument: for example, thesis 20 is what lies behind the normativity objection to dispositionalism. KW can perhaps be viewed as arguing that it is impossible to find any fact that could satisfy all of the main Fregean theses concerning sense: even if dispositional facts could determine the extension of "...+...", they would still fall down on the normativity requirement.

5.2 The sceptical solution and the argument against solitary language

Kripke distinguishes between two ways in which KW's sceptical argument might be responded to. One way he describes as a "straight solution". This would consist of a demonstration of the thesis that the sceptic called into question: the production of a suitable meaning-constituting fact of the sort the sceptic questions. On the other hand, there is what Kripke describes as a "sceptical solution". Such a solution would consist of two parts. First, an admission that the sort of fact questioned by the sceptic is in fact nonexistent. Secondly, in a more positive vein, an argument is then provided to the effect that the area of discourse does not have to be viewed as fact-stating in order for it to enjoy a tenable position within our lives. In other words, in the special case of, for example, meaning, it would be argued that our practice involving sentences that ascribe meaning and understanding does not require for its tenability the sort of justification that the sceptic demands, namely, an account of the facts that would render them true or false, or their truth-conditions. We can justify our practice of ascribing meaning and understanding in other terms. It is this latter sort of solution, a sceptical solution, that Kripke sees Wittgenstein himself advocating in the *Philosophical Investigations*.[14]

KW thus admits, at the outset of the sceptical solution, that sentences ascribing meaning do not have truth-conditions, that there are no facts or states of affairs in virtue of which such sentences have truth or falsity conferred upon them. As textual support for his claim that Wittgenstein rejected the idea that sentences had to be viewed as possessing truth-conditions in order for our practices with them to be deemed legitimate, Kripke cites Michael Dummett's claim that the emphasis in Wittgenstein's early work, the *Tractatus*, upon facts and truth-conditions was replaced in the later *Philosophical Investigations* by a completely different emphasis.[15] In the later work, the emphasis is on describing the conditions under which sentences are deemed to be *justified* or *assertable*, and on the *role or utility* that so deeming them assertable under those conditions has within our lives. As far as meaning goes, then, the change in emphasis that Kripke sees Wittgenstein as recommending is this: we are enjoined not to look for "entities" or "facts" corresponding to sentences ascribing meaning, but rather to look at the circumstances under which such ascriptions are actually made, and the utility that resides in ascribing them under these conditions. If these conditions and the corresponding role and utility can be specified adequately, then, KW suggests, we will have provided a sceptical solution to his own sceptical problem.

What are the relevant conditions, utility and role? Consider the sentence "Jones means *addition* by '+'". If Jones is considered in isolation from any linguistic community – as a speaker of a solitary language – then the conditions under which this will be asserted will correspond to those under which Jones himself would assert "I mean addition by '+'". There will thus be no distinction between the assertion conditions of "Jones believes that he means *addition* by '+'" and "Jones means *addition* by '+'". Thus, whatever seems right to Jones will be right, "and that only means that here we can't talk about 'right'".[16] Thus, in the case of an individual considered in isolation, the sceptical solution will be powerless to salvage any point to our practices with the notion of meaning, since any such reconstruction must respect the fact that the meaning an individual speaker attaches to an expression is normative with respect to his inclinations to apply it in certain ways. Kripke takes this to be the upshot of Wittgenstein's famous claim that "to think one is obeying a rule is not to obey a rule. Hence, it is not possible to obey a rule 'privately': otherwise thinking one was obeying a rule would be the same thing as obeying it".[17]

Matters stand differently when Jones is considered, not as a solitary individual, but as a member of a linguistic community. The utterance of "Jones means addition by '+'" is then considered to be justified when Jones has performed satisfactorily often enough with "+", where this is taken to involve nothing more than that Jones has satisfactorily often enough come up with the answer that most of the rest of his fellow speakers in the community are disposed to give. The utterance of the sentence thus marks the community's acceptance of Jones into its midst, and it marks also the community's conviction that Jones can generally be trusted to act as they do in transactions that involve the use of the "+" sign. The utility of uttering ascriptions of meaning under such conditions is clear. They allow us to discriminate between those people we can trust in our transactions involving "+" and those we cannot. More generally, they allow us to discriminate between people who are members of our general linguistic community and those who are not. A grocer who "means addition by '+'" is one who can be trusted to treat me as I expect when I go in to his shop to buy five apples. And note, crucially, that in the communal setting there is a distinction between the conditions under which it is assertable that Jones believes that he means addition, and the conditions under which it is assertable that he actually does mean this: it might indeed be the case that Jones believes that he means addition, but at the same time the rest of the community finds that his use of the "+" sign is out of step with theirs, so that the assertion conditions for "Jones means addition by '+'" are not in fact met.

To sum up then, the sceptical solution admits that discourse involving meaning is not fact-stating, but attempts to legitimize it by finding it a legitimate non-fact-stating role to play. This involves spelling out the assertability conditions of ascriptions of meaning, and showing that asserting them under these conditions plays a useful role in our lives. It emerges that these assertion conditions involve an essential reference to a linguistic community, since the community underwrites the "seems right/is right" distinction essential to any conception of meaning. The preservation of a legitimate role for ascriptions of meaning is thus claimed by KW to deliver a demonstration of the impossibility of a solitary language.[18]

5.3 Boghossian's argument against the sceptical solution

Two sorts of general criticism can be levelled against KW's "sceptical solution". First, that the sceptical solution does not succeed in establishing the impossibility of solitary language. Secondly, that such a sceptical solution about meaning is *internally incoherent*. We shall concern ourselves here only with criticisms of the second, more general, type.[19] We'll first look at an argument developed by Paul Boghossian, which purports to establish that the sceptical solution is incoherent. We'll argue that

Boghossian's argument is unsuccesful. In section 5.4, we'll look at an objection to the sceptical solution that has been raised by Crispin Wright, and suggest that it too is unsuccessful. We'll finish in section 5.5 by outlining José Zalabardo's (apparently successful) argument against the sceptical solution.

Boghossian's objection forms part of a general line of attack against what he terms *irrealist* conceptions of content:[20] against both *error-conceptions* of content – which claim that ascriptions of meaning possess genuine truth-conditions but are nevertheless *systematically false* – and against *nonfactualist* conceptions of content, according to which ascriptions of meaning do not even possess genuine truth-conditions.[21] KW's sceptical solution falls into the latter, nonfactualist, category of irrealist conception, so we'll concentrate here on Boghossian's argument against non-factualist accounts of meaning.

Boghossian notes that it is constitutive of nonfactualism about a given discourse that it denies that significant declarative sentences from that discourse have truth-conditions. He also notes that on a *deflationary conception of truth*, for a sentence to possess truth-conditions it is sufficient that it be disciplined by norms of correct usage, and that it possess the syntax distinctive of declarative sentences. It would seem to follow, therefore, that anyone wishing to advance a nonfactualist thesis about a given region of discourse would have to operate with a conception of truth richer than the deflationary: he would have to operate with what Boghossian terms a *robust conception of truth*, a conception "committed to holding that the predicate 'true' stands for some sort of language independent property, eligibility for which will not be certified purely by the fact that a sentence is significant and declarative".[22] For example, such sentences as "Jones means addition by '+'" are subject to norms of discipline, and are syntactically well-formed declaratives. So according to the deflationary conception they must have truth-conditions. But nonfactualism about meaning claims that they do not have truth-conditions. So nonfactualism about meaning presupposes that the deflationary conception of truth is false: nonfactualism presupposes, in the sense above, a robust conception of truth.

Boghossian now attempts to show that nonfactualism about meaning also entails that truth is *not* robust. It would then follow that nonfactualism about meaning presupposes both that truth is robust and also that truth is *not* robust, and this would demonstrate the incoherence of the nonfactualist position. Boghossian notes that nonfactualism consists in the following pair of claims. For any S, p:

(1) There is no property corresponding to the predicate "has truth-condition p",

and

(2) "S has truth-condition p" is not truth-conditional.[23]

Boghossian now argues that it follows from (1) that

(3) There is no property corresponding to the predicate "is true".

Why does this follow? Boghossian argues as follows. First of all, whether or not a sentence is true is a function of two things: the truth-condition it possesses and the way the world is. For example, the fact that the sentence "Grass is green" is true is a function of the fact that it has the following truth-condition:

(4) "Grass is green" is true iff grass is green

and of the fact that grass is, as a matter of fact, green. Secondly, if one of the things that determines whether a is F is nonfactual, then it will follow that there is no fact of the matter as to whether a is F either. This can be illustrated by using an example of Crispin Wright's:

> If among the determinants of whether it is worth while going to see a certain exhibition is how well presented the leading exhibits are, then, if questions of good presentation are not considered to be entirely factual, neither is the matter of whether it is worth while going to see the exhibition.[24]

If whether an exhibition (a) is worth while going to see (F) is determined in part by whether the leading exhibits are well-presented, and if there is no fact of the matter as to whether the leading exhibits are well-presented, then there will be no fact of the matter as to whether the exhibition is worth while going to see either (that is, no fact of the matter as to whether a is F). Applying this line of argument to the case of truth and truth-conditions: since the truth-value of a sentence is a function of its truth-condition, if there is no fact of the matter as to which truth-condition it possesses, it will follow that there is no fact of the matter as to its truth-value either. In other words, it follows from nonfactualism about meaning that, for any S,

(5) "S is true" is not truth-conditional.

But this is just to say that there is no property, truth, in virtue of the instantiation (or non-instantiation) of which sentences are true (or false). In other words, it follows that

(3) There is no property corresponding to the predicate "is true".

But if there is no property corresponding to the predicate "is true", then *a fortiori* there is no language-independent property corresponding to the predicate "is true". In other words, truth cannot be robust.

So the difficulty for nonfactualism about meaning is clear: it requires, via (2), the presupposition that truth is robust. But at the same time it entails, in the manner outlined above, that truth cannot be robust. Boghossian suggests that this constitutes a *reductio ad absurdum* of nonfactualism about meaning.

Since the publication of Boghossian's argument against nonfactualism about meaning, many responses to his argument have appeared in the literature (see the further reading section for a selection). We'll now attempt to add yet another response to this list. This response attempts to show that the nonfactualist about meaning can formulate his thesis in such a way that it does not entail the contradiction that Boghossian focuses on.

Jane Heal, in her book, *Fact and Meaning: Quine and Wittgenstein on the Philosophy of Language*, has suggested two conditions that a region of discourse has to satisfy in order for it to have a factual subject matter. First, the sentences of that region of discourse must satisfy the *law of non-contradiction*: it must not be possible for two incompatible sentences within that region to be equally fully acceptable. Secondly, the relevant sentences must satisfy a condition of *minimal doxastic independence*: the fact that a given sentence is true must not follow simply from the fact that some speaker believes it to be true. According to Heal, a demonstration that a region of discourse failed to satisfy either of these conditions would be sufficient to establish nonfactualism about the sentences of that discourse.

Interestingly, KW's sceptical argument does appear to take the form of a challenge to the claim that the law of noncontradiction is satisfied by sentences purporting to ascribe meaning. KW's claim is, after all, that there is no way of showing that the hypothesis that you mean *addition* is more acceptable than the incompatible hypothesis that you mean *quaddition*. Given Heal's necessary conditions on factuality, it follows straightforwardly that sentences ascribing meaning are nonfactual.

Is this way of viewing the route to the nonfactualism about meaning susceptible to Boghossian's argument? It seems not: it now appears that a nonfactualist about meaning can state his thesis without presupposing any commitment to a robust notion of truth. All the nonfactualist has to argue is that the significant, declarative sentences that constitute putative ascriptions of meaning do not satisfy the law of noncontradiction in Heal's sense. They are therefore nonfactual. Now where in this is the commitment to the view that truth is robust? *In arguing thus the nonfactualist does not seem to have become committed to the view that truth is some language-independent property.* Or at least, it requires some more substantial argument to show that they are so committed: at a minimum, Boghossian requires a substantial argument to show that a commitment to robust truth – in the form of a commitment to a view of truth as a language-independent property – emerges in any account of the rationale for taking nonsatisfaction of the law of noncontradiction to entail nonfactuality.

To put the point slightly differently, we can now represent KW as arguing in the following way:

(6) A discourse must satisfy Heal's law of noncontradiction in order to be factual.

(7) Discourse about meaning does not satisfy Heal's law of noncontradiction (the claim that you mean *addition* by "+" can no more be justified than the claim that you mean *quaddition* by "+").

So,

(8) Discourse about meaning is nonfactual.

Where does the commitment to a view of "true" as standing for a language-independent property surface in this formulation of KW's argument? (7) is just a statement of the conclusion of KW's sceptical argument, which we are supposed to be granting in order to evaluate his sceptical solution, so the only route open to Boghossian would seem to be to argue that the commitment to robust truth is contained implicitly in (6). And there is our unanswered question: why should laying down satisfaction of the law of noncontradiction as a necessary condition on factuality harbour a commitment to a view of truth as a language-independent property? The onus is on Boghossian to answer this question.

We can thus tentatively suggest that KW does have a way of stating his nonfactualist thesis about meaning in a manner that avoids the outright contradiction described by Boghossian. The internal incoherence of the sceptical solution has thus not yet been established.

5.4 Wright's objections to the sceptical solution

Perhaps the argument advanced by Boghossian, although not ultimately successful as it stands, does contain, in one of its steps, the resources for another argument that does undermine the sceptical solution. This is the argument, originally given by Wright, to the effect that if meaning is a nonfactual matter, it follows that the truth of sentences is likewise a nonfactual matter: in other words, it follows that no sentences whatsoever have a factual subject matter. Now this is quite striking: nonfactualism about meaning entails global nonfactualism, nonfactualism about all regions of discourse. Doesn't this show that there must be something wrong with nonfactualism about meaning?

There are (at least) two considerations that seem to suggest an affirmative answer to this question. First, if all sentences are nonfactual, this includes the conclusion of the sceptical argument itself together with the sentences that comprise KW's sceptical solution. Then the worry, as expressed by Wright, is that "a statement of the sceptical argument, for instance, is not itself to be projective".[25] Does this pose a genuine problem for KW? It is difficult to avoid agreeing with Boghossian's point that it is at least not transparent that there is a genuine difficulty here: "A global [non-factualism] would have to admit that it is no more than assertible that no sentence possess a truth condition. But what is wrong with that? If there is an instability here, it is not a transparent one."[26] Why cannot KW get by with the claim that, although the conclusion of the sceptical argument is itself lacking in truth-conditions, it is nevertheless assertable under certain conditions, and that its assertion has some point or role to play in our lives? At the very least, more substantial argument is required to show that this sort of story could not be sufficient for KW's purposes.

There is, however, perhaps a different line of argument lurking in Wright's objection. Surely the claim that sentences ascribing meaning are nonfactual is intended by KW to show that such sentences *compare unfavourably* with some other body of sentences, those that are genuinely factual and possess genuine truth-conditions. In other words, KW's argument depends on the existence of a *distinction* between factual and nonfactual sentences, and it is then supposed to emerge as a substantial conclusion that ascriptions of meaning fall on the nonfactual side of this divide. The suggestion would then be that if, as suggested by Wright's argument above, it follows that *no* sentences are factual, it is difficult to see what distinction there could be between factual and nonfactual sentences: KW, it would be suggested, owes us an account of what this distinction consists in, and the objection is that, given the consequences of his sceptical conclusion, he will be unable to do so. The sceptical conclusion and sceptical solution depend on a distinction that they themselves seem to obliterate.

Is this line of argument conclusive? It seems not. For one thing, someone claiming that there are no square circles can hardly be criticized if they are unable to give a substantial account of what it would be for a circle to be square. Why should it be any different for a sceptic who claims that there are no factual discourses? To be sure, in the case of square circles we can say that something would be a square circle if it satisfied a certain set of mathematical equations, which turn out to be *a priori* unsatisfiable. But likewise, in the case of the sceptic, we can say what it is for a predicate to have truth-conditions – for example, satisfying Heal's two conditions (section 5.3) on the factuality of a discourse – even though these turn out as an *a priori* matter never to be jointly satisfiable. Secondly, and perhaps more importantly, it seems in any case that the onus is not on KW to give substance to the factual/nonfactual distinction. All he has to do is take *our* favoured conception of factuality and show that on that conception ascriptions of meaning fail to be factual: if it follows from this that the notion of factuality in play has no instances, KW can simply reply – can't he? – that this is so much the worse for us, and that his argument not only shows that our notion of meaning vanishes into thin air, it goes further and shows that our notion of factuality vanishes with it. So it is by no means clear that the consequence of the sceptical solution Wright focuses on constitutes a difficulty for KW, rather than just an additional difficulty for someone concerned to avoid the conclusion of the sceptical argument. Again, the objection appears to leave the sceptical solution intact.

5.5 Zalabardo's objection to the sceptical solution

The final objection against the sceptical solution that we shall consider is perhaps more damaging. Curiously enough, it is suggested by an objection that KW himself raises in the course of giving his argument for the sceptical paradox. At one stage in that argument KW considers a reply to the sceptical argument that has it that a choice between the incompatible but apparently equally acceptable hypotheses that it was *addition* that was meant and that it was *quaddition* that was meant, could be made by some kind of appeal to the *simplicity* of the respective hypotheses: perhaps it is the simplest function that should be deemed to have been meant. KW, however, is scornful of this suggestion, but not merely because "simplicity is relative, or that it is hard to define, or that a martian might find the quus function simpler than the plus function".[27] These are indeed problems, but KW suggests that the difficulty with the suggestion is in fact more basic, and that it relies on a misunderstanding of the nature of the conclusion of the sceptical argument. The conclusion proper of the sceptical argument was not that there are two competing genuine hypotheses about what was meant: that conclusion was only supposed to be a "dramatic device", designed to facilitate the statement of the sceptical argument. The real conclusion of the sceptical argument was that no content can be attached to the hypothesis that a determinate meaning attached to a given expression. Keeping the real nature of the sceptical conclusion in mind then helps us to see how misplaced is the suggestion that appeal to simplicity considerations might help turn the trick. As Kripke puts it:

> Now simplicity considerations can help us to decide between competing hypotheses, but they can never tell us what the competing hypotheses are. If we do not understand what two hypotheses *state*, what does it mean to say that one is "more probable" because it is "simpler"? If two competing hypotheses are not genuine hypotheses, not assertions of genuine matters of fact, no "simplicity" considerations will make them so.[28]

In other words, if two ascriptions of meaning do not have truth-conditions, what does it mean to say that one of them is more probably true because it is simpler?

What we shall now suggest is that the sceptical solution offered by KW itself falls prey to a similar misunderstanding to that which apparently vitiates the appeal to simplicity considerations.[29] The objection has been forcibly made by José Zalabardo (though he fails to notice any similarity between his own objection and the one that KW makes against the simplicity suggestion). Zalabardo too points out that "the result does not concern an indeterminacy as to which rule is being followed, but the notion of rule itself".[30] If the problem were merely one of choosing between alternatives, then facts about agreement of communal responses, in the manner described by

KW, might indeed constitute a solution to that problem. But given that this is not the real sceptical problem, the crucial question is whether "Kripke's description of the assertibility conditions of content could provide the meaning of the ascriptions". And it would appear that the answer to this question has to be negative, for three reasons. First, if ascriptions of content amount to no more than claims about agreement of responses within the linguistic community, it would seem to follow that "all judgements would collapse into judgements about the ascribers' (or the whole community's) inclinations to consider certain situations as in some respect similar to each other".[31] In other words, and absurdly, that all our judgements would be about our fellow speakers' inclinations and the agreement or disagreement among them. Secondly, this would really only be another attempt at a straight solution, an attempt to spell out the truth-conditions of ascriptions of meaning in terms of communal responses, and the distinctive nature of the sceptical solution would be lost. Thirdly, this suggestion would itself be susceptible to KW's sceptical argument. This point has been well made by Crispin Wright:

> Could it yesterday have been true of a single individual that he associated with the sentence "Jones means addition by '+'" the sort of assertion conditions Kripke sketches? Well, if so, that truth did not consist in any aspect of his finite use of that sentence or its constituents; and, just as before, it would seem that his previous thoughts about that sentence and its use will suffice to constrain within uniqueness the proper interpretation of the assertion conditions he associated with it only if he is granted correct recall of the content of those thoughts – exactly what the sceptical argument does not grant. But would not any truths concerning assertion conditions previously associated by somebody with a particular sentence have to be constituted by aspects of his erstwhile behaviour and mental life? So the case appears no weaker than in the sceptical argument proper for the conclusion that there *are* no such truths; whence, following the same routine, it speedily follows that there are no truths about the assertion conditions that any of us presently associates with a particular sentence, nor, *a fortiori*, any truths about a communal association.[32]

It seems that the assertability conditions used in the sceptical solution must not be viewed as constituting the sense of ascriptions of meaning. But if KW makes no attempt to provide an account of what sense meaning ascriptions make – no account of their content – then it is difficult to see how the aim of the sceptical solution, that of rendering our practice of ascribing meanings explicable, could possibly be fulfilled. Given the absence of the kind of fact that the sceptic demands, we are still, in the sceptical solution, in the business of making sense of sentences that purport to ascribe content: this requires an account of the content of those ascriptions, but it would appear that the resources of the sceptical solution offer no plausible means of giving such an account. Giving a description of the conditions under which understanding is attributed to a speaker goes no way towards showing what content these attributions actually possess.

This, then, would appear to be the most powerful objection so far to KW's sceptical solution. The sceptical solution too is mistaken in taking the epistemic sceptical problem – the problem of knowing which ascription of meaning correctly describes a given speaker – to be more than a "merely dramatic device" used only *en route* to a more damaging and more pervasive constitutive sceptical conclusion: that ascriptions of meaning are themselves senseless.

In conclusion, we can say that although the objections discussed in sections 5.3 and 5.4 do not establish the implausibility of KW's sceptical solution, the objection discussed in the present section does suggest that the sceptical solution is a nonstarter. This means that we will have to think seriously about finding a *straight* solution to KW's sceptical paradox: an account of the fact that constitutes a speaker meaning one thing rather than another by an expression. We look at a number of attempts at such solutions in the next chapter.[33]

Further reading

The key text here is Saul Kripke, *Wittgenstein on rules and private language*. Further reading on responses to the sceptical paradox will be provided at the end of Chapter 6. Boghossian's objections to the sceptical solution can be found in "The rule-following considerations" (sections III–IV), *Mind* (1989), and "The status of Content", *Philosophical Review* (1990). For further discussion, see M. Devitt, "Transcendentalism about content", *Pacific Philosophical Quarterly* (1990), P. Boghossian, "The status of content revisited" (same issue), S. Blackburn, "Wittgenstein's irrealism", in L. Brandl and R. Haller (eds), *Wittgenstein: Eine Neubewehrung*, and C. Wright, *Truth and objectivity* (Ch. 6). Wright's own objections to the sceptical solution can be found in his "Kripke's account of the argument against private language", *Journal of Philosophy* (1984). Zalabardo's objection can be found in his "Rules, communities, judgements", *Critica* (1989). Other works of interest include S. Blackburn, "The individual strikes back", *Synthese* (1984), W. Goldfarb, "Kripke on Wittgenstein on rules", *Journal of Philosophy* (1985), and Chapter 4 of Colin McGinn's *Wittgenstein on meaning*. It should be pointed out that it is almost universally accepted that, whatever the philosophical merits of KW's arguments, they do not accurately reflect the views held by the actual, historical Wittgenstein. See Chapters 1 and 2 of McGinn for a good explanation of why not. We'll return to the question of Wittgenstein's own views on meaning in the next chapter.

Chapter 6

Saving sense: responses to the sceptical paradox

In the previous chapter, we outlined Kripke's Wittgenstein's sceptical paradox: there are no facts in virtue of which ascriptions of meaning, such as "Jones means addition by '+'", are either true or false. We also saw that KW's own attempt at rehabilitating meaning in the face of this conclusion – the sceptical solution – faces severe difficulties. We now look at a number of attempted "straight" solutions to the sceptical argument, solutions that try to meet the argument head on by giving an account of the facts that constitute meaning. In sections 6.2 and 6.3 we look at attempts to defend the sort of dispositionalist theories of meaning that we saw KW attacking in section 5.1. In section 6.4 we look at Jerry Fodor's "asymmetric dependency" account of meaning. In section 6.5 we look at McGinn's attempt to construe meaning and understanding in terms of the possession of *abilities or capacities*. In section 6.6 we outline Crispin Wright's attempt to respond to the sceptical argument by claiming that facts about meaning are "judgement-dependent". Finally, in section 6.7, we'll look at Wittgenstein's own response to the sceptical paradox. Before looking at these responses to KW's sceptical argument, we pause to make some brief comments on the relationship between scepticism about the notion of meaning as applied to expressions of public language and scepticism about the content of states of mind.

6.1 Linguistic meaning and mental content

So far in this book we have been concerning ourselves with questions about the meaning of expressions in a language. But it is not only linguistic expressions that are capable of possessing meaning. Some mental states – beliefs, desires, intentions and wishes, etc. – are also normally thought to possess meaning or content. For example, the content of my belief that Edinburgh is in Scotland is *that Edinburgh is in Scotland.* Just as the sentence "Edinburgh is less impressive than Glasgow" is *about* Edinburgh, and says it is less impressive than Glasgow, my belief is *about* Edinburgh, and is to the effect that it is in Scotland. This is also true of the other types of mental states mentioned. For example, I can have an intention with the content *that I will finish this book on time*; I can have a wish with the content *that the price of beer will be halved in the next budget*; and I can have a desire with the content *that I win next week's National Lottery*. Philosophers call mental states, such as beliefs, desires, wishes, intentions, hopes, and so on, *propositional attitudes.*[1] We can say that just as sentences have linguistic meaning, propositional attitudes have *mental content.*

Having made this observation, the following question now arises: what is the relationship between linguistic meaning and mental content? Do we have to explain the notion of linguistic meaning in terms of the notion of mental content? (that is, do we have to explain what it is for a linguistic expression to have meaning in terms of the propositional attitudes of speakers of the language?) or can we explain the notion of mental content in terms of the notion of linguistic meaning? (that is, can we explain what it is for a speaker to have a propositional attitude with a certain content in terms of the linguistic meaning of expressions of a language?). Philosophers of language have divided over the correct answers to these questions: Paul Grice has led philosophers who attempt to explain linguistic meaning in terms of the content of propositional attitudes, while Michael Dummett has been the main proponent of the view that the content of propositional attitudes must be explained in terms of the notion of linguistic meaning. In addition, philosophers like Donald Davidson have argued that there is no explanatory priority either way: linguistic meaning and mental content must be explained *together*, or not at all.

Deciding which of these three types of view on the relationship between language and thought is correct is an extremely difficult task, and in this book only a brief outline of some of the arguments for each type of position can be given (for the Gricean view, see Chapter 7; Davidson is discussed in Chapter 8; and Dummett in Chapter 9). In this section, our concern is with a more limited question: what is the relationship between scepticism about linguistic meaning and scepticism about mental content? For example, if KW's sceptical argument is cogent, does it carry over to the case of mental content? Would it follow that there are no facts of the matter in virtue of which we have propositional attitudes with one content rather than another? Alternatively, is there space for a sceptical argument about the contents of thoughts, which leaves the meanings of linguistic expressions alone?

The answer to the last of these questions is "yes", and the answer to the second is "no" regardless of what type of view on the explanatory priority issue is adopted. Suppose one adopted the Gricean account, on which linguistic meaning is to be explained in terms of the propositional attitudes possessed by speakers. Since linguistic meaning is explained *in terms of* mental content, KW's argument, which is targeted on linguistic meaning, will carry over to threaten the notion of mental content: if A is explained in terms of B, and the notion of A proves to be incoherent, then we cannot avoid the conclusion that B is incoherent also. For example, if the notion of responsibility is explained in terms of the notion of free will, then given the conclusion that the notion of responsibility is incoherent, we will be forced to the conclusion that the notion of free will is incoherent also.[2] Likewise for the Dummettian view, on which the content possessed by propositional attitudes is to be explained in terms of the use of language. If A is explained in terms of B, then any argument that B is incoherent will thereby threaten the coherence of A: if Divine Grace is explained in terms of God, and the latter notion proves to be incoherent, then there will be nothing left of the former. So, given the Dummettian view, KW's sceptical argument, in threatening the notion of linguistic meaning, will also threaten the notion of mental content. These points are well summarized by Paul Boghossian:

> There would appear to be no plausible way to promote a *language-specific* meaning scepticism. On the Gricean picture, one cannot threaten linguistic meaning without threatening thought content, since it is from thought that linguistic meaning is held to derive; and on the [Dummettian] picture, one cannot threaten linguistic meaning without *thereby* threatening thought content, since it is from linguistic meaning that thought content is held to derive. Either way, [mental] content and [linguistic] meaning must stand or fall together.[3]

The point is even clearer in the case of the Davidsonian view that there is no explanatory priority either way: if linguistic meaning and mental content must be explained together, or not at all, then any argument against the coherence of one notion is straightforwardly an argument against the coherence of the other.

In addition to the points above, there is another reason why it is difficult to restrict the conclusion of the sceptical argument to one or other of linguistic meaning and mental content. This concerns the nature of KW's argument itself: the argument turns, not on the fact that sentences belong to language, but just on the assumption that they possess meaning. All of the arguments that KW ran in section 5.1 could be rerun with mental items substituted for linguistic expressions, at no loss to the plausibility of the arguments. As Boghossian puts it:

> The real difficulty with the suggestion that one may sustain differential attitudes toward mental and linguistic content stems from the fact that the *best* arguments for the claim that nothing mental possesses content would count as *equally* good arguments for the claim that nothing linguistic does [and vice versa]. For these arguments have nothing much to do with the items being *mental* [or *linguistic*] and everything to do with

their being contentful: they are considerations of a wholly general character, against the existence of items individuated by content.[4]

Getting out of the predicament that we were left in at the end of Chapter 5 is thus all the more pressing. If KW's argument is successful, it follows that there is no fact of the matter as to whether we have propositional attitudes with certain contents. And this is a difficult conclusion to live with. Given that the content of propositional attitudes plays an essential role in the explanation of human *action* – for example, Jones reached for the fridge because he had a belief that there was beer in the fridge and a desire for a beer – the whole picture of human beings as *agents* comes under threat. So are there any plausible straight solutions to the sceptical paradox?[5]

6.2 Sophisticated dispositionalism

Recall that in section 5.1 KW argued against the idea that Jones's meaning addition by "+" could consist in his being disposed to respond to the relevant arithmetical queries with the sum of the numbers involved. First, our actual dispositions are finite, and so unable to determine a unique function as the semantic value of "+". Secondly, dispositional facts are facts about what we *will* do, not about what we *ought* to do, and as such cannot capture the normativity of meaning. In this section we'll consider whether a dispositionalist theory of meaning can offer any plausible responses to these objections.

The dispositional theory considered in section 5.1 was extremely crude. We arrive at a more serious dispositional theory if we follow Paul Boghossian in the reflection that "All dispositional properties are such that their exercise – the holding of the relevant counterfactual truth – is contingent on the absence of interfering conditions, or equivalently, on the presence of the ideal conditions."[6] For example, common salt possesses a disposition to dissolve when placed in water, but it will not dissolve in a sample of water that is already saturated; so to say that salt is water soluble is really to say that it is disposed to dissolve in water *under certain conditions*, one consequence of whose obtaining is that the water in question is not already saturated. The reflection suggests a sophisticated dispositionalism, the basic idea of which is that we can avoid the problems posed for the dispositional theory considered in section 5.1 if we concentrate on what we would be disposed to do *under some suitably specified set of ideal, or at least* ceteris paribus, *conditions*. The problem that the finiteness of our actual dispositions posed might then be avoided if we could include some specification in these conditions to the effect that the speaker lives long enough to hear out the relevant arithmetical enquiry: it seems plausible to say that if I were to live long enough, even for numerals "*n*" and "*m*" which are in fact too large for me to take in in my normal life span, I would, in response to an appropriate query, utter a numeral denoting the sum of the two numbers rather than "5". This would rule out the interpretation of "+" as standing for the skaddition function (see section 5.1). Moreover, it might also be plausible that such a sophisticated dispositionalism can provide us with something that captures the normativity of meaning: if the conditions specified are genuinely *ideal*, or at least conditions of *proper* functioning, then doesn't it follow from the fact that I would respond in a certain way under conditions of that type that I have a *reason* for responding in that fashion? For example, if someone in ideal conditions for appraising arithmetical claims were to say that a certain answer to an arithmetical problem was appropriate, and moreover, I know that the conditions are in fact ideal, doesn't it follow that I *ought* to accept the verdict given on the arithmetical problem? We also get the necessary distinction between competence and performance. Competence would be a matter of acting as one would act under ideal conditions; this could come apart from actual performance, in the cases where the ideal conditions fail to obtain. One could thus be systematically disposed to make a mistake, because the ideal conditions could systematically fail to obtain.

What is required, then, is a specification of the ideal conditions: a set of conditions such that *under those conditions* Jones is disposed to respond to the query "$x + y = ?$" with z, if and only if the numeral z stands for the *sum* of x and y. Since the dispositionalist is attempting to reduce facts about meaning to facts about dispositions, it is crucial that in spelling out the ideal conditions, no appeal is made to facts about meaning: this would put the cart before the horse, since the story about how speakers are disposed to behave under those conditions is supposed to tell us what constitutes the facts about meaning. So, no use of semantic or intentional materials is to be made in the specification of the ideal conditions.

In order to make the discussion simpler, we'll move away from the arithmetical example and consider a simple observational predicate, "magpie". Intuitively, "magpie" stands for *magpies*: bullfinches, sparrows, people and tables do not fall within its extension. Suppose that Jones means magpies by the predicate "magpie". The dispositionalist will say that this fact about Jones is constituted by the fact that he is disposed, under ideal conditions, to apply the predicate "magpie" to all and only those objects that are magpies. In other words, Jones's meaning *magpie* by "magpie" is constituted by the fact that he is disposed, under ideal conditions, to token the belief that x is a magpie, if and only if x is in fact a magpie. Can sophisticated dispositionalism spell out a set of ideal conditions such that this is true in a way that avoids the use of prior semantic and intentional materials?

Paul Boghossian has argued that it cannot, so that even sophisticated dispositionalism is ultimately bound to fail. Boghossian's objection takes off from the observation that the interpretation of a speaker's beliefs is a *holistic* affair. He writes: "Belief fixation is typically mediated by background theory – what contents a thinker is prepared to judge will depend upon what other contents he is prepared to judge … just about any stimulus can cause just about any belief, given a suitably mediating set of background assumptions."[7]

Boghossian notes that a speaker may token the belief *there is a magpie* when there is some other kind of bird present, due to the presence of a belief to the effect that there are no birds apart from magpies in the relevant neighbourhood, and so on. But, "A dispositional theorist has to specify, without use of semantic or intentional materials, a situation in which a speaker is disposed to think *lo, a magpie* only in respect of magpies."[8]

The sophisticated dispositionalist wishes to identify someone's meaning such and such with facts of the form: S *is disposed to token the belief* B *under conditions* C, where the C are to be specified nonsemantically and nonintentionally. Boghossian's argument focuses on the fact that these conditions will have to include some proviso to the effect that certain other clusters of background beliefs $B1, \ldots, Bn, \ldots$ are *absent*. Thus, in specifying the optimal conditions for the meaning-constituting disposition concerning "magpie", we will require nonintentional and nonsemantic optimal conditions for the range of background beliefs that figure in the clusters $B1, \ldots, Bn, \ldots$ otherwise we will not be able to stipulate, in nonintentional terms, the conditions under which each member of that range of beliefs is absent. Since "there looks to be a potential infinity of such mediating background clusters of belief", Boghossian claims that "what is needed is precisely what a dispositional theory was supposed to provide: namely, a set of naturalistic necessary and sufficient conditions for being a belief with a certain content", and concludes on this basis that "if there is to be any reductive story about meaning at all, it cannot take the form of a dispositional theory".[9]

Let's try to get clearer on what the problem here is supposed to consist in. Suppose we are trying to give an account of the conditions under which my forming the belief *lo, a magpie* covaries invariably with (and only with) the presence of magpies. In order to do so, we have to specify conditions under which each cluster in the potentially infinite set of clusters of beliefs $B1, \ldots, Bn, \ldots$ is absent. Then we require "a non-semantically, non-intentionally specified situation in which it is guaranteed that none of this potential infinity of background clusters of belief is present". And this requires just what we were supposed to be providing, namely, "a set of naturalistic necessary and sufficient conditions for being a belief with a certain content".[10]

Is the fact that the set of clusters of belief that have to be ruled out is *infinitely* large playing any significant role in Boghossian's argument? It looks as if the argument would go through equally well even if the set was finite. In order to give an account of the conditions under which my forming the belief *lo, a magpie* covaries invariably with (and only with) the presence of magpies, we have to specify conditions under which each cluster in the set of clusters of background beliefs $B1, \ldots, Bn$ is absent. Then we would require a nonsemantically and nonintentionally specified situation in which it is guaranteed that no member of this set of background clusters of beliefs is present. And this requires just what we were supposed to be providing, namely a set of naturalistic necessary and sufficient conditions *for being a belief with a certain content.* (This would seem to go through even if there was only *one* such cluster that had to be ruled out. In order to rule it out we would have to give naturalistic necessary and sufficient conditions for the various beliefs that appear in the cluster – in other words, naturalistic necessary and sufficient conditions for being a belief with a certain content. And this is just what we are in the process of attempting to provide).

So the argument doesn't seem to hinge on the *infinite* nature of the range of clusters of background beliefs, but rather on the fact that it is clusters of *beliefs* that have to be ruled out, so that the attempted reduction of facts about meaning to dispositional facts turns out to be viciously circular. If the belief *lo, a magpie* were itself a member of one of the sets of background beliefs whose absence was relevant for a member of one of the $B1, \dots ,Bn$, say B, then it would follow on the one hand that (a) we require non-semantic and nonintentional optimal conditions for B in order to specify the nonsemantic and nonintentional optimal conditions for *lo, a magpie*, while on the other hand that (b) we require non-semantic and nonintentional optimal conditions for *lo, a magpie* in order to specify the optimal conditions for B. The sophisticated dispositional account would thus be viciously circular.

If Boghossian's real objection to sophisticated dispositionalism is that it harbours a vicious circularity, then there is a move at the dispositionalist's disposal that will neutralize this worry about circularity. In the next section we describe this move, which consists in wedding a sophisticated dispositionalist account of meaning to a reductive analysis of the sort developed by David Lewis. The result is a form of what might be called *ultra-sophisticated dispositionalism*, a version of the dispositionalist view that is immune to the worry about vicious circularity we have just adumbrated. We'll then argue that although Boghossian does not consider the possibility of such a position in his original argument against sophisticated dispositionalism, that argument nevertheless possesses the resources for a rebuttal of even this ultra-sophisticated dispositionalism.

6.3 Lewis-style reductionism and ultra-sophisticated dispositionalism

There are reasons for thinking that the worry about vicious circularity *must* be surmountable. Isn't it an accepted fact that a similar problem arises when we consider the attribution of beliefs and desires to an agent? Simplifying somewhat, it is widely held that an intentional action in general requires both beliefs and desires to be present, so that when we attempt to give, for example, a constitutive account of the belief that partially rationalizes a certain action, we stand in need of a similar account of the appropriate desire; but when we attempt to give a constitutive account of the desire, we find that we stand in need of a similar account of the relevant belief. But we do not think that this signals the impossibility of providing a constitutive account either of belief or desire. We would instead perhaps attempt to give an account of what beliefs and desires there are that would break up into the following two components. (A) An account of how the various propositional attitude states relate to each other, consisting of an account of the platitudinous relations that constrain the relations that obtain between them. (B) An account of the interpretative principles which link the holistic system of propositional attitudes described in (A) to the nonintentional and nonsemantic facts which ground their ascription.[11]

The general method here is an example of David Lewis's style of reductive analysis.[12] Let's look at how Lewis's method applies to the case of colour terms. Just as the dispositionalist about meaning is attempting to give a reductive account of meaning, Lewis's method attempts to give us a reductive account of colour. Lewis's story takes off from the fact that there are a large range of *platitudes* about the colours, and that it is by virtue of coming to treat them as platitudes that we are enabled to master colour vocabulary. Examples of such platitudes would be "redness causes us, under certain circumstances, to have experiences of redness", "red is more similar to orange than to blue". Lewis has tried to show how we can obtain an analysis of the concept of being red from this range of platitudes. We first of all run through the various platitudes and rewrite them so that the references to colours appear in property name style. So the two platitudes mentioned above would be rewritten as "the property of being red causes us, under certain circumstances, to have experiences of the property of redness", "the property of being red is more similar to the property of being orange than it is to the property of being blue". Having done that for all of the colours, we go on to represent the result of conjoining the totality of platitudes as a relational predicate "T" true of all the various colour properties. That is, the conjunction will be represented by T[r g b...], where "r", "g", and so on stand for the properties of being red, green, and so on. Having done this we remove the property names of the various colours and replace them with free variables so that we get T[$x\,y\,z$ ...].[13] Then, if there actually are colours, there is a unique set of properties related to the world and to each other in exactly the way that the conjunction of platitudes we just formed says there are. In other words, if there actually are colours then it is true that

$$\exists x \,\exists y\, \exists z \,... \,\{T[x\,y\,z\,...] \,\& \,((\forall x^*)\,(\forall y^*)\,(\forall z^*)\,...\,T[x^*\,y^*\,z^*\,...]\text{ iff}$$
$$(x = x^*,\, y = y^*,\, z = z^* \,...))\}.$$

Then we could go on to say that the property of being red can be defined in the following manner: the property of being red is the x such that

$$\exists y\, \exists z\, ... \,\{T[x\,y\,z\,...] \,\& \,((\forall x^*)\,(\forall y^*)\,(\forall z^*)\,...\,T[x^*\,y^*\,z^*...]\text{ iff}$$
$$(x = x^*,\, y = y^*,\, z = z^* \,...))\}.[14]$$

This is a reductive analysis of red: it defines it in purely noncolour vocabulary, since no colour vocabulary appears on the right-hand side of the definition.

The important point for our purposes here is the ease with which Lewis's style of analysis achieves this, despite the fact that the platitudes that it uses as its data in the case of redness, for example, refer to *other* colours, such as blue and orange, in whose governing platitudes in turn reference is going to be made to redness. For example, the set of platitudes for orange is going to contain "the property of being orange is more similar to the property of being red than it is to the property of being blue". *But it is just this sort of circularity that Boghossian sees as fatal to the prospects of a reductive account of belief*: the objection was after all that the optimality conditions for one belief were going to refer to (the absence of) other beliefs, in the specifications of whose optimality conditions reference was going to have to be made to the (absence of) the original belief. *This shows that the sort of circularity that Boghossian points to needn't worry the sophisticated dispositionalist. It just shows that he will need to become an ultra-sophisticated dispositionalist and adopt the Lewis style analysis we've just sketched*: the worry about circularity can be avoided by treating the clauses that rule out certain background clusters of belief as akin to the various platitudes about colour that form the raw material for the Lewis-style reductive analysis of colour.

Is ultra-sophisticated dispositionalism plausible? Does it give us a plausible way of reducing facts about meaning to facts about dispositions? The answer to these questions is "no". We'll now see that even though the ultra-sophisticated dispositionalism can avoid the worry about circularity by adopting a Lewis-style method of reductive analysis, it is nevertheless open to a serious objection.

Recall that in our presentation of Boghossian's objection in section 6.2, the play with the fact that the range of defeating background beliefs was potentially infinite appeared to be idle. The real objection, it was suggested, concerns *vicious circularity*. The emphasis on circularity is predominant in the presentation of Boghossian's argument in "The Rule-Following Considerations". But in Boghossian's later paper, "Naturalizing Content", the emphasis switches from circularity to the fact that the range of combinations of background beliefs that have to be ruled out is potentially infinite. The worry now centres on our ability to *specify* the appropriate range of optimality conditions. Specifying the optimality conditions would involve giving an account of the various clusters of background beliefs which would have to be absent in order to ensure that the disposition to form the belief *lo, a magpie* really did covary with (and only with) the presence of magpies. This account would be of the form of

(*) – Bel 1 & – Bel 2 & – Bel 3 & ...

and Boghossian writes that

> Since, however, there looks to be a potential infinity of such mediating background clusters of belief, a non-semantically specified optimality condition would consist in the specification of a situation in which it has somehow been guaranteed that none of this potential infinity of background clusters of belief is present. And it appears utterly incredible that there should be such a specification ... The trouble is that proposition (*) is not finitely statable: there is no finite way to state what beliefs the [reductionist] must exclude before he may be assured of the desired concomitance of magpie beliefs and magpies. Literally any belief can frustrate the desired connection.[15]

Here it is clear that it is not so much the fact that the optimality conditions have to ensure the absence of *beliefs* that causes the trouble, but rather the fact that the range of items that have to be excluded is *potentially infinite*.

This does appear to be a damaging objection to sophisticated dispositionalism. But does it also apply to ultra-sophisticated dispositionalism? The Lewis-style analysis begins by writing out all of the platitudes about colour. But this presupposes that it is at least *in principle* possible to write out a *list* of the various platitudes, which presupposes in turn that the list of platitudes in question is not infinitely long. It may indeed be the case in the colour example that the list of platitudes is finite, but Boghossian's point about mediating background clusters of belief would seem to suggest that this will not be so in the case of content. The analogue of the platitudes about colour in the ultra-sophisticated dispositional analysis of meaning is the list of clauses ruling out awkward background clusters of belief. Since this list of clauses is not finitely stateable, the Lewis-style analysis will not even be able to get started in the case of meaning, because there will be no way of circumscribing the list of relevant platitudes that the analysis takes as its starting point.

Thus, even if switching to ultra-sophisticated dispositionalism can help the dispositionalist avoid Boghossian's worry about vicious circularity, it does nothing to solve the additional worry about the unspecifiability of its optimal conditions. No form of dispositionalism about meaning – crude, sophisticated or ultra-sophisticated – appears to constitute a successful response to KW's sceptical paradox.

6.4 Fodor's "asymmetric dependency" account of meaning

The problem posed by KW is as follows: what constitutes the fact that Jones means *horses* by "horse", or *cows* by "cow"? In this section we look at the straight solution to KW's problem that has been proposed by Jerry Fodor.

Fodor is happy to follow KW in his claim that the fact that Jones means *horses* by "horse" cannot be an irreducible, *sui generis*, sort of fact (see section 5.1):

> I suppose that sooner or later the physicists will complete the catalogue they've been compiling of the ultimate and irreducible properties of things. When they do, the likes of *spin, charm*, and *charge* will perhaps appear on their list. But *aboutness* surely won't; intentionality simply doesn't go that deep. It's hard to see, in face of this consideration, how one can be a realist about intentionality without also being, to some extent or other, a reductionist. If the semantic and the intentional are real properties of things, it must be in virtue of their identity with (or maybe their supervenience on?) properties that are themselves neither intentional not semantic. If aboutness is real, then it must really be something else.[16]

Recall that "semantic", "intentional" and "aboutness" are all phrases involving *meaning*. Fodor thus seeks to give an account of what it is for Jones to mean *horses* by "horse" which does not invoke any prior semantic or intentional materials.[17]

Before outlining Fodor's attempted solution, we'll pause to dispel a possible confusion that might be engendered by Tim Crane's recent presentation of it. Crane points out that one way in which Fodor could attempt to provide a straight solution to KW's sceptical problem would be to give naturalistically specified necessary and sufficient conditions for claims of the form " 'X' means Y". Fodor could be represented as attempting to find a principle of the form:

(R) "X" means Y if and only if ...

where what fills in the " ... " uses no semantic or intentional materials.

Now what is the nature of the "if and only if" as it appears in this principle? Crane distinguishes between two ways of reading it: on one reading (R), the *conceptual definition* reading, it expresses something like a conceptual or analytic truth; on the other reading, the *naturalistic definition* reading, it expresses something like a *nomological* truth.[18] Crane explicates the difference between the two readings by asking us to consider the case of colour and to compare:

(1) X is red if and only if X reflects light of wavelength N

and

(2) X is red if and only if X looks red to normal perceivers in normal circumstances.

Here, (1) attempts to provide at most a naturalistic definition of red, while (2) attempts to provide a conceptual definition of red. Fodor is then represented as attempting to provide a naturalistic definition of " 'X' means Y". Another difference between (1) and (2) is that (1) is reductive, in the sense that the concept being defined appears nowhere on the right-hand side; whereas (2), since it contains "red" on its right-hand side, is nonreductive. Fodor is represented as trying to provide a reductive definition of " 'X' means Y".

It appears that Crane's discussion harbours some confusions. First of all, one gets the impression from reading Crane that he takes (1) and (2) to be *competitors*. But in fact they are not: so long as (1) is read as expressing only some empirical law-like regularity, it is perfectly compatible with the conceptual definition (2). (1) and (2) only start to compete with each other when they are both regarded as conceptual definitions. The claim that what determines, as a matter of conceptual necessity, that a certain object is red is its disposition to appear red to normal observers in normal circumstances is perfectly consistent with the claim that, *as a matter of empirical fact*, there is some complex physical property that all red things have in common. Secondly, there is something odd in Crane's interpretation of the notion of a naturalistic definition: if the "if and only if" is read as expressing only a nomological correlation, by what right can we call this a *definition* at all? It is no more a definition than the claim that water is identical to H_2O; that is to say, no definition at all. It seems to me that Crane has made the following mistake in his exposition of Fodor: he has confused two different senses of "naturalistic definition". On one reading, the naturalism of the definition resides in the fact that the "iff" expresses at most a nomological rather than a conceptual correlation. If our claim above is correct, it is misleading to call this a definition. On another reading, the naturalism of the definition resides, not in the fact that the "iff" is read as expressing a merely nomological correlation, for it is now read as expressing a conceptual correlation, but rather in the fact that the right-hand side of the definition refers only to nomological or causal facts. *Crane appears to be confusing the nature of the biconditional involved with the nature of what features on its right-hand side.* It seems to me that Fodor is attempting to provide a naturalistic definition of meaning in the *latter* of these two senses: Fodor is attempting to provide a conceptual definition of content, but a conceptual definition whose right-hand side concerns only nomological or causal facts.

Having clarified this, we should now turn to consider the analysis of meaning that Fodor actually proposes.

One way to try to obtain a conceptual definition of the sort Fodor is seeking would be to fill out (R) as follows:

(R) "X" means Y if and only if it is a law that Y's cause tokenings of "X".

Now obviously there are going to be lots of predicates that have a content ill-suited to being captured by (R), since they concern things that don't, or cannot, cause anything: predicates intuitively denoting nonexistent things (perfect students, unicorns, etc.), or things that are nonspatiotemporal (numbers and other mathematical entities). But the idea here is to see how we get on with the simpler cases, such as "horse" and "cow", where there appears to be no such problem. If we can get (R) to work in these cases, then maybe we can somehow extend our account to include the more esoteric cases; while if we cannot get (R) to work in even these easy cases, we can rest assured that there is no chance it will work in the hard cases anyway.

The main problem for this construal of (R) is that it appears to leave no scope for a notion of *error*: it leaves no room for a notion of *mistaken* application of "*X*", and hence leaves no room for the idea of *correct and incorrect application* of "*X*". To see this, consider the case of "horse". (R) then claims that

(R) "Horse" means horses if and only if it is a law that horses cause tokenings of "horse".

Now one immediate problem is that if it is a law that horses cause tokenings of "horse", horses cannot *fail* to cause tokenings of horse. But this seems to preclude the possibility of misrepresentation: encountering a sheep and tokening "horse", so that the tokening of "horse" thereby misrepresents, or represents falsely. (R) seems to imply that false representation is impossible: but if this is the case then it follows all applications of predicates are correct, so that the distinction between correct and incorrect application that is essential to meaning is lost.

Another problem is that there are going to be occasions when I do in fact misapply the predicate "horse": perhaps on dark nights, the cows in the field across from the pub look deceptively like horses, so that when I stagger out at closing time I invariably token "horse" on encountering them on the pastures opposite. Since the conditions under which this occurs are systematic and uniform – the same thing would happen again, given similar animals, similar conditions of illumination and similar levels of alcohol in the bloodstream – it will be a law that horsey-looking-cows-on-dark-nights, etc. cause tokenings of "horse". It will then follow from (R) that "Horse" means horsey-looking-cow-on-a-dark-night. Or actually, not quite: there will be some sets of background circumstances in which horses do cause tokenings of "horse" (good conditions of illumination, etc.). So the class of things that sustain a lawlike connection with tokenings of "horse" will actually be *disjunctive*: it is a law that horses-in-good-conditions-of-illumination or horsey-looking-cows-on-dark-nights, etc. cause tokenings of "horse". Then it follows from (R) that the predicate "horse" actually has a disjunctive meaning: according to (R) it means *horses-in-good-conditions-of-illumination* or *horsey-looking-cows-on-dark-nights*. Thus, applying "horse" to horsey-looking-cows-on-a-dark-night will not be a misapplication, since anything that is a horsey-looking-cow-on-a-dark-night is *ipso facto* a horse-in-good-conditions-of-illumination or a horsey-looking-cow-on-a-dark-night. Again, there seems to be no scope left for incorrect application of the predicate. This problem is known as the *disjunction problem.*

According to Fodor, this is the main problem facing naturalistic accounts of meaning. One way of trying to solve this problem would be to alter (R) along the following lines:

(R*) "X" means Y if and only if it is a law that Y's cause tokenings of "X" under optimal conditions.

Of course, the optimal conditions would have to be specified purely naturalistically, in nonsemantic and nonintentional terms. Now it is plausible that the optimal conditions for tokening the predicate "horse" do not include conditions under which it is dark, etc. This would mean that since horsey-looking-cows-on-a-dark-night do not cause tokenings of "horse" under optimal conditions, we avoid the disjunction problem. (R*) does not deliver the conclusion that "Horse" means horse-in-good-conditions-of-illumination or horsey-looking-cow-on-a-dark-night, so that tokenings of "horse" that occur on encountering a horsey-looking-cow on a dark night could after all count as false or incorrect.

The problem, of course, is the characterization of a suitable set of optimal conditions in nonsemantic and nonintentional terms. Note that (R*) is basically the same idea as lay behind sophisticated dispositionalism. To say that sugar is disposed to dissolve in water is basically to say that it is a law that if sugar is placed in water it will dissolve. So

Jones means horse by "horse" iff Jones is disposed to apply "horse" to horses under ideal conditions

basically says the same thing as

Jones means horse by "horse" iff it is a law that horses cause Jones to token "horse" under optimal conditions.

This means that the arguments we developed in sections 6.2–6.3 against sophisticated dispositionalism also apply to any attempt to solve the disjunction problem that relies on something like (R*).[19]

Fodor's aim is therefore to provide a naturalistic solution to KW's sceptical problem that does not require the formulation of naturalistic optimal conditions in the manner required by (R*). To this end he develops his "asymmetric-dependency" account of meaning.[20]

If we are not allowed to appeal to naturalistically specified optimal conditions, how can we distinguish between *correct* tokenings of "horse" in response to the presence of horses, and *incorrect* tokenings of "horse" in response to the presence of horsey-looking-cows-on-dark-nights? Fodor's idea is that the latter sort of tokening is incorrect because the causal relationship between tokenings of "horse" and horsey-looking-cows is *asymmetrically dependent* upon the causal relationship between tokenings of "horse" and horses.

What does this mean? Consider the fact that horsey-looking-cows sometimes cause tokenings of "horse". This is dependent +upon the fact that horses sometimes causes tokenings of "horse", since it is plausible that *if it were not the case that horses sometimes cause tokenings of "horse", it would not be the case that horsey-looking-cows sometimes cause tokenings of "horse" either.* And the dependence is asymmetric since it does not hold the other way round: it is false that if it were not the case that horsey-looking-cows sometimes cause tokenings of "horse", it would not be the case that horses sometimes cause tokenings of "horse". *"Horse" means horses, and not horses or horsey-looking-cows, because the causal relation between horsey-looking-cows and tokenings of "horse" is asymmetrically dependent upon the causal relation between horses and tokenings of "horse".* In general, the causal relation between Y's and tokenings of "X" can be said to constitute the fact that "X" means Y if for every Z the causal relation between Z's and tokenings of "X" is asymmetrically dependent upon it.

How plausible is Fodor's account? It is difficult to avoid sympathizing with the following worry, raised by Crane:

[It is difficult] to see how asymmetric dependence goes any way towards *explaining* mental representation. I think that the conditions Fodor describes probably are true of mental representations. But I do not see how this helps us to understand how mental representation actually works. In effect, Fodor is saying: error is parasitic on true belief. But it's hard not to object that this is just what we knew already. The question rather is: what is error? Until we can give some account of error, then it does not really help us to say that it is parasitic on true belief.[21]

But the objection is hard to assess. KW asked us to specify some fact that constitutes an expression meaning one thing rather than another, and it seems that Fodor has specified such a fact in purely causal and nomological terms. What is the additional demand for explanation? and how is it motivated? What sort of explanation is being asked for? and what are the constraints on its acceptability? Unfortunately, we cannot pursue these questions here, but must end this section by noting that Fodor's attempted solution is far from obtaining universal acceptance among philosophers of mind and language.[22]

6.5 McGinn on normativity and the ability conception of understanding

In his book *Wittgenstein on Meaning*, Colin McGinn makes a number of suggestions as to how KW's sceptical paradox might best be responded to. One suggestion is that viewing understanding as consisting in the possession of an *ability* or a *capacity* might provide us with a plausible straight solution to the sceptical argument. A move to viewing linguistic understanding in this way is quite explicitly apparent in the work of the later Wittgenstein, as the following quotes illustrate:[23]

The grammar of the word "knows" is evidently closely related to that of "can", "is able to". But also closely related to that of "understands". ("Mastery" of a technique.)[24]

To understand a language means to be master of a technique.[25]

Only in the practice of a language can a word have meaning.[26]

In short, facts about what I mean are constituted by facts about which capacities I possess. This solution, it is claimed, avoids the sorts of pitfalls that allegedly vitiate dispositional responses to the sceptical argument. In particular, where dispositionalism has difficulty accounting for the *normative* aspects of meaning and understanding, the capacity response does not:

> One important way in which capacities and dispositions can come apart is through the possibility of *mistake*: two people could both have the capacity to classify red things on the basis of their appearance, but one of them fails to do so when presented with a red object because he believes his senses to be functioning abnormally – he is then *able* to do what he is not *disposed* to do. Or again, I have the capacity to dial telephone numbers, but in some circumstances I make mistakes: it is not a necessary condition of possessing an ability that one *always* exercise it correctly. [Likewise, a] disposition is not sufficient for having an ability: we can conceive of set-ups in which a person is disposed to ψ in conditions C but he has not the ability to ψ – he gets the disposition from some source other than the possession of the ability.[27]

McGinn thinks that the capacity/ability response can avoid the problems faced by dispositionalism because it can fulfil the condition whose satisfaction is sufficient for accommodating the normativity of meaning. The condition is that we provide: "(a) an account of what it is to mean something at a given time, and (b) an account of what it is to mean the same thing at two different times".[28] And the capacity suggestion easily satisfies these desiderata: "to mean addition by '+' at t is to associate with '+' the capacity to add at t, and to mean the same by '+' at t^* is to associate with '+' the same capacity at t^* as at t".[29]

Now this conception of what is required for an account of normativity is obviously suggested by some aspects of KW's presentation of the sceptical argument: the challenge was to cite some fact that would establish that what you *now* mean by '+' is the *same* as what you meant in the past. The sceptic "puts the challenge in terms of a sceptical hypothesis about a change in my usage", and the challenge is to produce a fact that rules out the hypothesis that such a change has in fact occurred. The challenge is set up in this way to allow the sceptical problem to be intelligibly formulated: in order to be able to converse with me, the sceptic allows that I presently mean addition by "+" and proposes a sceptical hypothesis that suggests that I meant something incompatible in the past. As Kripke himself puts it, "Only past usages are to be questioned. Otherwise we will be unable to formulate our problem."[30]

However, Paul Boghossian points out that the notion of normativity McGinn is working with here cannot be the notion of normativity at stake in KW's discussion. This is apparent because it places no substantial constraints on the choice of a meaning-constituting fact: "The requirement defined by McGinn could hardly act as a substantive constraint on theories of meaning ... Any theory of meaning that provided an account of what speakers mean by their expressions at arbitrary times – however crazy that theory may otherwise be – would satisfy McGinn's constraint."[31] For instance, the dispositionalist response, which KW attacks precisely because he claims it cannot leave room for the normativity of meaning, easily satisfies McGinn's condition. Since Kripke's discussion does not suggest that we can have no criteria for the transtemporal identity of dispositions, we might just as easily say that to mean addition by "+" at t is to associate with "+" the disposition to add at t, and to mean the same thing by "+" at t^* is to associate with "+" at t^* the same disposition as at t.

Clearly something has gone wrong in McGinn's characterization of normativity, and Boghossian succinctly explains where. Properly viewed, normativity does not concern the relation between *past* meaning and *present* meaning, *but rather between meaning something by an expression at a time and the use that is made of the expression at that time*. What I mean now by an expression determines what uses I now make of that expression are correct or incorrect, and this is the normative constraint that the sceptic is challenging us to account for. As Boghossian puts it, "The normativity of meaning turns out to be, in other words, simply a new name for the familiar fact that, regardless of whether one thinks of meaning in truth-theoretic or assertion-theoretic terms, meaningful expressions possess

198

conditions of correct use."[32] The question as to how conditions of correct use can be so much as possible is what is at issue, not the question concerning the possibility of transtemporal identity conditions for meaning.

This leaves us with a problem, however: given that McGinn's reading of the normativity requirement was naturally suggested by KW's presentation of the sceptical argument in terms of a hypothesis about a change in usage, and given KW's claim that this is the only way in which the sceptical problem can be intelligibly formulated, we have to find some new way of framing the sceptical problem consonant with the proper understanding of the normativity requirement. Fortunately, this is not very difficult. As Boghossian puts it, "Having a meaning is essentially a matter of possessing a correctness condition. And the sceptical challenge is to explain how anything could possess *that*."[33] The challenge – to explain what it is for a linguistic expression to possess conditions of correct usage – can be set out without even mentioning the sceptic. Bringing in the sceptic is only a device – a dispensable device – for setting out the challenge. We should not take the dialogic setting in which Kripke introduces the challenge too seriously: "The constitutive problem about meaning – how could there so much as be a correctness condition – can be stated quite forcefully without the actual provision of a convincing global reinterpretation of a person's words."[34] Once we appreciate this, we can see that the sceptical challenge can be framed in a way that avoids McGinn's confusions about the nature of normativity.

Where do these considerations leave McGinn's capacity/ability solution to KW's sceptical problem? McGinn's claim that the capacity solution could avoid the worries faced by dispositionalism rests upon a mistaken conception of the normativity requirement, so to that extent McGinn's suggestion is severely weakened. Moreover, there are other worries that suggest that the capacity suggestion cannot constitute an adequate response to KW's sceptical challenge.

Wright says,

> If we ask, what capacity is constitutively associated with an understanding of "green"?, the natural answer is: the capacity to use the word correctly. And here "correctly" means, roughly: in ways which are appropriately sensitive to its meaning.[35]

The mere claim that understanding consists in the possession of a capacity thus appears to get the cart before the horse, at least so far as a response to KW is concerned. For example, in the case of "green", a competent speaker possesses the capacity to suit his use with the expression to its meaning. But this – the meaning of green – is precisely what KW is challenging us to characterize! So we need to go further and say what the capacity in question is a capacity to do:

> Well, what then is the capacity, allegedly constitutive of an understanding of "green", a capacity, most fundamentally, to *do*? McGinn's discussion contains, so far as I have been able to see, no clear suggestion about how a proponent of his "straight solution" should respond to this question.[36]

This is perhaps a *little* unfair on McGinn, as he does attempt to characterize the relevant capacities in more detail:

> In Kripke's favourite example, the suggestion would be that it is the concept of *addition* that I exercise when I do computations involving "+" and not the concept of *quaddition*, because the capacity that gets brought to bear is the capacity to *add* and not to *quadd*, where the former capacity is conceived as a capacity to recognise what is the *sum* of pairs of numbers.[37]

McGinn's suggestion is thus that meaning addition by "+" consists in associating with "+" the capacity to *add*, and meaning quaddition by "+" consists in associating with "+" the ability to *quadd*. Unfortunately, this is a very weak response to KW's challenge, for KW can simply reformulate the challenge in terms of capacities: in virtue of what does Jones possess the capacity to *add*, rather than the capacity to *quadd*? All of the arguments of section 5.1 can be brought back in to suggest that there is no plausible answer to *this* question.[38]

The problem McGinn's suggestion faces is thus as follows. Just as a speaker will have a range of dispositions associated with a given expression, he will also have a range of capacities associated with it. So McGinn must give us some account of which capacities are constitutive of understanding in a way that does not simply put the cart before the horse and that does not fall prey to a simple reformulation of KW's original sceptical problem. And it seems that the provision of such an account is no easier than the dispositionalist's task of spelling out a suitable set of optimal conditions:

> The relevant capacities have to be singled out somehow, and the problem is structurally reminiscent of – indeed, in no way interestingly different from or more promising in outcome than – the problem, confronted by the dispositional response, of saying what puts a particular disposition in the idealized, meaning-constituting class which it is obliged to define.[39]

6.6 Wright's "judgement-dependent" account of meaning

Wright's response attempts to meet KW's sceptical challenge by identifying and challenging an extremely important methodological assumption that underlies the presentation of that challenge. That assumption is this: that if semantic facts are to be legitimately countenanced then they must be *reducible* to some *other* class of facts that can be fully and adequately described *without the use of semantic and intentional notions (i.e. notions involving meaning)*. Wright's response questions this assumption: when faced with a demand for an account of the kind of fact that constitutes my meaning addition by "+", why is it not sufficient simply to reply "my meaning addition by '+'"? As Wright says, "it cannot *always* be possible to justify a presumed genre of knowledge 'from without' in the way the sceptic is here demanding".[40] This means that the onus is on KW to provide us with a *positive* argument against nonreductionism about meaning (the view that facts about meaning are irreducible and *sui generis*). As we saw in section 5.1, KW does gesture in the direction of such an argument. Recall that KW writes of the claim that meaning such and such by an expression is an irreducible state that

> Such a move may in a sense be irrefutable, and taken in an appropriate way Wittgenstein may even accept it. But it seems desperate: it leaves the nature of the postulated primitive

state – the primitive state of meaning addition by "plus" – completely mysterious. It is not supposed to be an introspectible state, yet we are supposedly aware of it with some fair degree of certainty whenever it occurs. For how else can each of us be confident that he *does*, at present, mean addition by "plus"?[41]

How can nonreductionism respond to this charge of desperation and mystification? Is it really mysterious and desperate to postulate the existence of a kind of state with the sorts of properties possessed by our intuitive conception of meaning? Colin McGinn responds that, far from being mysterious and desperate, the properties in question are possessed by certain of our everyday psychological states, such as beliefs, thoughts, intentions, hopes, and so on. For example, introspection reveals that there is no state of consciousness, with its own affective phenomenology, which could *be* a given intention, and yet we are ordinarily taken to have *authoritative* and *noninferential* access to the contents of our own intentions. Suppose I ask you whether you intend to travel to London next weekend. Your answer, whatever it is, will normally be given automatically: you will not have to *infer* that you have (or don't have) the intention to visit London from some other fact about you (say, from your behaviour). Moreover, your judgement that you intend (or don't intend) to visit London is authoritative in the sense that it is ordinarily taken to be the highest court to which one can appeal over the matter as to what you intend or do not intend to do. It is only *ordinarily* the highest court of appeal in such matters, because there are circumstances, for example, when there is independent evidence that you are self-deceived, or lying, or have misunderstood the question, in which it can be overturned. But the important point is that the onus is on someone who wants to overturn your judgement to bring such evidence forward: in the absence of this sort of evidence, you do not have to *justify* your judgement as to what you intend.[42] Intention, moreover, displays the same sort of "disposition-like theoreticity" as our intuitive conception of meaning: just as the ascription of an intention to a person may be withdrawn if he behaves in certain ways in the future, the ascription of understanding to him may be withdrawn if he applies the expression in certain bizarre ways in future situations. How can the properties possessed by our intuitive conception of meaning be mysterious and desperate when they are possessed by a whole range of psychological states that figure constantly in our everyday mental lives and in our explanations of each other's actions? McGinn thinks these observations sufficient to rebut the sceptical argument at this point:

> How to give a philosophical *theory* of this kind of knowledge is of course a difficult and substantial question, but the lack of a theory of a phenomenon is not in itself a good reason to doubt the existence of the phenomenon. I therefore see no mystery-mongering in the claim that there are primitive non-experiental states which display a distinctive first-person epistemology.[43]

It is difficult not to agree with Wright's claim that this reply of McGinn's is, as it stands, "about as flagrant an instance of philosophical stone kicking as one could wish for".[44]

In order to provide a satisfying response to the sceptic we may not need to provide a detailed philosophical *theory* of the nature of our first-person knowledge of meaning, but we surely do require at least a *sketch* of the epistemology of meaning, a sketch that would show how a state could possess both (a) a first-person epistemology of the sort described and nevertheless (b) "have to answer ... to what one says and does in situations so far unconsidered". The feature (a) pulls us in the direction of a *Cartesian* conception of meaning. The first-person epistemology would be explained if we could view understanding as some qualitative introspectible state possessing its own distinctive phenomenology: the noninferential nature of our knowledge of our intentions would be explained because when we possess an introspectible state with its own qualitative phenomenology we do not have to infer this, and the first-person authority of intention would be explained because we have special privileged access to our conscious, introspectible states. But, of course, KW has shown that that sort of view of meaning is a nonstarter. The feature (b) pulls us in the direction of a *dispositional* conception of meaning. Just as an ascription of brittleness to a glass has to answer to how that glass would behave (crucially, whether it would shatter) in unactualized situations, so an ascription of understanding to a speaker has to answer to how that speaker would go on to apply the relevant expression (certain patterns of application would lead us to withdraw the original ascription of understanding, just as certain patterns of behaviour by the glass would lead us to withdraw the ascription of brittleness). Taking understanding to be constituted by a disposition would explain this. But, of course, the dispositional conception of meaning and understanding is also thrown into doubt by KW's arguments. These two features thus seem to pull in two different directions, and the same ambivalent pull permeates the psychological states whose first-person epistemology McGinn adverts to in his attempted response to KW. So, the upshot is that *a nonreductionist response to the sceptical challenge is not acceptable unless it can be shown how it accommodates both of these apparently incompatible properties of meaning – its first-person epistemology and "disposition-like theoreticity" – and in a way that avoids the pitfalls both of crude Cartesianism and the dispositional conception of meaning.*[45] McGinn makes no attempt at all to do this, and his nonreductionism is inadequate because of it.[46] Wright, however, does attempt to develop a form of nonreductionism that explicitly takes on this task. Wright argues that predicates such as "means addition by '+'" are *judgement-dependent*, and that viewing them as judgement-dependent allows us to explain *both* the first-person epistemology of meaning and its "disposition-like theoreticity". We must now explain Wright's conception of judgement-dependence.[47]

Suppose that we are considering a particular region of discourse. Consider the opinions formed by the practitioners of that discourse, formed under conditions that are, for that discourse, *cognitively ideal*. Call such opinions *best opinions*, and the cognitively ideal conditions the *C-conditions*. To take colour discourse as an example, if we consider the predicate "red", the C-conditions would be "conditions of illumination like those which actually typically obtain at noon on a cloudy summer's day out of doors and out of shadow". We cannot find conditions *better* than these for determining whether an object is red.[48]

Suppose we find that the best opinions formed by the practitioners *covary* with the facts about the instantiation of a predicate "red", so that it is true that if the C-conditions obtain, a suitable subject will judge that x is red if and only if x is red. Wright suggests that there are two broad ways in which we might seek to explain this covariance. On the one hand, we might take best opinions to be playing at most a *tracking* role: best opinions about redness are just extremely good at *tracking* independently constituted facts about redness. In such a case, best opinion plays merely an *extension-reflecting* role, serving merely to *reflect* the independently determined extension of "red". On the other hand, we might try to explain the covariance of best opinion and fact by assigning to best opinion an altogether different sort of role. Rather than viewing best opinion as merely tracking the facts about the extension of "red", we can view them as themselves *determining* that extension. Best opinion, on this sort of view, does not serve merely to track independently constituted states of affairs that determine the extensions of colour predicates: rather, best opinion serves to *determine* those extensions and so to play an *extension-determining* role. When the covariance of best opinion and the facts about the instantiation of the central predicates of a region of discourse admit of this latter sort of explanation, the predicates of that region are said to be *judgement-dependent*; when it admits only of the former sort of explanation, the predicates are said to be *judgement-independent*.[49]

How do we determine whether colours, for example, are judgement-dependent ? Wright's discussion proceeds by reference to what he terms *provisional equations*. These have the following form:

(PE) $(\forall x)$ (C → ((A suitable subject S judges that x is red) ↔ x is red))

where "C" denotes the cognitively ideal C-conditions. Redness is then said to be judgement-dependent if and only if the provisional equation is *a priori* true, if the C-conditions can be specified *nontrivially* and in such a way that the question as to whether they are satisfied is *independent* of facts about redness, and if there is no better explanation as to why the covariance between best opinion and fact is *a priori* and substantial in this way.[50,51]

Wright now argues that in the case of self-ascriptions of intention best opinions can be viewed as playing an extension-determining role. The C-conditions are roughly as follows: *the subject* S *is not lying, is prey to no material self-deception, is not making a simple slip of the tongue, has an adequate grasp of the concepts requisite for the expression of the intention, and is adequately attentive to the question of the content of his intention.* Under these conditions a speaker's first-person avowal of an intention is authoritative, in the sense that there is ordinarily no higher authority to which we can appeal in order to overthrow his judgement that he so intends. Rejecting the subject's opinion requires showing that at least one of these conditions is not satisfied in the given instance. Equally, when these conditions obtain, the subject's opinions about the contents of their intentions, and the truth about the contents of the relevant intentions, match perfectly. And, crucially, when the C-conditions are specified in this way the provisional equation INTENTION (below) is plausibly *a priori* and nontrivial:

INTENTION. ($\forall$ S) (C $\rightarrow$ ((Subject S judges that he intends to ø) iff (he intends to ø)).

There appear to be no worries about INTENTION satisfying the conditions required for intentions to be judgement-dependent: it is *a priori* because all that is required to know the truth of INTENTION is mastery of the concept of intention, the conditions don't seem to amount to a "whatever it takes" clause and so are not trivially specified, and the satisfaction of the C-conditions is logically independent of the truth of "S intends to ø". There is no better explanation of this substantial *a priori* covariance between best opinion and fact unless "full-blown Cartesianism" is plausible – and as we saw above Wright agrees with KW that full-blown Cartesianism is not an option.[52]

If Wright is justified in his claim that self-ascriptions of intention are judgement-dependent the payoff is as follows. First, a solution to the problem of the first-person epistemology of intention seems to be immediate: a subject's knowledge of the contents of his own intentions is noninferential and authoritative because it is his *own* judgements about the contents of his own intentions that determine the extensions of the predicates that self-ascribe those intentions. And such knowledge is easily accomplished because it is easy enough to get oneself into the appropriate conditions. We also appear to have a nice solution to the problem of the relationship between a subject's possession of an intention and the so far unactualized behaviour that serves in part to determine whether he possesses that intention:

> Suppose a subject believes that he has formed an intention to continue the series – 2, 4, 6 ... – in a certain way and he writes – 8, 10, 12. He need have given no thought yet to what he will write after "12", but when he comes to that point he confidently continues – 14, 16, 18 – and judges that he is following out his former intention, that he is, in Wittgenstein's phrase, "going on in the same way". Wright's idea is that just as his original judgement that he had that particular intention constitutively determined that he did indeed have that intention, so his later judgement that writing "14, 16, 18" implemented rather than frustrated that intention constitutes the fact that such behaviour does implement that particular intention. So best opinion ... as to what current behaviour implements a former intention determines what behaviour implements that former intention.[53]

So Wright accounts for the fact that the ascription of an intention to someone has to answer to how they would behave in as yet unactualized situations: it explains the "disposition-like theoreticity" of intention.

We can thus explain the features that might incline us, respectively, either in the direction of a Cartesian account of intention, or in the direction of a purely dispositional construal, without succumbing to the problems faced by either of those types of theory. Suppose that Wright's account of intention is successful. What are the prospects for giving a similar account in the case of meaning and understanding? If meaning such and such by an expression can be taken to consist in the possession of a certain sort of intention, then the application of Wright's judgement-dependent account of intention to the case of meaning will be straightforward. But even if this is not the case, we can still construct something like the story we constructed about intention for the case of meaning. As Wright says, responding to the sceptical argument via an account like his "does not require construal of meaning as a kind of intention; it is enough that the concepts are relevantly similar – that both sustain authoritative first-person avowals, and that this circumstance is to be explained in terms of [judgement-dependence]."[54] How plausible is Wright's claim that self-ascriptions of meaning and intention are judgement-dependent? This question has received a lot of discussion in the literature, with many philosophers raising doubts about whether intention is plausibly viewed as judgement-dependent. We'll end this section by looking briefly at one objection to Wright's account, that proposed by Paul Boghossian.[55]

Consider again the kind of provisional biconditional central to Wright's account:

If C then (S believes that he means addition by "+" if and only if he means addition by "+").

The problem is this. We want to view S's best beliefs as determining the extension of predicates such as "S means ... by '+'". But as Boghossian argues, we cannot view S's best *beliefs* (or *judgements* or *opinions*) as playing an extension-determining role with respect to ascriptions of meaning without violating the condition that the question as to whether the C-conditions are satisfied is independent of prior facts about meaning. This is because we have to take for granted at least the *content* of the beliefs that figure in the provisional equation. Best opinions cannot constitutively determine the extension of predicates ascribing meaning or content, because we have to assume some *prior* determination of the content or meaning possessed by those best opinions themselves. It follows that meaning cannot be judgement-dependent, since the judgement-dependent account itself presupposes prior facts about meaning. As Boghossian puts it himself:

> It is already clear that there is a serious difficulty seeing how facts about mental content could conceivably satisfy the stated requirements on judgement-dependence. For it is inconceivable, given what *judgement-dependence* amounts to, that the biconditionals in the case of mental content should satisfy the requirements that their left-hand sides be free of any

assumptions about mental content. For, at a minimum, *the content of the judgements* said to fix the facts about mental content have to be presupposed. And that means that any such biconditional will always presuppose a constitution of mental content quite independent of constitution by best judgement.[56]

No doubt Wright has a reply to Boghossian's worry.[57] But at the very least it shows that Wright's solution to KW's sceptical paradox, appealing though it is, faces considerable problems of its own. We'll leave the evaluation of Wright's account to the reader and proceed in the next section to consider a final solution to KW's paradox, one that was arguably advocated by Wittgenstein himself.

6.7 Wittgenstein's dissolution of the sceptical paradox?

The sceptical paradox about sense which has been at the centre of this chapter was inspired, as we have seen, by Wittgenstein's later writing, especially certain sections of the *Philosophical Investigations*. KW advances the sceptical paradox and attempts to neutralize its effect by developing a "sceptical solution", an account that tries to legitimize our practice of ascribing meaning and understanding in the absence of meaning-constituting facts. But what is KW's relationship to the actual, historical Wittgenstein? Does KW accurately reflect his views, and if not, what *are* his views on the topics we have been considering? The interpretation of Wittgenstein's later works is a matter of extreme controversy in contemporary philosophy, and any interpretation is likely to face serious objections from those wishing to defend their own favoured interpretations. But having said that, one must make a choice, and it seems to me that the interpretation of Wittgenstein that sits best with a reading of the texts is that which has been proposed by John McDowell. It would be impossible to defend this exegetical claim in the present work, so I limit myself here to a description of McDowell's Wittgenstein's views, and to remarks about their philosophical import.

Recall that Wright sees Wittgenstein as pointing to a problem that any nonreductionist conception of meaning and understanding must face: how is it possible for there to be states of mind, such as meaning and intention, that are noninferentially and authoritatively known to their possessors, but which also display "disposition-like theoreticity"? However, although Wittgenstein's writings bring this question sharply into focus, "it is probably in vain to search Wittgenstein's own texts for a concrete positive suggestion"[58] about how to answer it. This is a reflection of the later Wittgenstein philosophical method, which is conditioned by a mistrust of such "constitutive" questions. Wittgenstein thought that philosophy's job was not to give *explanations: a fortiori* it was not philosophy's job to explain how there could be states of mind with the features mentioned.

> Philosophy may in no way interfere with the actual use of language; it can in the end only describe it. For it cannot give it any foundation either. It leaves everything as it is.[59]

> Philosophy simply puts everything before us, and neither explains nor deduces anything.[60]

What, then, should we say about our practice of ascribing meaning and understanding, if we are not to attempt to explain how it is possible? Wittgenstein's view is that the job of philosophy is only to dispel possible misunderstandings of these practices:

> The results of philosophy are the uncovering of one or another piece of plain nonsense and of bumps that the understanding has got by running its head up against the limits of language.[61]

> What is your aim in philosophy? – To show the fly the way out of the fly-bottle.[62]

Once the false views of meaning and understanding have been destroyed, there is no further *constructive* contribution philosophy can make. Philosophy's job is to provide *therapy*, to prevent us from slipping back into the bad old ways of thinking:

> The philosopher's treatment of a question is like the treatment of an illness.[63]

The philosopher should not try to provide a constructive *answer* to the question: rather, he should try to *cure* the temptation to think that there was a genuine question in the first place.[64] We can thus say nothing constructive or explanatory about our practices (or "language-games", as Wittgenstein puts it) of ascribing meaning and understanding:

> Our mistake is to look for an explanation where we ought to look at what happens as a "proto-phenomenon". That is, where we ought to have said: *this language-game is played.*[65]

> The question is not one of explaining a language-game by means of our experiences, but of noting a language-game.[66]

Wittgenstein is thus a nonreductionist about meaning, but also a *philosophical quietist* who thinks that once we have pointed out the errors in other conceptions of meaning, there is nothing constructive left for us to say:

> If I have exhausted the justifications I have reached bedrock, and my spade is turned. Then I am inclined to say: "This is simply what I do."[67]

The philosopher cannot justify our practices of ascribing meaning and justification: all he can do is dispel misunderstandings of what those practices involve. After that, all he can say is "This game is played" or "This is what we do".

Wright is sceptical about this quietistic aspect of Wittgenstein's philosophy. *Should* we just accept that meaning, intention and the like exhibit both first-person authority and "disposition-like theoreticity" and content ourselves with refuting mistaken conceptions of what meaning and intending consist in? Wright thinks that we should not give up too easily:

> It is an important methodological precept that we do not despair of giving answers to constitutive questions too soon; if the accomplishments of analysis in philosophy often seem meagre, that may be because it is difficult, not impossible.[68]

> I suspect that [Wittgenstein] did not succeed in representing to himself a sound theoretical basis for declining rather than ... rising to the challenge posed by his own thought which I have tried to describe. In any case, we now confront a challenge: make out the constitutive answer which Wittgenstein ... does not deliver ... or make out the necessary theoretical basis for the analytical quietism which, "officially", he himself adopted.[69]

As we saw in section 6.6, Wright himself does try to deliver an answer to the constitutive question, via his "judgement-dependent" conception of meaning.

McDowell rejects this view of Wittgenstein, which represents him as raising some perfectly good philosophical questions but then declining to attempt to answer them:

> Wright takes Wittgenstein to have uncovered some good philosophical problems about meaning and understanding, [and as appealing to] an adventitiously negative view of philosophy's scope to justify not engaging with those tasks.[70]

Moreover, McDowell thinks that Wittgenstein himself would have been totally out of sympathy with something like Wright's "judgement-dependent" conception of meaning. There are two main reasons for this.

First, on Wright's "judgement-dependent" conception of meaning or intention, there is no inner state of meaning such and such or intending to so and so that our judgements about our meanings or intentions access or track. As Wright puts it:

> There is no essential inner epistemology of rule-following. To express the matter dangerously, we have nothing "in mind".[71]

McDowell thinks that Wittgenstein himself had no inclination to deny that having an intention is a matter of having something in mind:

> *Certainly* all these things happen in you. – And now all I ask is to understand the expression we use. – The picture is there. And I am not disputing its validity in any particular case. – Only I want to understand the application of the picture.[72]

Wittgenstein does not want to deny that having an intention is a matter of having something "in mind": he only wants to destroy *certain misleading conceptions* of *what it is* to have something "in mind".

Secondly, McDowell thinks that some of the implications of the judgement-dependent conception are actually destructive of our everyday conceptions of meaning and understanding. The judgement-dependent conception of intention implies that

> There is nothing for an intention, conceived as determining subsequent conformity and non-conformity to it autonomously and independently of its author's judgements on the matter, to be.[73]

Likewise, the judgement-dependent conception of meaning implies that

> The meaning, say, of an instruction for extending a numerical series [does not determine] what is correct at any point in the series in advance of anyone's working out the series to that point.[74]

McDowell thinks that in each case we have a dramatic departure from our ordinary, common sense conceptions of meaning and intention. The idea

> that the meaning reaches forward in the series ahead of anyone who actually works the series out, and is so to speak already there waiting for such a person, ready to stand in judgement over her performance, at any point in the series that she reaches ... is just part of the idea of meaning's normative reach.[75]

The move to a judgement-dependent conception of meaning cannot preserve the idea that the meaning of an expression lays down a normative constraint on future uses of that expression. And the departure from common sense is even clearer when we consider intention:

> Suppose I form the intention to type a period. If that is my intention, it is settled that only my typing a period will count as

executing it. If that is indeed the intention which I form, nothing more than the intention itself is needed to determine what counts as conformity to it. Certainly it needs no help from my subsequent judgements. So there is something for my intention to type a period, conceived as determining what counts as conformity to it autonomously and independently of my judgements on the matter, to be: namely, precisely, my intention to type a period. An intention to type a period is exactly something that must be conceived in that way. This is common-sense.[76]

McDowell thinks that it is unlikely that Wittgenstein – who thought that "philosophy leaves everything as it is" – would accept an account of meaning and intention that implies the falsity of these common sense views.

How, then, does Wittgenstein justify his philosophical quietism while at the same time leaving our everyday conceptions of meaning and intention intact? Intuitively, the fact that someone grasps a certain meaning is a fact about that person's mind. Suppose that one accepted a conception of the mind (call it the "master-thesis") according to which "it is populated exclusively with items that, considered in themselves, do not sort things outside the mind, including specifically bits of behaviour, into those that are correct or incorrect in the light of those items".[77] The master-thesis has it that, considered in themselves, mental states and acts just "stand there like a signpost".[78] A signpost, considered in itself, does not sort episodes of behaviour into those that constitute following the signpost correctly or incorrectly. So, if you accepted this conception of the mind, you would have to give some account of what *does* sort episodes of behaviour into those that constitute following the signpost correctly, or as acting in accord with the meaning that is grasped. A tempting answer would be that

What does sort behaviour into what counts as following the sign-post and what does not is not an inscribed board fixed to a post, considered in itself, but such an object *under a certain interpretation* – such an object interpreted as a sign-post pointing the way to a certain destination.[79]

But according to Wittgenstein this idea is hopeless. Recall the passage from section 198 of *Philosophical Investigations* that we quoted on p. 158: " ... any interpretation still hangs in the air along with what it interprets, and cannot give it any support. Interpretations by themselves do not determine meaning." Suppose that meaning such and such by an expression was a matter of putting a certain interpretation on it. Then what is required for competence is that the *correct* interpretation is put on it. But, according to the master-thesis, acts of mind, such as putting an interpretation on an expression, just "stand there like a sign-post". So, we require that the interpretation of the expression *itself* be interpreted. And now we are off on a regress: the interpretation of the interpretation in its turn just "stands there like a sign-post", and so will require interpretation, and so on *ad infinitum*.

Now according to Kripke, at this point Wittgenstein accepts that there is no such thing as a fact about what anyone means and intends, and attempts to develop a sceptical solution to preserve meaning and intention in the light of this conclusion:

> This was our paradox: no course of action could be determined by a rule, because every course of action can be made out to accord with the rule. The answer was: if everything can be made out to accord with the rule, then it can also be made out to conflict with it. And so there would be neither accord nor conflict.[80]

But as many commentators have pointed out, the paragraph in *Philosophical Investigations* that follows this one shows that, contrary to what Kripke claims, Wittgenstein does *not* accept the sceptical paradox that there is no such thing as a fact about meaning:

> It can be seen that there is a misunderstanding here from the mere fact that in the course of our argument we give one interpretation after another; as if each one contented us at least for a moment, until we thought of yet another standing behind it. What this shows is that there is a way of grasping a rule which is *not* an *interpretation*, but which is exhibited in what we call "obeying the rule" and "going against it" in actual cases.[81]

McDowell suggests that what this shows is that Wittgenstein does not accept the master-thesis plus the consequent need for interpretation and then proceed to draw the conclusion that, since interpretations do not determine meaning, there is no such thing as meaning an expression in one way rather than another; rather, *Wittgenstein blocks the route to the sceptical paradox by refusing to accept the master-thesis in the first place.*

Is Wittgenstein's refusal to accept the master-thesis justified? According to McDowell, the master-thesis is an extremely unintuitive piece of philosophical theory, and as such the onus is on its defenders to justify their adherence to it. Consider a mental occurrence, like the having of the thought *that people are talking about me in the next room.* Only a state of affairs in which people are talking about me in the next room will be in accord with this thought; if another state of affairs obtains, such as a state of affairs in which the next room is empty, this will not be in accord with that thought. The master-thesis then implies

> that whatever I have in my mind on this occasion, it cannot be something to whose very identity that normative link to the objective world is essential ... that what a person has in mind, strictly speaking, is never, say, *that people are talking about her in the next room* but at most something that *can* be interpreted as having that content, although it need not.[82]

And McDowell finds this at worst an extraordinary idea, and at best highly counterintuitive and unmotivated:

> Once we realise that, the master-thesis should stand revealed as quite counterintuitive, not something on which a supposed need for constructive philosophy could be convincingly based.[83]

Wright, because he (perhaps unwittingly) accepts the master-thesis ends up denying that meaning and intending can be a matter of having something "in mind", and this leads him to a piece of "constructive philosophy", the judgement-dependent conception of meaning and intention. But once the master-thesis is revealed as an unintuitive and unmotivated philosophical

216

invention, the need for such a piece of constructive philosophy simply falls away. Since there is no need for a judgement-dependent conception of meaning and intention, we can simply hold on to the common-sense idea that meaning "reaches ahead" and determines in advance, independently of anything we go on to say and do, what patterns of behaviour accord with it and which do not. Everything is left as it was:

> The question "How is it possible for meaning to reach ahead of any actual performance?" is just a specific form of the question "How is it possible for the concept of accord to be in place in the way that the idea of meaning requires it to be?" The Wittgensteinian response is not that these are good questions, calling for constructive philosophy to answer them. The Wittgensteinian response is to draw attention to the way of thinking that makes it look as if there are problems here.[84]

> Questions like "How is meaning possible?" express a sense of spookiness, and Wittgenstein's point is that we should not indulge the sense of spookiness, but rather exorcize it. The question looks like an urgent one from the standpoint of a world-view that is inhospitable to meaning: a standpoint from which it looks like a task for philosophy to shoehorn the world into something as close as we can get to our previous conception of meaning. But philosophy's task is rather to dislodge the assumptions that make it look difficult to find a place for meaning in the world.[85]

Does Wittgenstein really succeed in exorcizing the spookiness that a range of irreducible, *sui generis* facts about meaning and intention can make us feel? Or is Wright correct that the questions raised are good ones requiring constructive (as opposed to merely therapeutic) philosophy to answer them? And what of the call for an explanation of the first-person authority of ascriptions of meaning and intention? Can Wittgenstein exorcize the temptation we feel to make such a call? These are the questions that must be answered if we are to have a true estimate of Wittgenstein's contribution to the study of meaning.[86]

Further reading

Paul Boghossian's literature survey "The rule-following considerations", *Mind* (1989), is extremely useful in relating KW's arguments to themes in contemporary philosophy of language and mind. Two papers that attempt to defend versions of sophisticated dispositionalism are G. Forbes, "Scepticism and semantic knowledge", *Proceedings of the Aristotelian Society* (1984) and C. Ginet, "The dispositionalist solution to Wittgenstein's problem about understanding a rule", *Midwest Studies in Philosophy* (1992). For criticism, see Boghossian, "The rule-following considerations", section V, and "Naturalizing content", in G. Rey and B. Loewer (eds), *Meaning in mind*. For details of David Lewis' account of reductive analysis, see his "How to define theoretical terms", *Journal of Philosophy* (1970) and "Psychophysical and theoretical identifications", *Australasian Journal of Philosophy* (1972).

For J. Fodor's views, see "Meaning and the world order", which is Chapter 4 of his *Psychosemantics*; and "A theory of content (I and II)" in his *A theory of content and other essays*. For discussion of Fodor, see T. Crane, *The mechanical mind*, Chapters 4 and 5, J. Zalabardo, "A problem for information theoretic semantics", *Synthese* (1995), and Boghossian "Naturalizing content".

C. McGinn's views on Wittgenstein are contained in his book *Wittgenstein on meaning*. This contains some extremely useful material but should be read in conjunction with C. Wright's "Critical notice of McGinn" in *Mind* (1989) and Boghossian's review, in the *Philosophical Review* (1989).

Wright's "judgement-dependent" account of meaning and intention is outlined in his "On making up one's mind: Wittgenstein on intention", in P. Weingartner and G. Schutz (eds), *Logic, science, and epistemology*, and "Wittgenstein's rule-following considerations and the central project of theoretical linguistics", in A. George (ed.), *Reflections on Chomsky*. Other useful exposition is provided in his "Moral values, projection, and secondary qualities", *Proceedings of the Aristotelian Society* (1988), and in *Truth and objectivity*, appendix to Chapter 3. For criticism of Wright, see R. Holton, "Intention detecting", *Philosophical Quarterly* (1993); A. Miller and J. Divers, "Best opinion, intention detecting, and analytic functionalism", *Philosophical Quarterly* (1994); A. Miller, "An objection to Wright's treatment of intention", *Analysis* (1989); M. Johnston, "Objectivity disfigured", appendix on "Two distinctions", in J. Haldane and C. Wright (eds), *Reality, representation and projection*; P. Sullivan, "Problems for a construction of meaning and intention", *Mind* (1994); J. Edwards, "Secondary qualities and the *a priori*", *Mind* (1992), and "Best opinion and intentional states", *Philosophical Quarterly* (1992); S. Blackburn, "Circles, finks, smells, and biconditionals", *Philosophical Perspectives* (1993). For a "response-dependent" solution which contrasts with Wright's, see Philip Pettit "The Reality of Rule-following" *Mind* (1990), and the first four chapters of his *The common mind*.

L. Wittgenstein's key texts on rule-following are *Philosophical investigations* (especially sections 138–242) and *Remarks on the foundations of mathematics* (especially section VI). McDowell's interpretation of Wittgenstein is most accessible in "Meaning and intention in Wittgenstein's later philosophy", *Midwest Studies in Philosophy* (1992). Other important papers are "Intentionality and interiority in Wittgenstein", in K. Puhl (ed.), *Meaning scepticism*, and "Wittgenstein on following a rule", *Synthese* (1984). The debate between Wright and McDowell on the import of Wittgenstein's rule-following considerations is alive and kicking, and continues in Wright, "Self-knowledge: the Wittgensteinian legacy", and J. McDowell "Reply to Crispin Wright", in C. McDonald, B. Smith, and C. Wright (eds), *Self-knowledge and externalism*. See also McDowell's *Mind and world*, Wright's critical study, "Human Nature?", in *Inquiry* (1997), and A. Miller "Rule-following, response-dependence, and McDowell's debate with anti-realism", *European Review of Philosophy* (1997).

For more general discussions of Wittgenstein, see N. Malcolm, *Nothing is hidden*, and O. Hanfling, *Wittgenstein's later philosophy*.

Chapter 7

Sense, intention and speech-acts: Grice's programme

In the previous three chapters we have considered various versions of scepticism about meaning, and we have suggested a number of lines of response to such scepticism. Our discussion of attempts to save sense in the light of semantic scepticism has been far from exhaustive. Rather than discuss further responses to scepticism about sense, we return in the final three chapters to questions about the nature of sense and the relationship of issues in the theory of meaning to metaphysical issues in philosophy in general.

7.1 Homeric struggles: two approaches to sense

In his inaugural lecture, delivered in Oxford in 1969, P. F. Strawson began by asking a number of questions: "What is it for anything to have a meaning at all, in the way, or in the sense, in which words or sentences or signals have meaning? What is it for a particular sentence to have the meaning or meanings it does have?"[1] These questions have been central to the present book.

Recall that in section 2.6 we distinguished, very roughly, between *sentence-meaning* and *speaker's-meaning*. Sentence-meaning concerns the strict and literal meaning of a given sentence type. So the following would be a statement of the sentence-meaning of "Jones is an efficient administrator":

(1) "Jones is an efficient administrator" means that Jones is an efficient administrator.

Recall that on the Fregean account of meaning developed in Chapter 2 this could be cashed out as

(2) "Jones is an efficient administrator" is true if and only if Jones is an efficient administrator.

Now we said that speaker's-meaning is, roughly, a matter of the information someone uttering a particular token of an expression intends to convey by means of the utterance of that expression. In the example in section 2.6, the speaker's-meaning of my utterance of a token of "Jones is an efficient administrator" is that Jones is an uninteresting philosopher.

This raises the question of the relationship between sentence-meaning and speaker's-meaning. Do we explain sentence-meaning in terms of speaker's-meaning, or vice versa? In the Fregean account outlined in Chapter 2, questions of sentence-meaning are dealt with by semantics, and questions about speaker's-meaning are dealt with by pragmatics. The central question that pragmatics must answer, on the Fregean picture, is: *given that a type of sentence has a particular sentence-meaning*, what determines the speaker's-meaning of utterances of tokens of that type? So according to the Fregean picture, the explanation of sentence-meaning – in terms of truth-conditions – comes first, with the explanation of speaker's-meaning coming afterwards. In his inaugural lecture, Strawson notes that there is a struggle between philosophers who align themselves with Frege and seek to explain speaker's-meaning in terms of sentence-meaning and truth-conditions, and philosophers who argue that this gets matters upside down: according to these latter philosophers, sentence-meaning must be explained in terms of speaker's- meaning rather than vice versa:

A struggle on what seems to be such a central issue in philosophy should have something of a Homeric quality; and a Homeric struggle calls for gods and heroes. I can at least, though, tentatively, name some living captains and benevolent shades: on the one side, say, Grice, Austin, and the later Wittgenstein; on the other, Chomsky, Frege, and the earlier Wittgenstein.[2]

Strawson terms Grice, Austin and the later Wittgenstein "theorists of communication-intention": speaker's-meaning, a matter of what speakers *intend to communicate* in uttering particular linguistic tokens or in performing particular speech-acts, is the fundamental notion, and the notion of sentence-meaning is explained (in part) in terms of it. Strawson, aligning himself with these theorists, sums their viewpoint up thus: "As theorists, we know nothing of human *language* unless we understand human *speech*."[3] Or in the words of Searle, another communication-intention theorist:

> It is not, as has generally been supposed, the symbol or word or sentence, or even the token of the symbol or word or sentence, which is the unit of linguistic communication, but rather it is the *production* of the token in the performance of the speech-act that constitutes the basic unit of linguistic communication.[4]

Frege and the others, on the other hand, might be called "truth-conditional theorists": sentence-meaning, the possession of truth-conditions, is the fundamental notion, and it is only after explaining this that we are able to proceed to the explanation of speaker's-meaning. Language is explained first, speech afterwards.

The debate between the theorists of communication-intention and the truth-conditional theorists is of such fundamental interest because it promises an answer to the question about the relationship between *language* and *thought*. We have already touched on this in section 6.1. If the theorists of communication-intention are right, sentence-meaning, or linguistic-meaning, can be explained in terms of the contents of speakers' mental states: in this sense, the content of mental states will be *explanatorily prior* to linguistic meaning. In this chapter, we concentrate on one of the most famous theorists of communication-intention, Paul Grice.

7.2 Grice on speaker's-meaning and sentence-meaning

In his short but crucially important article "Meaning", Grice begins by distinguishing between two senses in which the expressions "means", "means something", "means that" may be taken. The first of these is the *natural* sense, exemplified by

(3) "Those spots mean measles."
(4) "Those spots didn't mean anything to me, but to the doctor they meant measles."
(5) "The recent budget means that we shall have a hard year."

This type of meaning is sometimes referred to as *indicator-meaning*, since the idea is that spots *indicate* the presence of measles and so on. Grice points out that one feature of natural meaning is that if x means that p (where x is an object or objects, p a proposition) in the sense of natural meaning, it follows that p. Where natural meaning is concerned, it makes no sense to say, for example, "Those spots meant measles, but he hadn't got measles" or "The recent budget means that we shall have a hard year, but we shan't have".

This sense of meaning contrasts with *nonnatural* meaning, exemplified by

(6) "Those three rings of the bell (of the bus) mean that the bus is full."
(7) "That remark, 'Smith couldn't get on without his trouble and strife', meant that Smith found his wife indispensable."

Unlike the natural sense of meaning, there is no entailment from x means that p to p: it makes perfect sense to say that "Those three rings of the bell mean that the bus is full, but the conductor is mistaken and it isn't actually full" or "That remark … meant that Smith found his wife indispensable, but in fact he deserted her seven years ago." (Why does Grice call these latter cases cases of *nonnatural* meaning? It is not a matter of *convention* that spots mean measles, whereas it is in some sense a matter of convention that three rings mean that the bus is full: in other countries, for example, the convention might be different [three rings of the bell might mean that the bus is stopping].)

Grice is concerned purely with the nonnatural sense of meaning, and he uses the abbreviation "means$_{NN}$" to distinguish this sense. Grice proceeds in two steps. *First, he aims to explain speaker's-meaning$_{NN}$ in terms of the intentions of the utterer. Secondly, he aims to explain sentence-meaning$_{NN}$ in terms of speaker's-meaning, so that ultimately we have an account of sentence-meaning$_{NN}$ in terms of utterers' intentions.* So, in the first stage he is concerned with such locutions as

(8)   Speaker A meant$_{NN}$ something by sentence x (on a particular occasion of use).

Given an account of this sense of means$_{NN}$ in terms of A's intentions, Grice goes on to attempt to explain sentence-meaning by explaining means$_{NN}$ as it appears in such locutions as

(9)   Sentence x means$_{NN}$ (timeless) something (that so-and-so).

Let's work towards Grice's account of (8) and speaker's-meaning. Concentrate on the case where the sentence x is a declarative or "informative" sentence, such as "Jones is an efficient administrator" (as opposed to "noninformative" sentences or imperatives, such as "Close the window"). We are looking for a set of necessary and sufficient conditions for the truth of

(10) Miller meant$_{NN}$ that Jones is an efficient administrator by his utterance of "Jones is an efficient administrator".

Suppose that I direct this utterance to my colleague Divers, so that Divers constitutes the "audience" for this remark. A first stab at a sufficient condition for (10) might be

(a)   Miller intends his utterance of the sentence to induce the belief that Jones is an efficient administrator in Divers.

But as Grice points out, the intention to induce a belief in the audience is not on its own sufficient for a case of meaning$_{NN}$:

> I might leave B's handkerchief near the scene of a murder in order to induce the detective to believe that B was the murderer; but we should not want to say that the handkerchief (or my leaving it there) meant$_{NN}$ anything or that I had meant$_{NN}$ by leaving it that B was the murderer.[5]

The problem here is that I do not intend the detective to *recognize the intention* behind my leaving the handkerchief near the scene of the murder (this would be self-defeating in this case). So we can add, to the condition (a) that Miller intends his utterance of the sentence to induce the belief that Jones is an efficient administrator in Divers, the condition

(b)   Miller also intends Divers to recognize the intention behind his utterance.

Do we now have a sufficient condition for the truth of (10)? Grice thinks not and that we need to add a further condition. He brings this out by considering the following two cases:

(11)   I show Mr X a photograph of Mr Y displaying undue familiarity to Mrs X.
(12)   I draw a picture of Mr Y behaving in this manner and show it to Mr X.

Grice suggests that whereas we would want to say that by drawing the picture in the case of (12) I mean$_{NN}$ that Mr Y had been unduly familiar with Mrs X, we would not want to say this in the case of my producing the photograph. Why not? Because my intention that Mr X form the belief that Mr Y had been unduly familiar with Mrs X, and my intention that Mr X recognize this intention of mine, do not play any part in the explanation of why Mr X forms this belief: even if I had not had these intentions – if Mr X had stumbled on the photograph by accident, for example – Mr X would still have formed this belief. This is not so in the example of the drawing. So, in addition to my intention that Mr X form this belief, and my intention that Mr X recognize this intention of mine, *I must also intend that Mr X's recognition of this intention of mine plays a part in the explanation of why Mr X forms the belief.* Thus, the following three conditions are jointly sufficient (and individually necessary) for the truth of (10):

(a) Miller intends his utterance of "Jones is an efficient administrator" to induce the belief that Jones is an efficient administrator in Divers.

(b) Miller intends Divers to recognize the intention behind his utterance of "Jones is an efficient administrator".

(c) Divers recognition of Miller's intentions plays a part in the explanation of why Divers forms the belief that Jones is an efficient administrator.

This account can be generalized to deal with "noninformative" cases. Suppose we are at a department meeting trying to decide who has sufficient administrative acumen to be a good examinations officer. I want my colleagues to choose Jones. Then the meaning$_{NN}$ of my utterance of "Jones is an efficient administrator" is Jones's being picked as examinations officer if: I intend to induce my colleagues to pick Jones as examinations officer by means of my utterance, and I intend to induce them to pick Jones *via* their recognition of this intention.

Grice sums up his account of speaker's-meaning$_{NN}$ as follows:

"A meant$_{NN}$ something by x" is (roughly) equivalent to "A intended the utterance of x to produce some effect in an audience by means of the recognition of this intention"; and we may add that to ask what A meant is to ask for a specification of the intended effect.[6]

Having accounted for speaker's-meaning, Grice goes on to consider sentence-meaning. We are looking for a necessary and sufficient condition for the truth of

(13) The sentence "Jones is an efficient administrator" means$_{NN}$ (timeless) that Jones is an efficient administrator.

Grice suggests that (13) is true if and only if tokens of "Jones is an efficient administrator" are *regularly* or *conventionally* associated with the speaker's-meaning$_{NN}$ that Jones is an efficient administrator.[7] The conventional way for a speaker A to mean$_{NN}$ that Jones is an efficient administrator is to utter a token of the type "Jones is an efficient administrator". Of course, there are other uses of this token: a speaker can use it to mean$_{NN}$ that Jones be picked as examinations officer, or to mean$_{NN}$ that Jones is an uninteresting philosopher. But these uses are *nonconventional*, the exception rather than the rule, as it were.

Thus, the notion of sentence-meaning is explained in terms of the notion of speaker's-meaning and the notion of convention, where the notion of speaker's-meaning is explained in terms of utterers' intentions. This is why Grice's account is sometimes known as a "convention plus intention" account of sentence-meaning. Note that Grice's analysis of sentence- or linguistic-meaning is intended to be a *reductive analysis*: the notion of speaker's-meaning is defined in terms of utterers' intentions, in a way that requires no use of the notion of sentence-meaning; and the notion of sentence-meaning is defined in terms of speaker's-meaning and convention in a way which requires no use of the notion of sentence-meaning. The meaning of language is non-circularly analyzed in terms of mental content.

7.3 Searle's modifications: illocutionary and perlocutionary intentions

Needless to say, many counterexamples to Grice's analysis have been suggested, both by philosophers opposed to his analysis and by philosophers wishing to refine it. This has led to an extremely complicated series of epicycles that we shall not attempt to review here. Rather, we look only at two suggested counterexamples and one suggested refinement.

The first counterexample is due to Paul Ziff:

> On being inducted into the army, George is compelled to take a test designed to establish sanity. George is known to be an irritable academic. The test he is being given would be

appropriate for morons. One of the questions asked is: "What would you say if you were asked to identify yourself?". George replied to the officer asking the question by uttering:

(14)   Ugh ugh blugh blugh ugh blug blug.[8]

George intends the officer to be offended, and, moreover, he intends to induce the officer being offended by means of the officer's recognition of this intention. So according to Grice's analysis, George means$_{NN}$ something by (14). But according to Ziff, this is implausible. George does not mean *anything* by (14) (that is the whole point of his uttering it in this situation).

The second counterexample is due to John Searle:

Suppose that I am an American soldier in WW2 and that I am captured by Italian troops. And suppose also that I wish to get these troops to believe that I am a German officer in order to get them to release me. What I would like to do is to tell them in German or Italian that I am a German officer. But let us suppose that I don't know enough German or Italian to do that. So I attempt to put on a show of telling them that I am a German officer by reciting those few bits of German that I know, trusting that they don't know enough German to see through my plan. Let us suppose I know only one line of German, which I remember from a poem I had to memorize in a high school German course. Therefore I, a captured American, address my Italian captors with the following sentence: "Kennst du das Land, wo die Zitronen blühen?"[9]

Here, the soldier intends to induce the belief that he is a German officer in the Italians, and he intends that they form this belief in virtue of their recognition of this intention. So, according to Grice's account the following is true:

(15)   The soldier means$_{NN}$ that he is a German officer by "Kennst du das Land, wo die Zitronen blühen?"

But according to Searle this is implausible:

229

In this case it seems plainly false that when I utter the German sentence what I mean is "I am a German officer", or even "Ich bin ein deutscher Offizier", because what the words mean is, "Knowest thou the land where the lemon trees bloom?" Of course, I want my captors to be deceived into thinking that what I mean is "I am a German officer", but part of what is involved in the deception is getting them to think that that is what the words which I utter mean in German.[10]

The diagnosis of why Grice's account is susceptible to counterexamples like the two we have considered is, according to Searle, that it suffers from two defects:

First of all, it fails to distinguish the different kinds of effects – perlocutionary versus illocutionary – that one may intend to produce in one's hearers, and it further fails to show the way in which these different kinds of effects are related to the notion of meaning. A second defect is that it fails to account for the extent to which meaning is a matter of rules or conventions. That is, [Grice's] account of meaning does not show the connection between one meaning something by what one says and what that which one says actually means in the language.[11]

In order to explain how Searle attempts to amend Grice's account so that it is freed of these defects, we must first explain the distinction between *illocutionary* and *perlocutionary* effects.

Note that in our final quote from Grice in section 7.2, he said that to ask what A meant by x is to ask for a specification of the effect of his utterance of x. Of course, not all effects of the utterance of x are relevant to its speaker's-meaning, and we looked at Grice's attempt to narrow down the effects to those that *are* relevant to speaker's-meaning: the effects must be intended, induced in an audience, and be the upshot of the audience's recognition of the relevant intention. *Searle suggests that we narrow down even further the class of effects relevant to speaker's-meaning. In addition to the conditions just mentioned, the effects must be illocutionary rather than perlocutionary.* An illocutionary effect is one that is in part the content of an illocutionary intention, *where an illocutionary intention is an intention that is fulfilled simply on the basis of the audience's recognition of the presence of the intention.*

Examples of illocutionary effects include: Jones is given a report, Jones is given a warning, Jones is given a promise, Jones is given a proposal, Jones is given an order, Jones is thanked. In each case, all that is required for the occurrence of the effect is Jones's recognition that the speaker has the relevant intention: if Jones recognizes my intention to warn him in uttering "I warn you", then he is thereby warned; if Jones recognizes my intention to thank him in uttering "I thank you", then he is thereby thanked; if Jones recognizes my intention to issue him with an order in uttering "I order you", then he is thereby ordered.

A perlocutionary effect, on the other hand, is one which is in part the content of a perlocutionary intention, *where a perlocutionary intention is an intention that is* not *fulfilled simply on the basis of the audience's recognition of the presence of the intention.* Examples of perlocutionary effects include: Jones forms a certain belief, Jones is amused, Jones is impressed, Jones is embarrassed. In each case, Jones's recognition that the speaker has the relevant intention does not guarantee the occurrence of the effect: if Jones recognizes my intention to induce him to form a certain belief by means of an utterance, he may nevertheless fail to form the belief in question; if Jones recognizes my intention to amuse him by means of an utterance, he may nevertheless fail to be amused; if Jones recognizes my intention to impress him by means of an utterance, he may nevertheless be unimpressed; and if Jones recognizes my intention to embarrass him by means of an utterance, he may fail to be embarrassed.

Searle thus adds to Grice's three conditions on speaker's-meaning$_{NN}$ the conditions

(d) that the speaker's intentions be illocutionary and
(e) that he intends to respect the conventions governing the use of the relevant expression in the language concerned:

In the performance of an illocutionary act the speaker intends to produce a certain effect by means of getting the hearer to recognize his intention to produce that effect, and furthermore, if he is using words literally, he intends this recognition to be achieved in virtue of the fact that the rules for using the expressions associate the expressions with the production of that effect.[12]

How does this modification deal with the two counterexamples we described earlier? The first counterexample is taken care of, since the speaker's intention to offend the officer is not illocutionary: the officer's recognition that the speaker intends to offend him by means of the utterance does not guarantee that he will actually take offence. So the modified account can accommodate the thought that the speaker's utterance of (14) does not mean$_{NN}$ anything. In the second counterexample, the intention is not illocutionary either, since someone's recognizing that you intend to induce a belief in them by means of a given utterance does not guarantee that they will form this belief. Moreover, the American soldier does not intend the Italians' recognition of his intention to be achieved in virtue of the fact that in German the effect of inducing the belief that one is German is conventionally associated with the utterance of "Kennst du das Land, wo die Zitronen blühen?" In German this sentence is conventionally associated with an altogether different sort of effect (that which consists in certain questions being answered). So, the modified account can accommodate the thought that the utterance of "Kennst du das Land, wo die Zitronen blühen?" does not mean$_{NN}$ "I am a German officer".

It is worth noting that the second part of Searle's modification – dealing with the rules that conventionally govern the use of the expressions concerned – is necessary. Because the intention is to induce the belief in the Italians that one is a German officer, it might seem as if the first condition – requiring that the speaker's intentions be illocutionary – is enough to deal with this example. But consider the following example. The intention to announce that so and so is an illocutionary intention: mere recognition on the part of the audience that one intends to announce so and so is enough to guarantee that one *has* announced so and so. So suppose that the example is as before, except that the American soldier intends to *announce* to the Italians that he is German by means of uttering "Kennst du das Land, wo die Zitronen blühen?" Then condition (d) will not kick in. But condition (e) will kick in, since in German the sentence "Kennst du das Land, wo die Zitronen blühen?" is not conventionally associated with the illocutionary act of announcing that one is a German officer.

However, this shows that there is a problem with Searle's modified version of Grice's analysis. The problem is that the analysis now appears to be circular. Recall that Grice's central idea is that we can noncircularly define a notion of speaker's meaning in terms of speaker's intentions, and then noncircularly define the notion of sentence-meaning in terms of speaker's-meaning and convention. The result is supposed to be a noncircular analysis of sentence-meaning. *But the second condition introduced in Searle's modification seems to presuppose the notion of sentence-meaning: that is, the speaker's-meaning conventionally associated with tokens of a sentence-type.* This renders the account of sentence-meaning circular: we define this in terms of speaker's-meaning, the definition of which presupposes an account of sentence-meaning. Is there any way Searle can respond to this charge of circularity? We must leave this as an exercise for the reader. In the next section we go on to look at further problems faced by Gricean analyses.

7.4 Objections to Gricean analyses

In this section, we'll look at two objections to Gricean accounts that have been developed by Mark Platts. We'll see that, although the first of these objections fails, the second objection does pose a very serious problem for Gricean accounts. We'll then develop a couple of further worries for Grice. In the next section we'll look at Simon Blackburn's response to Platts's objection, and argue that Blackburn's response fails to solve the problem.

Platts's first objection also concerns an alleged circularity in Gricean accounts. It starts with the observation that to find out what intentions a person has typically involves knowing what the expressions of their language mean:

> Utterers' intentions are not recognised by unfailing intuition, nor do Acts of God figure large. It is perhaps possible that very simple intentions be detected quasi-behaviouristically; but for

intentions of any fair degree of complexity, this is simply implausible, the behavioural guide being too *inexact*. Any explanation of how such intentions are recognised will inevitably rely upon the audience's recognition of the literal meaning of the sentence; that meaning is the route to the speaker's intentions, the reverse journey usually being impossible.[13]

My meaning$_{NN}$ that Jones is an efficient administrator by my utterance of "Jones is an efficient administrator" requires that I have certain intentions and that I intend that my audience should recognize those intentions. So my audience recognizing that I mean$_{NN}$ that Jones is an efficient administrator requires that they recognize that I have these intentions. But this recognition will usually have to proceed via their understanding some verbal expression of these intentions, which in turn requires their knowledge of the meanings of those expressions. Speaker's-meaning$_{NN}$ cannot be elucidated in terms of speaker's intentions, because knowledge of speaker's intentions *presupposes* knowledge of speaker's-meaning$_{NN}$.

But this objection actually misses the mark. To see this, we have to appreciate the nature of the Gricean claim that mental content is prior to linguistic meaning. As Martin Davies has pointed out

> The kind of priority that concerns us here is priority in the order of philosophical analysis or elucidation. To say that the notion of X is *analytically prior* to the notion of Y is to say that Y can be analysed or elucidated in terms of X, while the analysis or elucidation of X itself does not have to advert to Y.[14]

Grice is claiming that the notion of speakers intending such and such is *analytically prior* to the notion of sentence-meaning. In addition to analytic priority there is another notion of priority, epistemic priority:

> To say that X is *epistemologically prior* to Y is to say that it is possible to find out about X without having to proceed via knowledge about Y, whereas finding out about Y has to go by way of finding out about X.[15]

But analytic priority is one thing, epistemological priority another: the two notions are logically independent. So it does not follow from the fact that X is analytically prior to Y, that X is epistemologically prior to Y. For example, although the details are controversial and complicated, most philosophers would accept that the notion of personal identity should be analyzed in terms of the notions of physical and psychological continuity: but it doesn't follow from this analysis that when I meet you in the street I need to advert to these complex facts about continuity in order to know that you are the same person I was talking to yesterday (I do that by *looking* at you). So Grice in particular, who is committed to the claim that speaker's intentions are analytically prior to sentence-meaning, is not committed to the claim that it is possible to find out about speaker's intentions without having to proceed via knowledge of facts about sentence-meaning. Platts's first objection thus fails to touch the claim of analytic priority which is definitive of Gricean accounts.

Platts's second objection is more damaging:

> On Grice's theory, sentence-meaning is defined in terms of the intentions with which the sentence is uttered, along, perhaps, with the response standardly secured in an audience by that utterance. Now, as an account of the meanings of sentences in natural languages this will not do for a simple reason: the majority of such sentences, natural languages containing a denumerable infinity of sentences, will never be uttered. They will therefore not be uttered with any intentions, nor will their utterance induce any response in an audience. What, then, can Grice say about these unuttered sentences?[16]

Given that these sentences have never actually been uttered with any intentions, it seems that Grice's only option is to try to account for their meaning in terms of the intentions with which they *would* be uttered, and the responses they would elicit, were that ever to happen. That is, Grice can attempt to account for the meanings of unuttered sentences in terms of *hypothetical intentions*. But not *all* hypothetical intentions can be relevant to meaning; so Platts asks what *constraints* are there on the hypothetical intentions that constitute the meaning of a particular sentence? If there are *no* such constraints, "the meanings of unuttered sentences will be left completely indeterminate: they *could* mean anything, so they *do* mean nothing".[17] On the other hand, if there are constraints, what are they? Platts argues that the only answer available to Grice at this point is that the hypothetical intentions are constrained by the meaning of the sentence, thus rendering the analysis circular:

> Generally, the constraint upon the hypothetical intentions with which a sentence can be uttered, and upon the audience's responses to such an utterance, is precisely the meaning of the sentence ... If this is correct, the attempt to define the meanings of unuttered sentences in terms of hypothetical intentions and responses is hopeless: for it presupposes a prior notion of sentence-meaning.[18]

This difficulty is a reflection of the problems Gricean analyses face in attempting to account for the *compositionality* of meaning: that the meaning of a given sentence, for example, is determined by the meanings of its constituent words and their mode of combination. Consider how the Fregean position developed in Chapters 1 and 2 can deal with the meanings of unuttered sentences by means of theses 2 and 11:

THESIS 2. *The semantic value of a complex expression is determined by the semantic values of its parts.*

THESIS 11. *The sense of a complex expression is determined by the senses of its constituents.*

Theses 2 and 11 – the principles of compositionality for semantic value and sense, respectively – tell us how the meaning of a complex sentence is determined, regardless of whether that sentence has been uttered or not. The problem for the Gricean position is that it is difficult to see how it can contain analogues of these theses. The Gricean would in some sense have to mimic the simple Fregean semantic theory that we sketched in section 1.7, and correlate intentions (or more generally intentional states) of speakers with the axioms of that theory. The idea would then be that the intentions corresponding to complex unuttered sentences could be generated systematically from the intentions corresponding to the theory's axioms. The intentions corresponding to whole sentences – dealt with by theorems in the semantic theory – would be determined by the intentions corresponding to words and modes of combination – dealt with by the theory's axioms.

There are two main problems with this idea. First of all, there are good reasons for thinking that if there are states of speakers that correspond to the axioms of a semantic theory for their language, they cannot be intentions (or propositional attitudes of any sort). This is because there is a constraint on propositional attitudes, such as intentions, which the states of speakers corresponding to semantic axioms do not satisfy. This point has been well made by Gareth Evans and Crispin Wright. Evans and Wright argue that there is a necessary condition that all genuine intentional states must satisfy to qualify as such, and that the states of speakers that correspond to semantic axioms do not satisfy this condition. In order to motivate this condition they ask us to contrast, on the one hand, the belief that a man might have to the effect that a certain substance is poisonous, with the disposition that a rat might have to avoid a similarly contaminated substance. Can we describe the rat as having a genuine *belief* that the substance is poisonous? Evans and Wright suggest not: for whereas in the case of the man the belief is, to use Evans's phrase, "at the service of many distinct projects", and can interact with others of his beliefs and desires to produce new beliefs and desires, none of this obtains in the case of the rat's disposition. In the case of the man, for instance, the belief could be at the service of such projects as killing an adversary, retaining good health, getting out of an obligation by taking a small dose, to name but a few. None of this is possible in the case of the rat: the putative "belief" is harnessed to the single "project" of avoidance of the substance. This is supposed to be a reflection of the fact that propositional attitudes and intentional states, such as beliefs, desires and intentions, come in articulated systems or holistic networks. And it is because genuine beliefs come in such networks and can thus interact with other beliefs that they can indeed be at the service of many distinct projects. For example, the man's belief that the substance is poisonous can be at the service of the project of getting out of a particular obligation because that belief can, together with the beliefs that a small amount of the substance causes only a mild illness and that a mild illness will release him from the obligation, lead to the belief that taking a small amount of the substance will enable him to avoid fulfilling the obligation.

A crude version of the constraint suggested by the Evans–Wright discussion might therefore run as follows:

> A state P of an agent W is a genuine propositional attitude or intentional state only if P can interact with others of W's propositional attitudes and intentional states to produce new propositional attitudes – thus putting P at the service of many distinct projects of the agent.

Evans and Wright both claim that states of speakers corresponding to semantic axioms violate the above constraint. Far from being at the service of many distinct projects the speaker's possession of such a state is, says Evans,

> Exclusively manifested in speaking and understanding a language; the information is not even potentially at the service of any other project of the agent, nor can it interact with any other beliefs of the agent (whether genuine beliefs or other "tacit" beliefs) to yield further beliefs.[19]

While Wright puts it like this:

> The (implicit) knowledge of a meaning-theoretic *axiom* would seem to be harnessed to the single project of forming beliefs about the content of sentences which contain the expression, or exemplify the mode of construction, which it concerns

and he asks the following (rhetorical) question:

> What is supposed to be the role of *desire*? What is the (implicit?) desire which explains why the subject puts his axiomatic beliefs to just this use, and what are the different uses to which they might be put if his desires were different?[20]

No plausible answers to these questions suggest themselves, so the conclusion is that states of speakers corresponding to semantic axioms cannot plausibly be viewed as propositional attitudes. *A fortiori*, they cannot be viewed as intentions, and this surely bodes ill for the Gricean attempt to accommodate compositionality.

Even if the Gricean can deal with this worry, there is a further problem. Suppose that speakers could have intentions, or intentional states, corresponding to the axioms of a semantic theory. What would the content of such intentions and intentional states be? What intention, for example, would correspond to the axiom dealing with the proper name "Plato"? The only plausible answer seems to be something along the following lines: *the speaker intends to use the word "Plato" to refer to Plato and only to Plato.* But from a Gricean point of view this is hopeless: the content of the intention explicitly concerns the *semantic properties of a linguistic expression,* so that Grice's attempt to give a noncircular analysis of the semantic notions applicable to linguistic expressions is scuppered.[21]

7.5 Response to Blackburn

Simon Blackburn has attempted to respond to Platts's dilemma concerning "hypothetical intentions" that we outlined in the previous section. He argues that Platts's objection is confused:

> It is certainly true that although a speaker will at any time only have understood a certain set of sentences which he has been exposed to, he is equipped to go on and understand new ones, and will standardly do so in just the way other speakers would as well. That is fortunate. But it is not some mysterious thing, the meaning of the new sentence which "constrains" the speakers and explains this identity in psychology ... nothing constrains a group ... except their training and the way they find it natural to take that training.[22]

Blackburn thus thinks that Grice can steer through the horns of Platts's dilemma by viewing the hypothetical intentions in question as being constrained by training and the ways speakers naturally react to such training.

But this surely gets matters back to front. Training no doubt constrains the verbal behaviour of speakers, but it can only do the work necessary to avoid Platts's dilemma if it is training relevant to the grasp of sentence-meaning. Just as Platts asked after the constraints on hypothetical intentions, we can go further and ask after the constraints on training. Platts's dilemma simply re-emerges further down the line for Blackburn. If a speaker's training with a given sentence is unconstrained, then "the meanings of that sentence will be left completely indeterminate: it *could* mean anything, so it *does* mean nothing". On the other hand, if there is a constraint, what is it? As before, the only available answer seems to be the literal meaning of the sentence concerned, and the circularity of this is again evident.

Blackburn's response to Platts thus fails. But in addition to the response to Platts, Blackburn also has a positive suggestion about how the Gricean can accommodate compositionality. The passage in which he develops this suggestion is worth quoting at length:

One of the merits of a convention-belief approach is that it concentrates upon the total act of communication – the whole desire or belief communicated by a whole sentence. The presence of a word is subsidiary – a word is something whose presence is a meaning-determining feature of a sentence. We can illustrate this in the figure of the radical interpeter. His initial hypothesis is that some native utterance communicates some whole judgement or command – that *p*. From a number of such hypotheses he can start to extract the features which recur and whose presence seems to be determining the interpretation to be given to any sentence; once this is done he can predict the way in which new sentences will be taken. A convention-belief approach will see the second stage as one of correlating recurrent *features* of utterances with recurrent *features* of beliefs which natives seem to be displaying. The presence of the word "fish" may indicate, for instance, that the speaker is displaying a belief about fish. Once there is regularity in the features of sentences which indicate features of beliefs, there is the possibility of using those features in new combinations to display new beliefs, and we have the elasticity of language. Here, then, we have the place of system according to one natural view of language.[23]

Blackburn's idea seems to be that we can reach an interpretation of a body of native beliefs and utterances and then "project" a structure into the language, a structure that determines the meanings of complex sentences. But it is difficult to see what comfort this can give the Gricean. The discernment of structure acts as a *constraint* on the process of interpretation: as such, the process of interpreting whole sentences *presupposes* rather than *delivers* compositionality. The fact that structure constrains interpretation is well made by Elizabeth Fricker:

> Insofar as interpretation is determinate, the primary feature ensuring this is the fact that the assignment of a meaning to one sentence constrains and is constrained by the assignments made to other sentences ... Some principle for discerning structure in sentences is essential to interpreting a language, and the correctness of an interpretation cannot be considered to be independent of facts about their structure.[24]

This bears some fleshing out. Suppose that we are out to interpret the speech of some previously unmet tribe. We observe one of the natives pointing to a nearby mountain and uttering "Lo, monadi kel guro". What does he mean? We will no doubt initially take the native to be saying something about the nearby peak, and let's suppose, for the sake of argument, that this is in fact what he is trying to do. He might have been saying any number of things about it, maybe that it is icy, that it would be exciting to climb it, that it would command a good view of the neighbouring terrain, and so on. What enables us to decide which of these interpretations is the correct one is the contribution the predicate "guro" makes to the meanings of other sentences in which it appears. For example, suppose at some later time after his utterance of the above sentence we observe the native picking up a glass of milk containing ice cubes and uttering "Lo pazo kel guro"; then the most plausible interpretation of the earlier sentence will be that the mountain in view is icy. There may be alternative interpretations – we might interpret him as having said that the mountain is white – but the method whereby such interpretations are eliminated should be clear enough (we can check to see what he says about a glass of coca-cola filled with ice cubes, for example). Now the crucial point is that we can only employ this method of narrowing

241

down the possible interpretations on the assumption that the predicate "guro" makes the same systematic contribution to the meanings of the sentences in which it figures. And to say that the language contains expressions that make *systematic* and *recurring* such contributions is just to say that the language is semantically structured. The interpretation of one sentence constrains, and is constrained by, the interpretation of others via the presence of such expressions, and so via the presence of semantic structure.

Interpretation thus *presupposes* a principle for discerning structure: it cannot by itself deliver such a principle. Interpretation *assumes* that expressions make systematic and recurring contributions to the meanings of the sentences in which they figure: it therefore cannot explain the possibility of such systems. So it is difficult see how Blackburn's story really can afford the Gricean an explanation of the place of system in language.

Our conclusion is thus that Blackburn's attempt to respond to the central problems facing Gricean accounts of meaning is a failure. Given this, the prospects for a communication-intention account of sentence-meaning appear bleak. We now leave communication-intention accounts of meaning and return, in the next chapter, to work in the alternative truth-conditional tradition.

Further reading

Grice's classic paper "Meaning", as well as many other relevant articles, can be found in his collected papers *Studies in the ways of words*. Strawson's views are set out in his "Meaning and truth", in his *Logico-linguistic papers*. Searle's modification of Grice is contained in his "What is a speech-act?", in M. Black (ed.), *Philosophy in America*. See also Searle's book *Speech-acts*. Stephen Schiffer's book *Meaning* is an attempt to develop a systematic Gricean approach to language, although Schiffer has more recently come to the conclusion that Grice's programme is a failure (see his *Remnants of meaning*). See also Martin Davies, *Meaning, quantification, and necessity*, Chapter 1. For criticism of Grice, see P. Ziff "On H. P. Grice's account of meaning", *Analysis* (1967), and Mark Platts, *Ways of meaning*, Chapter 3. Blackburn's response to

Platts can be found in *Spreading the word,* Chapter 3. The Evans–Wright argument used in section 7.4 can be found in G. Evans, "Semantic theory and tacit knowledge", in S. Leich and S. Holtzmann (eds), *Wittgenstein: to follow a rule*; and C. Wright, "Theory of meaning and speakers' knowledge", in his *Realism, meaning and truth.* For further discussion of the Evans–Wright argument, see A. Miller, "Tacit knowledge", in *The Blackwell companion to the philosophy of language.*

Chapter 8

Sense and truth: Tarski and Davidson

Recall that in sections 1.7 and 2.5 we introduced the idea of a systematic semantic theory in the formal sense: a theory that delivers, for each well-formed declarative sentence of a particular language, a theorem that gives the meaning or sense of that sentence. Recall also that for Frege the sense of a sentence can be given by stating its truth-condition: "Every [sentence] expresses a sense, a thought. It is determined by what we have laid down under what conditions every such [sentence] designates The True. The sense of this [sentence], the thought, is the sense or thought that these conditions are fulfilled."[1] This is an idea which has been taken up by the influential contemporary American philosopher, Donald Davidson: "To give truth-conditions is a way of giving the meaning of a sentence."[2] In this chapter, we explain Davidson's idea that a systematic theory of meaning for a natural language can be provided by a theory that generates, for each declarative sentence, a theorem that states its truth-conditions.

8.1 Davidson and Frege

Davidson makes it clear that when he speaks of a theory of meaning, he is primarily interested in the notion that Frege termed sense:

> Frege held that an adequate account of language requires us to attend to three features of sentences: reference [semantic value], sense, and force. Elsewhere I have argued that a theory of truth patterned after a Tarski-type truth-definition tells us all we need to know about sense. Counting truth in the domain of reference [semantic value], as Frege did, the study of sense thus comes down to the study of reference [semantic value].[3]

As we'll see, Davidson says that the study of sense comes down to the study of semantic value, because he thinks that we can – and must – provide a theory of meaning for natural languages that does not involve the invocation of senses as objects or entities. But what about the Fregean semantic theory we sketched in section 1.7? We saw that this theory works by assigning only semantic values to expressions, and displays not only how the semantic value of a sentence is a function of the semantic values of its constituents, but also how specifications of sentences' *truth-conditions* can be generated purely on the basis of assignments of semantic values. It might seem, then, that so far as a systematic theory of meaning in the formal sense is concerned, Frege has already shown us how to bring the study of sense down to the study of semantic value or reference. In fact, however, Davidson thinks that Frege's model for a theory of semantic value (and thereby for a systematic theory of sense) is unsatisfactory, because it provides no useful or explanatory account of how sentence-meaning can be a function of word-meaning. Suppose we were to ask for the meaning of the sentence "Theaetetus flies":

> A Fregean answer might go something like this: given the meaning of "Theaetetus" as argument, the meaning of "flies" yields the meaning of "Theaetetus flies" as value. The vacuity of this answer is obvious. We wanted to know what the meaning of "Theaetetus flies" is; it is no progress to be told that it is the

meaning of "Theaetetus flies". This much we knew before any theory was in sight. In the bogus account just given, talk of the structure of the sentence and the meanings of words was idle, for it played no role in producing the description of the meaning of the sentence.[4]

Frege's semantic theory works by assigning "unsaturated" or "incomplete" entities – namely, functions – to predicates and quantifiers as their semantic values, and "saturated" or "complete" entities – The True or The False – to sentences as their semantic values. Davidson finds this type of theory completely unexplanatory, and he writes that "it seems to label a difficulty rather than solve it".[5] Davidson's task, therefore, is to find a model for the construction of systematic theories of meaning that does not work by postulating incomplete entities as the semantic values of predicates or quantifiers. Davidson argues that such a model is provided by a theory of truth along the lines of the definition of truth constructed by the Polish logician, Alfred Tarski. We'll now attempt to get clear on Davidson's motivation for this claim, and then we'll explain the workings of Tarskian theories of truth.

8.2 Davidson's adequacy conditions for theories of meaning

In broad outline, Davidson's strategy is relatively simple. First of all, he lays down a number of general conditions that any adequate theory of meaning for a natural language must satisfy. It then emerges that one way of providing a theory that meets each of these conditions would be to adapt a theory of truth, in the style of Tarski, for the natural language concerned. We'll concentrate on three general conditions of adequacy of theories of meaning:

(a) *The Extensional Adequacy Condition*: The theory of meaning must generate a theorem which "gives the meaning" of each sentence of the language under consideration.

(b) *The Compositionality Condition*: The theory should be *compositional*. A theory of meaning is compositional if and only if (i) it has only finitely many axioms, and (ii) each of the meaning-giving theorems is generated from the axiomatic base in such a way that the semantic *structure* of the sentence concerned is thereby exhibited. What motivation is there for seeking compositional semantic theories in preference to their more readily available non-compositional counterparts? Why should the construction of a semantic theory be constrained by the requirement that it reflect the semantic structure of the language concerned? Davidson's answer is that the construction of specifically compositional theories will take us some way towards providing answers to each of the following three questions:[6]

(i)   How is it possible, given the finitude of their capacities, for speakers of a natural language to understand a potential infinity of sentences?
(ii) How is it possible to understand utterances of previously unencountered sentences?
(iii) How is it possible for a natural language to be learnable? (That is, how is it possible for explicit training with only a relatively small number of sentences to secure competence with a possibly very large set of sentences outwith that initial set?)

Briefly, the axioms of a theory of meaning deal with the semantic properties of the words or subsentential expressions of a language, while the theorems, which are generated from these axioms, deal with the semantic properties of the sentences of the language. A compositional theory of meaning will therefore show how the meanings of sentences are systematically dependent upon the semantic properties of their constituent words and the way they are put together. Since there are only finitely many words, dealt with by only finitely many axioms in a compositional theory of meaning, we will have an insight into how (i), (ii) and (iii) can be answered: speakers with finite capacities will be able to understand a potential infinity of sentences because, on the basis of a finite set of axioms, we will be able to generate a potential infinity of meaning-giving theorems; we understand unfamiliar sentences via understanding the familiar words out of which they are composed and their mode of composition, as this will be modelled on the way in which a meaning-giving theorem for an unfamiliar sentence can be derived from axioms dealing with familiar words; and the way in which meaning-giving theorems can be derived from axioms for familiar words and modes of combination also provide insight into the learnability of natural languages.[7]

(c) *The Interpretation Condition*: The theory of meaning must allow us *correctly* to *interpret* the speakers of that language, in accordance with constitutive principles governing interpretation (such as the *principle of charity*). We'll explain this condition in section 8.7.

In short, a theory of meaning must be extensionally adequate and compositional, and it must enable us to interpret the speech of its speakers.[8] Before working towards the sort of theory of meaning that Davidson favours, we'll look at two types of theory he rejects.

8.3 Intensional and extensional theories of meaning

What sort of theorem "gives the meaning" of a sentence? Davidson first of all considers a theory of meaning that yields, for each sentence of the language, a theorem of the form

(1) *s* means *m*

where "*s*" is replaced by a name of a sentence, and "*m*" is replaced by a term which refers to or denotes the meaning of that sentence. Meanings are thus conceived as entities, and the job of the theory of meaning is to pair sentences with such entities. Now just as Davidson rejected Frege's semantic theory on the grounds that the assignment of entities to predicates and quantifiers as their semantic values was completely unexplanatory, he also rejects theories of meaning that assign entities to expressions as their meanings or senses:

> The one thing meanings do not seem to do is oil the wheels of a theory of meaning – at least as long as we require of such a theory that it non-trivially give the meaning of every sentence in the language. My objection to meanings in the theory of meaning is not that they are abstract or that their identity

conditions are obscure, but that they have no demonstrated use.[9]

We can perhaps view Davidson as applying a version of *Ockham's Razor* – "that entities are not to be multiplied beyond necessity" – to meanings: Davidson will show that everything we want from a theory of meaning can be achieved without bringing in meanings as entities, so that Ockham's Razor tells us that we should not postulate the existence of such entities.

But what about a theory of meaning that attempts to satisfy the Extensional Adequacy condition by generating theorems of the form

(2) *s* means that *p*

where "*s*" is replaced by a name of a sentence and "*p*" is replaced by some sentence that gives its meaning. Such a theory does not require the postulation of meanings as entities, and would appear to satisfy the Extensional Adequacy condition in the most direct way possible. But Davidson rejects the idea that (2) is the correct form for a meaning-giving theorem of a theory of meaning. Davidson's reason for rejecting theories of this form has been well spelled-out by Mark Platts. Platts notes that "... means that ..." creates what is known as an *intensional context*, a context in which the substitution of expressions having the same semantic value need not preserve the semantic value (truth-value) of the original sentence. (An intensional context is thus a context in which thesis 3 (see section 1.4) is violated). To see the intensionality of " ... means that ..." consider the true sentence

(3) "Snow is white" means that snow is white.

Now, the sentence "Snow is white" has the same semantic value (truth-value) as the sentence "Grass is green". But when we substitute the latter for the former in (3), we obtain the false sentence

(4) "Snow is white" means that grass is green.

The problem now is that "The only systematic account of intensional contexts that survives even the most cursory glance explains the intensionality by reference to the notion of *meaning*."[10] The reason that the move from (3) to (4) is invalid is precisely that the sentences "Snow is white" and "Grass is green" *do not have the same meaning*. This contrasts with the move from

(5) "Jones is an oculist" means that Jones is an oculist

to

(6) "Jones is an oculist" means that Jones is an eye-doctor,

which is valid, because the sentences "Jones is an oculist" and "Jones is an eye-doctor" do in fact have the same meaning.

This shows that a theory of meaning that yielded theorems of the form of (2) would really only presuppose the very notion that it is the purpose of a theory of meaning to elucidate. As Platts puts it,

> The general explanation of intensional contexts requires reference to meanings; and explanation of the properties of any given intensional construction requires reference to the meanings of the particular expressions occurring within it. If this is correct, there is no point to the employment of intensional idioms within the systematic, axiomatic component of a theory of meaning.[11]

A theorem of the form of (2) creates a context the general explanation of which requires the use of the notion of meaning; a theory of meaning that generates theorems of the form of (2) therefore cannot provide a genuinely explanatory account of meaning.

In addition, the logical machinery required in a theory of meaning that is itself couched in a language that contains intensional constructions will be immensely complicated. As we'll see, the logical machinery required in a theory of meaning that is couched in a purely extensional language can be provided by the familiar and relatively simple Fregean logic we described in Chapter 1.

The upshot of these considerations is that a theory of meaning should be extensional in the sense that it does not postulate intensional entities, such as meanings or senses, and that it should be couched in a language which itself contains no intensional constructions. But how is it possible to give a theory of meaning in purely extensional terms – in other words, to show that the study of sense comes down to the study of semantic value?

8.4 Extensional adequacy and Tarski's convention (T)

Davidson's answer to this question is that a theory of meaning is extensionally adequate if it yields, for each sentence of the language under consideration, a theorem of the form

(7) s is true if and only if p

where "s" is replaced by a name of the sentence and "p" by the sentence in question itself. Thus, a meaning-giving theorem for the sentence "snow is white" would be

(8) "Snow is white" is true if and only if snow is white.

This is a case where we are trying to give a theory of meaning for English in English itself. The language *for* which we are trying to give a theory of meaning is called the *object-language*, and the language *in* which that theory is given is called the *meta-language*. Thus, in the case of a theory yielding (8) the object-language is English, and the meta-language is English also. But of course, there is no reason why the object- and meta-languages have to be identical. For example, we could give a theory of meaning for French (the object-language) in English (the meta-language). Such a theory would yield not (8), but rather

(9) "La neige est blanche" is true if and only if snow is white.

Likewise, a theory of meaning for German (the object-language) could be given in English as the meta-language. Such a theory would yield

(10) "Schnee ist weiss" is true if and only if snow is white.

Obviously, in cases such as these, where the object- and meta-languages are different, we cannot require that "p" in (7) be replaced by the sentence concerned itself, because the sentence will not belong to the meta-language in which the theory is couched. For example, in the case where the object-language is German and the meta-language is English, we cannot require that "p" be replaced by "Schnee ist weiss" itself because this sentence does not belong to the meta-language, English. What we require in this sort of case is rather that "p" be replaced by a sentence of the meta-language that *translates* it.

In general, then, Davidson requires that the theory of meaning yield a theorem of the form (7) for each sentence of the object-language, where "s" is replaced by a name of the relevant sentence, and "p" by that sentence itself (in the case where the object-language is contained within the meta-language) or by a translation of that sentence into the meta-language (in the case where the object-language is not contained within the meta-language).

That is simply a statement of Davidson's condition of Extensional Adequacy. But how did Davidson reach it? And how is the connection with Tarskian theories of truth forged? Platts suggests that Davidson's argument for taking the condition of Extensional Adequacy in this way is contained in the following passage:

> Anxiety that we are enmeshed in the intensional springs from using the words "means that" as a filling between description of sentence and sentence, but it may be that the success of our venture depends not on the filling but on what it fills. The theory will have done its work if it provides, for every sentence s in the language under study, a matching sentence (to replace "p") that, in some way yet to be made clear, "gives the meaning" of s. One obvious candidate for matching sentence is just s itself, if the object-language is contained in the meta-language; otherwise a translation of s in the meta-language. As a final bold step, let us try treating the position occupied by "p" extensionally: to implement this, sweep away the obscure "means that", provide

the sentence that replaces "*p*" with a proper sentential connective, and supply the description that replaces "*s*" with its own predicate.[12]

Following Platts, we can break the argument down into six separate stages:

Stage 1. The condition of Extensional Adequacy, in its most general form, states that for each sentence of the language under consideration, the theory of meaning must generate a theorem that in some sense "gives its meaning".

Stage 2. Requiring that the theory of meaning generate a theorem of the form of either (1) or (2) is no good as a way of cashing out extensional adequacy: such theories would be obscure and unexplanatory.

Stage 3. Since we are aiming for a theorem that spells out an equivalence in point of meaning, we could try replacing "means that" with the biconditional "if and only if", familiar from Fregean logic. This would produce something of the form

(11) *s* if and only if *p*.

Stage 4. But (11) is not syntactically well-formed, for the expression on the left-hand side is not a sentence, but rather a *name* of a sentence. Remember that when you enclose a sentence in quotation marks, as in "Snow is white", what you get is a name of the enclosed sentence, not another sentence. When we have

(12) "Snow is white" if and only if snow is white

we actually have something like

(13) Peter if and only if snow is white

which is simply a piece of ungrammatical nonsense.

Stage 5. One way to render (12) grammatical would be to make the left-hand side into a sentence by concatenating the name with a predicate. What we require for extensional adequacy is thus that for each sentence it yield a theorem of the form

(14) s is X if and only if p

where "s" is replaced by a name of that sentence, and "p" is replaced by that sentence itself (if the object-language is contained within the meta-language), or by a translation of that sentence into the meta-language (if the object-language and the meta-language are distinct).

Stage 6. In his paper "The Semantic Conception of Truth", Tarski wrote:

> We shall call any equivalence of the form
>
> (T) s is true if and only if p
>
> (with "p" replaced by any sentence of the language to which the word "true" refers, and "s" replaced by a name of this sentence) an "equivalence of the form (T)" ... Now at last we are able to put into a precise form the conditions under which we will consider the usage and the definition of the term "true" as adequate from the material point of view: we wish to use the term "true" in such a way that all equivalencies of the form (T) can be asserted, and we shall call a definition of truth "adequate" if all these equivalencies follow from it.[13]

Tarski is here laying down the following as a condition of adequacy on any proposed definition of "is true": any acceptable definition of truth should have as a consequence all instances of the (T) schema

(T) s is true if and only if p

where "s" is replaced by a name of any sentence of the language for which truth is being defined (the object-language), and "p" is replaced by that sentence or a translation thereof, depending on whether or not the object-language is contained in the meta-language.

This is Tarski's condition of *material adequacy* on definitions of "is true" (sometimes known as Convention [T]).[14] Given this condition, we know that the predicate "X" in (14) will at least be co-extensive with the truth-predicate for the object-language. So we might as well take "X" in (14) to be the truth-predicate for the object-language. The condition of Extensional Adequacy on theories of meaning is thus that for each sentence of the object-language, they yield a theorem of the form

(7) s is true if and only if p

where "s" is replaced by a name of the relevant sentence, and "p" by that sentence itself (in the case where the object-language is contained within the meta-language) or by a translation of that sentence into the meta-language (in the case where the object-language is not contained within the meta-language).

Interpreting the Extensional Adequacy condition in this way has a number of interesting consequences. A theorem of the form of (7) gives the *truth-conditions* of the sentence named on the left-hand side. We have thus arrived, by an independent route, at Frege's conclusion that the sense of a sentence can be given by stating its truth-condition. Also, given this interpretation, Davidson's condition of Extensional Adequacy on theories of meaning is identical to Tarski's Convention (T), his condition of material adequacy on theories of truth. *Importantly, Tarski provided a formal account that shows how a theorem of the form of (7) can be generated for each sentence of a formal language – basically, the language of Frege's predicate calculus – in a way that respects the compositionality constraint (b).* What this suggests is that we can use systematic truth-theories of the sort developed by Tarski as models for compositional theories of meaning for natural languages. This is exactly what Davidson proposes to attempt: given any stretch of natural language, we first of all attempt to formalize it into Frege's logical language, and once it is in this form we construct a Tarski-style theory that shows how the truth-conditions of sentences are systematically dependent upon the semantic properties of their parts.

Before examining further Davidson's proposal to use a Tarski-style truth theory as a model for a theory of meaning, we must pause to see how Tarski-style truth-theories actually work.

8.5 Tarskian truth-theories

We'll first of all sketch a truth-theory for a very simple form of the language of propositional logic, a language whose sytnax is given by the rules stated in section 1.2. In such a language (call it L), we distinguish between *atomic sentences*, represented by individual propositional variables, such as P, Q, R and so on, and *complex sentences*, such as P & Q, P v Q, –P, and so on, which result from combining the sentential connectives and the atomic sentences (there will be infinitely many of these). In order to keep things simple, we'll suppose that this language has only three atomic sentences, P, Q and R, and we'll ignore the conditional and biconditional connectives. What we are after is a theory which shows how the truth-conditions of complex sentences can be derived systematically from the truth-conditions of the atomic sentences and clauses governing the connectives. This theory can actually be stated quite simply:

(1a) "P" is true if and only if snow is white.
(1b) "Q" is true if and only if grass is green.
(1c) "R" is true if and only if penguins waddle.
(2a) For any sentences A, B, "A & B" is true if and only if "A" is true and "B" is true.
(2b) For any sentences A, B, "A v B" is true if and only if "A" is true or "B" is true.
(2c) For any sentence A, "–A" is true if and only if "A" is not true.[15]

Given these axioms, we can generate, for any complex sentence of the language, a theorem that which specifies its truth-condition. Take "P & –Q", for example. By step (2a)

"P & –Q" is true if and only if "P" is true and "–Q" is true.

By step (2c)

"P & –Q" is true if and only if "P" is true and "Q" is not true.

By steps (1a) and (1b)

"P & –Q" is true if and only if snow is white and grass is not green.

Thus, we have derived a truth-condition for "P & $-Q$" from axioms spelling out the semantic properties of its parts. Note that the truth-condition of the complex sentence is derived from the truth-conditions of its constituents "P", "$-Q$", with the truth-condition for "$-Q$" in turn derived from the truth-condition for "Q".

Now, suppose we wanted to use the above truth-theory as a model for a theory of meaning for a fragment of a natural language, such as English. The first thing we would have to do would be translate the sentences of this fragment of English into the language L. Having done that, we could then go on to apply the truth-theory. But as we saw in Chapter 1, the capacity of a simple propositional language like L to translate sentences of natural language is very limited. In order to capture the validity of even quite simple argument forms, we need the more complicated language of *predicate* logic. So can we give a truth-definition for the language of predicate logic? Immediately, there appears to be a problem with simply copying the truth-theory for L. The truth-theory for L derives the truth-conditions of a complex sentence of L from the truth-conditions of its constituents, but in many cases the constituents of the complex sentences of the language of predicate logic won't even *have* truth-conditions. For example, consider

(15) $(\forall x)(Fx$ & $Gx)$.

Suppose we wanted to spell out the truth-conditions of (15) in a way that reflects the contributions made by the semantic properties of its constituents. The constituents of (15) are the open sentences Fx, Gx, and because the variables in these sentences are unbound, Fx and Gx are neither true nor false. The complex sentences of the language of predicate logic are composed out of open sentences; open sentences are neither true nor false, and therefore do not have truth-conditions. So giving a truth-theory for the language of predicate logic cannot consist in showing how the truth-conditions of complex sentences are a function of the truth-conditions of their constituents.

What we require is some analogue, for open sentences, of the notion of truth as applied to closed sentences (sentences, such as

($\forall x)Fx$, in which the variables are bound by quantifiers).
Tarski suggests that the analogue of truth for open sentences
is *satisfaction*: just as closed sentences are either true or false,
open sentences are either satisfied or not by objects. For
example, the open sentence Fx, where we take "F" to represent the
predicate " ... is a philosopher", is satisfied by Socrates and
Plato,but not by Clint Eastwood or Hilary Clinton. Tarski's
suggestion regarding the construction of a truth-theory for
the language of predicate logic is therefore as follows: first of
all define the notion of satisfaction, and then define the notion
of truth in terms of this notion of satisfaction. This will allow
us to derive the truth-conditions of complex sentences of
predicate calculus in terms of the semantic properties of their
constituents.

For technical reasons, which we need not go into here, Tarski
takes satisfaction to be a relation not between open sentences and
individual objects, but rather between open sentences and *infinite
ordered sequences of objects*. An example of an ordered sequence of
objects would be <Socrates, Plato, London, John Major, ...>.
Because we are dealing with *ordered* sequences, this would count
as different from <Plato, Socrates, London, John Major, ...>. The
convention is that an open sentence with n variables is satisfied by
a sequence just in case it is satisfied by the first n members of that
sequence: the subsequent members of the sequence are simply
ignored. Thus, the open sentence Fx above would be satisfied by
both <Socrates, Plato, London, John Major, ...> and <Plato,
Socrates, London, John Major, ...> (since there is only one variable
in Fx, the crucial question is whether the first member of these
sequences satisfies F, which they do in this case). Likewise, the
open sentence Gx_1x_2 where "G" is " ...wrote about ...", would be
satisfied by <Plato, Socrates, London, John Major,...> but not by
<Socrates, Plato, London, John Major,...> (since Plato wrote about
Socrates, but not vice versa).

We'll now show how Tarski's account of truth in terms of
satisfaction works for an extremely simple predicate language $L*$.
This language contains a one place predicate "F", translating "...is
a philosopher", a one-place predicate "G", translating "... is Greek",
variables, the universal quantifier, and the existential quantifier.
We first of all give the definition of satisfaction for $L*$.[16]

8.5.1 Definition of satisfaction for L*

We take X, Y, and so on to range over infinite ordered sequences of objects, and A, B, and so on to range over open sentences of L^*. X_i denotes the ith member of the sequence X (so, for example, for $X =$ <Socrates, Plato, Rod Stewart, Bjork, ... >, X_2 = Plato, X_3 = Rod Stewart, and so on).

(i) $\forall X$: X satisfies "Fx_1" if and only if X_1 is a philosopher.

(ii) $\forall X$: X satisfies "Gx_1" if and only if X_1 is Greek.

(iii) $\forall X$, A: X satisfies "$-A$" if and only if X does not satisfy "A".

(iv) $\forall X$, A, B: X satisfies "$A \& B$" if and only if X satisfies "A" and X satisfies "B".

(v) $\forall X$, A: X satisfies "$(\exists x_1)A$" if and only if there is a sequence Y, differing from X in at most the first place, such that Y satisfies "A".

(vi) $\forall X$, A: X satisfies "$(\forall x_1)A$" if and only if every sequence Y, differing from X in at most the first place, is such that Y satisfies "A".

Clauses (i) – (iv) are pretty obvious, but (v) and (vi) are far from obvious. We'll explain why Tarski spells them out as he does very shortly. Before doing so, though, we now define truth for closed sentences in terms of the notion of satisfaction just defined (again, we'll see why Tarski does it in this way in due course):

DEFINITION *of "true" for* L^*: A closed sentence of L^* is true if and only if it is satisfied by all sequences.

The main reason for spelling out clauses (v) and (vi) and the definition of truth for closed sentences in this way is that they work: given these definitions we can generate the intuitively correct truth-conditions for the closed sentences of L^*. We'll illustrate this by means of a few examples.

First, though, note that, given our definition of satisfaction, a closed sentence is satisfied by all sequences if and only if it is satisfied by at least one sequence. The left-to-right side of this is trivial, but what about the right-to-left side? Why is it the case that if a closed sentence is satisfied by at least one sequence, it is satisfied by all sequences? Suppose that there is one sequence X

which satisfies $(\exists x_1)Fx_1$. By (v), this means that there is some sequence X^*, differing from X in at most the first place, such that X^* satisfies the open sentence Fx_1. Since X^* satisfies Fx_1, X_1 will be a philosopher (Kant, say, for the sake of argument). Now choose an arbitrary sequence X^{**}: <London, Sydney, Stan Laurel, Alfred Hitchock, ... >. Does X^{**} satisfy $(\exists x_1)Fx_1$? Is there a sequence, differing from X^{**} in at most the first place, such that that sequence satisfies Fx_1? The answer is that there is: simply take the first member of X^{**} and replace it with the first member of X^* (Kant): the resulting sequence satisfies Fx_1, since Kant is a philosopher, so by (v), X^{**} also satisfies $(\exists x_1)Fx_1$. So, on the assumption that there is one sequence that satisfies the closed sentence $(\exists x_1)Fx_1$ it follows that an arbitrary sequence satisfies $(\exists x_1)Fx_1$: in other words, if a closed sentence is satisfied by one sequence, then it is satisfied by all sentences. (The reader should verify that the same thing holds when the closed sentence is a universally quantified sentence).

EXAMPLE 1: $(\forall x_1)Gx_1$

Intuitively, this sentence is true if and only if everything is Greek. We can derive this truth-condition as follows:

(a) "$(\forall x_1)(Gx_1)$" is true if and only if it is satisfied by all sequences (from the definition of "true").

(b) "$(\forall x_1)(Gx_1)$" is true if and only if it is satisfied by at least one sequence (from above).

(c) "$(\forall x_1)(Gx_1)$" is satisfied by a sequence X if and only if every sequence X^*, differing from X in at most the first place, satisfies "Gx_1" (from [vi]).

(d) Every such sequence X^* satisfies "Gx_1" if and only if everything is Greek (if everything is Greek, every choice for X^*_1 will be Greek, so that every X^* will satisfy "Gx_1"; conversely, if there is something which is not Greek, choosing it as X^*_1 will result in a sequence X^* which does not satisfy "Gx_1").

Putting all of these together gives:

(e) "$(\forall x_1)(Gx_1)$" is true if and only if everything is Greek.

EXAMPLE 2: $(\exists x_1)\text{--}Fx_1$

Intuitively, this sentence is true if and only if there is something that is not a philosopher. We can derive this truth-condition as follows:

(a) "$(\exists x_1)\text{--}Fx_1$" is true if and only if it is satisfied by all sequences (from the definition of "true").
(b) "$(\exists x_1)\text{--}Fx_1$" is true if and only if it is satisfied by at least one sequence (from above).
(c) "$(\exists x_1)\text{--}Fx_1$" is satisfied by a sequence X if and only if there is some sequence X^*, differing from X in at most the first place, which satisfies "$\text{--}Fx_1$"(from [v]).
(d) There is such a sequence X^* if and only if there is a sequence X^* such that X^*_1 does not satisfy "Fx_1"(from [iii]).
(e) There is a sequence X^* such that X^*_1 does not satisfy "Fx_1" if and only if there is at least one object that is not a philosopher (if there is such a person, say Plato, we can take X^*_1 to be this person; if there is no such person, there will be no appropriate X^*_1).

Putting all these together gives:

(f) "$(\exists x_1)\text{--}Fx_1$" is true if and only if there is at least one thing that is not a philosopher.

EXAMPLE 3: $(\exists x_1)(Fx_1 \ \& \ Gx_1)$

Intuitively, this sentence is true if and only if there is something that is both Greek and a philosopher. We can derive this truth-condition as follows:

(a) "$(\exists x_1)(Fx_1 \ \& \ Gx_1)$" is true if and only if it is satisfied by all sequences (from the definition of "true").
(b) "$(\exists x_1)(Fx_1 \ \& \ Gx_1)$" is true if and only if it is satisfied by at least one sequence (from above).
(c) "$(\exists x_1)(Fx_1 \ \& \ Gx_1)$" is satisfied by a sequence X if and only if there is some sequence X^*, differing from X in at most the first place, that satisfies "$Fx_1 \ \& \ Gx_1$" (from [v]).

(d) There is such a sequence X^* if and only if there is a sequence X^* such that X^*_1 satisfies both "Fx_1" and "Gx_1"(from [iv]).

(e) There is a sequence X^* such that X^*_1 satisfies both "Fx_1" and "Gx_1" if and only if there is at least one thing that is both Greek and a Philosopher (if there is such a person, say Plato, we can take X^*_1 to be this person; if there is no such person, there will be no appropriate X^*_1).

Putting all of these together we get:

(f) "$(\exists x_1)(Fx_1 \ \& \ Gx_1)$" is true if and only if there is something that is both Greek and a philosopher.

In each case, we have shown how the truth-conditions of a closed complex sentence depend systematically on the semantic properties of the sentences' constituents, even though those constituents are not themselves capable of truth or falsity.[17] This shows that if we can translate the sentences of a fragment of natural language into a language like L^* – the language of predicate logic – we can provide a Tarskian truth-theory for that fragment. Given the argument of the previous section, it would follow that we can provide a systematic theory of meaning for that fragment of language. Theories of meaning in this style do not contain intensional constructions, and

> They make no use of meanings as entities; no objects are introduced to correspond to predicates or sentences; and from a finite set of axioms it is possible to prove, for each sentence of the language to be interpreted, a theorem that states the truth-conditions of that sentence.[18]

We now return to Davidson's idea that Tarskian theories of truth can serve as theories of meaning for natural languages.

8.6 Truth and translation: two problems for Davidson

Platts argues[19] that there is a problem with the six-stage Davidsonian argument rehearsed in section 8.4, stemming from

Davidson's use of the notion of *translation*. Tarski spelled out his condition of material adequacy in the course of attempting to give a definition of "true": so there is no problem about his stipulating that in the instances of the (T) schema the sentence replacing "*p*" should be a translation of the sentence named by "*s*". However, Davidson, unlike Tarski, cannot help himself to the notion of translation in spelling out his condition of Extensional Adequacy. Translation means *correct translation*, and correct translation is essentially *meaning-preserving* translation: the reason that "Snow is white" is a correct translation of "Schnee ist weiss" is that the former preserves the *meaning* of the latter. It is legitimate for Tarski to presuppose this notion because his project is that of defining truth: but Davidson's project is that of providing a theory of meaning, so if he wants to avoid a damaging circularity in his theory he will have to avoid using the notion of a meaning-preserving translation in the adequacy conditions on a theory of meaning (deciding whether the adequacy condition was satisfied would itself presuppose that we had an adequate theory of meaning). But if Davidson drops the condition that "*p*" be replaced by a translation of the sentence named by "*s*", the six-stage argument appears to falter at stage 6: there will be no guarantee that the predicate "*X*" will be co-extensive for "is true", and so no reason for thinking that a theory of truth can serve as a theory of meaning. In effect, Davidson is faced with a dilemma. If he uses the notion of correct translation in the condition of Extensional Adequacy, then his account simply presupposes the notion – meaning – it is attempting to elucidate; if he does not use the notion of correct translation, the route to forging the connection between theories of meaning and Tarskian truth-theories is blocked.

Another problem that Davidson faces is this. Davidson's theory of meaning issues in theorems of the form

(7) *s* is true if and only if *p*.

In (7) the "if and only if" is taken to be the *material biconditional* of propositional logic. Indeed, Davidson takes this to be an advantage of his theory of meaning: it can be framed using the familiar materials of basic, truth-functional logic. But this leaves us with a problem. Recall that the truth-table for the material biconditional is as follows:

P	Q	$P \leftrightarrow Q$
T	T	T
T	F	F
F	T	F
F	F	T

In other words, a material biconditional is true, just in case the two sentences flanking it have the same truth-value. Now, given this, it certainly follows that

(16) "Snow is white" is true if and only if snow is white

is true: "'Snow is white' is true" and "Snow is white" have the same truth-value (true), so the overall biconditional is true also. But so are

(17) "2 + 2 = 4" is true if and only if there are nine planets in the Solar System
(18) "Fish swim" is true if and only if dogs bark

for the same reason: in each case the sentence on the left-hand side of the biconditional has the same truth-value as the sentence on the right. But surely we would not conclude from this that the sentence "2 + 2 = 4" means *that there are nine planets in the Solar System* or that the sentence "Fish swim" means *that dogs bark*? Again, Davidson appears to be faced by a dilemma: either he strengthens "if and only if" so that it is stronger than the material biconditional, in which case his aim to give a theory of meaning in a purely extensional language is endangered; or he is committed to totally implausible claims about what certain sentences mean.

How can Davidson respond to these worries? In the next section, we'll see that the answer to this question turns on a constraint on theories of meaning that we have so far paid little attention to: the interpretation condition.

8.7 Radical interpretation and the principle of charity

In fact, Davidson is perfectly aware of the need to say something in response to the two problems we raised in the previous section. The first problem is addressed in the following quote:

> In Tarski's work, T-sentences are taken to be true because the right branch of the biconditional is assumed to be a translation of the sentence truth-conditions for which are being given. But we cannot assume in advance that correct translation can be recognised without pre-empting the point of radical interpretation; in empirical applications, we must abandon the assumption. What I propose is to reverse the direction of explanation: assuming translation, Tarski was able to define truth; the present idea is to take truth as basic and to extract an account of translation or interpretation.[20]

The key here is obviously the third adequacy constraint on theories of meaning, the interpretation condition: the theory of meaning must allow us *correctly to interpret* the speakers of that language, in accordance with constitutive principles governing interpretation. Davidson's idea, very roughly, is as follows. We lay down a set of constitutive constraints on the interpretation or translation of the utterances of the speakers of the language for which we are attempting to provide a theory of meaning. These constitutive constraints can be spelled out *without* presupposing the notion of correct translation. If a theory of meaning satisfies these constraints, the sentence on the right-hand side of one of its theorems will effectively provide a translation of the sentence named on its left-hand side. The notion of translation is not *presupposed*; rather, the notion of correct translation is *yielded* by the constitutive constraints on interpretation. The upshot of this is that Davidson's condition of Extensional Adequacy can be spelled out without using the notion of translation, as follows: for each sentence of the object-language, a theorem of the form

(7)   *s* is true if and only if *p*

"gives the meaning" of the sentence named by "*s*" if and only if it is delivered by a theory that satisfies the constitutive constraints on interpretation. Thus, we need to explain Davidson's views on interpretation. What is interpretation and what are the constitutive constraints that govern it?

Davidson is attempting to spell out what is involved in constructing systematic theories of meaning for natural languages. Two distinctive features of natural languages that we have thus far ignored are that (a) they are spoken, and (b) they contain indexical expressions, such as "I", "here" and "now". The truth-values of sentences containing indexical expressions change according to context: for example, "It is raining here now", as uttered by AM in Birmingham on 27 August 1996 would be true, whereas the same sentence uttered by AM in Nottingham on 18 August 1996 would be false. Davidson's way of coping with this, in a way that takes (a) into account as well, is to view truth as a relation between a sentence, a speaker and a time. The theorems of a theory of meaning will thus have the following form:

(19) "It is raining here now" as uttered by AM at time t is true if and only if it is raining in the vicinity of AM at time t.

If the theory of meaning which issues in (19) is correct, it will allow us to *interpret* AM's utterance of the sentence "It is raining here now" as an act of saying *that it is raining in the vicinity of AM at time* t:

> We interpret a bit of linguistic behaviour when we say what a speaker's words mean on an occasion of use. The task may be seen as one of redescription. We know that the words "Es schneit" have been uttered on a particular occasion and we want to redescribe this uttering as an act of saying that it is snowing.[21]

Call a theory of meaning that allows us to do this correctly "interpretative". Now the problem facing us can be stated as follows: how can we say what it is for a theory of meaning to be "interpretative" other than saying that it issues in correct translations or interpretations of speakers' utterances? *Davidson's answer to this is that a theory of meaning will be interpretative if it satisfies a number of constitutive constraints on interpretation, principally, the principle of charity.*

Suppose that Kurt utters the sentence "Es regnet" and that we wish to interpret his utterance: we wish to describe his uttering that sentence as an act of saying that such and such. What sort of evidence are we allowed to go on in attempting to construct such an interpretation? The evidence allowed by Davidson concerns what Kurt *holds true:* the idea is that we use

(20) Kurt holds true "Es regnet" if and only if it is raining in Kurt's vicinity

as evidence for

(21) "Es regnet", as uttered by Kurt, is true if and only if it is raining in Kurt's vicinity.

Two points should be made about the selection of facts concerning what speakers hold true as evidence for interpretation. First, such evidence is semantic, since holding a sentence true is believing that the sentence is true. Since the evidence allowed is semantic, Davidson is *not* attempting to give an account of how interpretation can proceed on a nonsemantic basis (in this respect he differs from Quine; see section 4.7). Secondly, although the evidence is semantic, it is still *thinner* than the notion of an utterance being an act of saying that such and such: one can know that a speaker holds a sentence true without knowing what that sentence means. So even though we start from semantic evidence, we can still make progress in our attempt to understand other, richer, semantic notions:

> A good place to begin is with the attitude of holding a sentence true, of accepting it as true. This is, of course, a belief, but it is a single attitude applicable to all sentences, and so does not ask us to make finely discriminated distinctions among beliefs. It is an attitude an interpreter may plausibly be taken to be able to identify before he can interpret, since he may know that a person intends to express a truth in uttering a sentence without having any idea *what* truth.[22]

Davidson's plan is to impose constraints on the selection of evidence in the form of (20) such that (21) will allow us to interpret Kurt's utterance of "Es regnet" as an act of saying *that it is raining*.

We need such constraints because on its own (20) does *not* provide evidence for (21). This is because of the interdependence of belief and meaning:

> A speaker who holds a sentence to be true on an occasion does so in part because of what he means, or would mean, by an utterance of that sentence, and in part because of what he believes. If all we have to go on is the fact of honest utterance, we cannot infer the belief without knowing the meaning, and have no chance of inferring the meaning without the belief.[23]

Suppose that it is a rainy afternoon in Berlin. Suppose also, that for some strange reason, Kurt does *not* believe that it is raining (perhaps he is under the influence of a drug, or suffering from some other sort of perceptual malfunction). Then we cannot take the fact that Kurt holds the sentence "Es regnet" true as evidence for (20). Likewise, suppose that "Es regnet" actually means something different, say, it is Tuesday. Then we could not take the fact that Kurt holds this true as evidence for the claim that he believes that it is raining. In order to move from a claim about what sentences Kurt holds true to a claim about what he believes to be the case, we need to know the meanings of those sentences; and in order to move from a claim about what sentences Kurt holds true to a claim about what he means, we need to know what he believes to be the case. We are thus faced with a problem: we want to move from evidence concerning what Kurt holds true to a claim about what he means; in order to do this we need to know what he believes; but in order to get to what he believes from what he holds true, we need to know what he means. How can we break out of this circle?

Davidson's answer is that we break out of the circle via an application of the *principle of charity*: we assign to Kurt the beliefs that we would have in the circumstances in question, and then go on to move from these beliefs, together with the facts about what sentences Kurt holds true, to conclusions concerning what those sentences mean. In other words, we break out of the circle by assuming that in the circumstances in question Kurt has the beliefs which, by our lights, are true:

> [We] solve the problem of the interdependence of belief and meaning by holding belief constant as far as possible while solving for meaning. This is accomplished by assigning truth-conditions to [native] sentences that make native speakers right when plausibly possible, according, of course, to our own view of what is right.[24]

To take the simple example above. If we were to find ourselves in Berlin in the middle of a downpour, among the beliefs we would have would be the belief that it is raining. So, by the principle of charity, we assume that Kurt has this belief. We can then move from (20) to (21).

Let's sum up the story so far. In order to avoid the problem about presupposing the notion of correct translation, we impose the interpretation condition as a condition of adequacy on theories of meaning: the theory must allow us *correctly to interpret* the speakers of that language. In order correctly to interpret the speakers of the language, we must take as evidence facts about which sentences they hold true. But this evidence only counts as evidence if we make assumptions about what they believe. The principle of charity licenses such assumptions: we ascribe to the natives, by and large, the beliefs that we would deem to be appropriate in the relevant circumstances. Thus, for Extensional Adequacy, we do not require that in theorems of the form of

(7) s is true if and only if p

the sentence replacing "p" translates the sentence named by "s". *The work done by this circular specification of Extensional Adequacy is now done by the noncircular requirement that the theorem be generated by a theory that satisfies the constitutive constraints on interpretation, principally, the principle of charity.* This is how Davidson proposes to take truth as basic and to *extract* an account of translation and meaning: we can after all forge a connection between theories of meaning and Tarskian truth-theories without begging the question by invoking a notion of correct translation. The second horn of the dilemma posed for Davidson in section 8.6 is thus neutralized.[25]

At this stage, a few clarificatory notes are in order:

Note 1: It might seem as if the principle of charity used above leaves it impossible to interpret a speaker as ever having a belief which is, by our own lights, false. But this was only a very crude version of the principle. Properly construed, the principle of charity is a *holistic* constraint applying, not to individual beliefs, but rather to *systems* of belief: we must interpret a speaker so that *most* of the beliefs in his system are, by our lights, true. This leaves room for us to ascribe *some* false beliefs to him. In fact, there is an even more sophisticated version of the principle according to which we interpret speakers not as necessarily having beliefs that are true by our own lights, but as having beliefs that are *intelligible* by our own lights. This allows us to attribute false beliefs to a speaker, so long as the source of his error is, by our own lights, *explicable* or *intelligible.* Davidson sums this up in the slogan "The aim of interpretation is not agreement but understanding."[26]

Note 2: According to Davidson, the principle of charity is not merely a useful heuristic principle that we can rely on to facilitate the practical process of interpretation. The adoption of the principle is rather *constitutive* of the whole process of interpretation:

> The methodological advice to interpret in a way that optimizes agreement [or minimizes inexplicable disagreement, in the more sophisticated version] should not be conceived as resting on a charitable assumption about human intelligence that might turn out to be false. If we cannot find a way to interpret the utterances and other behaviour of a creature as revealing a set of beliefs largely consistent and true by our own standards [or not inexplicably inconsistent and wrong by our own standards], we have no reason to count that creature as rational, as having beliefs, or as saying anything.[27]

Note 3: The necessity of applying the principle of charity stems from the constitutive interdependence of belief and meaning. This shows where Davidson stands on the question raised in section 6.1 concerning the relationship between linguistic meaning and mental content. Davidson holds a "no-priority" view: linguistic meaning – the meaning of sentences – and mental content – the content of such propositional attitudes as belief – must be explained *together*, or not at all.

Note 4: Although we have written as if there was only one constitutive constraint governing interpretation, the principle of charity, this principle is only one of a *range* of such constitutive principles. As Hookway puts it, "Interpretation rests upon a number of normative standards. We are constrained to look for true beliefs, to look for rationally coherent bodies of belief, to avoid ascribing inexplicable ignorance, to look for reasonable desires, to look for coherent patterns of preferences, and so on."[28]

Note 5: Davidson writes that it is unlikely that the constraints on theories of meaning – Extensional Adequacy, Compositionality and Interpretation – will constrain the choice of a correct theory of meaning to within uniqueness. There will probably be different theories of meaning satisfying all of the relevant constraints:

> It is not likely that only one theory will be found satisfactory. The resulting indeterminacy of interpretation is the semantic counterpart of Quine's indeterminacy of translation. On my approach, the degree of indeterminacy will, I think, be less than Quine contemplates ... But in any case the question of indeterminacy is not central [to my concerns]. Indeterminacy of meaning or translation does not represent a failure to capture significant distinctions; it marks the fact that certain apparent distinctions are not significant. If there is indeterminacy, it is because when all the evidence is in, alternative ways of stating the facts remain open.[29]

Davidson writes that the amount of indeterminacy left open will be less than that envisaged by Quine because his use of the principle of charity is more wide-ranging than Quine's (who takes it to apply only to the translation of the logical constants) and because "the uniqueness of quantificational structure is apparently ensured if Convention T is satisfied".[30] Presumably, the fact that Davidson allows a richer sort of evidence than Quine to count in the process of interpretation will also contribute to the reduction of indeterminacy. But what is the source of Davidson's confidence that any residual indeterminacy will be "insignificant"? He writes,

> A rough comparison may help give the idea. A theory of measurement for temperature leads to the assignment to objects of numbers that measure their temperature. Such theories put formal constraints on the assignments, and also must be tied empirically to qualitatively observable phenomena. The numbers assigned are not uniquely determined by the constraints. But the *pattern* of assignments is significant. (Fahrenheit and Centigrade temperature are linear transformations of each other; the assignment of numbers is unique up to a linear transformation.) In much the same way, I suggest that what is invariant as between different acceptable theories of truth is meaning.[31]

And what is invariant between different acceptable theories of truth is the role they assign to the sentences of the language under consideration:[32]

> The meaning (interpretation) of a sentence is given by assigning the sentence a semantic location in the pattern of sentences that comprise the language. Different theories of truth may assign different truth conditions to the same sentence ... while the theories are (nearly enough) in agreement on the roles of the sentences of the language.[33]

Whereas in Quine's case that which is invariant between different translation manuals – stimulus-meaning – does not amount to anything even resembling our intuitive concept of meaning, in Davidson's account that which is invariant between different acceptable theories of truth is conceived as approximating to our intuitive conception of meaning.

8.8 Holism and T-theorems

Thus far we have been considering only Davidson's response to the first of the worries raised in section 8.6. But what about the second worry that was raised? How can Davidson rule out "rogue"

T-theorems, such as

(18) "Fish swim" is true if and only if dogs bark

from the theory of meaning? Recall that the dilemma Davidson faced was as follows: either he strengthens "if and only if" as it appears in the T-theorems so that it is *stronger* than the material biconditional, in which case his aim to give a theory of meaning in a purely extensional language is endangered; or he is committed to totally implausible claims about what certain sentences mean (for example, that the sentence "Fish swim" means *that dogs bark*).

Davidson's strategy in responding to this dilemma is similar to that discussed in the previous section. He attempts to neutralize the second horn of the dilemma by showing that we can stick to an extensional theory of meaning whose theorems are couched in terms of only material equivalencies, but invoke the holistic constraints on interpretation to rule out theories of meaning containing "rogue" T-theorems.

Let's go back to our rainy afternoon in Berlin, and Kurt's utterance of "Es regnet". Suppose that there is also an aeroplane passing overhead at the time of the utterance. Then the following material biconditional will be true, since both its left- and right-hand sides have the same truth value:

(22) "Es regnet", as uttered by Kurt, is true if and only if there is an aeroplane passing overhead.

Now given that this is true, how can we rule it out from the theory of meaning we are attempting to construct for Kurt's language? Can we say that, although it is true, it nevertheless corresponds to a false statement about what Kurt holds true? The relevant statement would be

(23) "Es regnet" is held true by Kurt if and only if there is an aeroplane passing overhead.

But this sentence (call it an H-sentence) is actually true as well: at the time of utterance it is true that Kurt holds true the sentence "Es regnet" and it is also true that there is an aeroplane passing overhead.

What this shows is that what supports the claim that (21) gives the meaning of "Es regnet" is not the truth of the individual H-sentence (20): *rather, it is the fact that (21) is a theorem of a theory of meaning none of whose T-theorems correspond to false H-sentences.* The idea is then that we can say that although (22) is true, it does not give the meaning of "Es regnet", because a theory of meaning containing it would at some point generate a theorem corresponding to a *false* H-sentence. The constraints on interpretation are holistic in the sense that they apply to the theory as a whole, not to individual theorems considered in isolation. As Hookway puts it,

> The empirical test supports the theory as a whole; we accept the statement about what "Es regnet" means because the theorem follows from an empirically adequate theory of meaning. Statements of truth-conditions cannot be verified singly: utterances and actions always reflect the influence of many of an agent's beliefs and desires – there are no straightforward links between belief and behaviour.[34]

So why is it likely that a theory of meaning containing (22) would at some point generate a theorem corresponding to a *false* H-sentence? Well, given that "regnet" is being treated as a subsentential expression that coincides in extension with "aeroplane", the theory is likely to include a clause like the following in its axiomatic base:

(24) $(\forall x)(x$ satisfies "Regnet" if and only if x is an aeroplane).

Now such a theory is also likely to generate a T-theorem like

(25) "Das ist regnet", as uttered by Kurt, is true if and only if the demonstrated object is an aeroplane.

But what H-sentence corresponds to this? It will be

(26) Kurt holds true "Das ist regnet" if and only if the demonstrated object is an aeroplane.

And this is plausibly false. If we get Kurt to focus his attention on the aeroplane, we will find that he does not hold true "Das ist regnet". The left-hand side of (26) is false, while the right-hand side is true: so by the truth-table for the material biconditional, (26) itself is false. Since the theory of meaning containing (22) in this way leads to a T-theorem that corresponds to a false H-sentence, we are justified in rejecting this theory of meaning, even though (22) itself is true. This contrasts with the theory containing (20), which, because it does not contain (24), has no such implication.

This shows how the holistic constraints on interpretation, and the holistic process of confirming a theory of meaning, allow us to rule out theories of meaning containing "rogue" T-theorems without requiring anything more than material equivalence in our statements of truth-conditions: the second horn of the dilemma is thus neutralized.[35]

8.9 Conclusion: theories of meaning and natural language

As we have seen, Davidson thinks that a theory of meaning for a natural language can be provided by a theory of truth in the Tarskian style that satisfies the conditions of Extensional Adequacy, compositionality and interpretation. Given a fragment of·natural language, what we require in order for a theory of meaning of this sort to be constructed is that the sentences of this language be couched in a form that renders them amenable to Tarskian treatment. In effect, what this requires is that the sentences be translatable into the language of Frege's symbolic logic. Now many of the sentences of natural language do easily translate into this formal notation: any student who has taken an elementary logic course at university will be familiar with this process (see also section 1.1). But there are many regions of natural language that resist straightforward translation into Frege's logical language. Both Frege and Tarski are pessimistic about providing systematic semantic theories or theories of truth for natural languages, and limit themselves to constructing theories for formal languages and the language of mathematics: natural languages are simply too amorphous and paradox-ridden for this to be a viable project. Davidson, however, is more optimistic about the prospect of constructing a systematic theory of meaning for a natural language. He ends one of his most important papers, "Truth and Meaning", with the following comment:

> Since I think there is no alternative, I have taken an optimistic and programmatic view of the possibilities for a formal characterisation of a truth-predicate for a natural language. But it must be allowed that a staggering list of difficulties and conundrums remains. To name a few: we do not know the logical form of counterfactual or subjunctive sentences; nor of sentences about probabilities and about causal relations; we have no good idea what the logical role of adverbs is, nor the role of attributive adjectives; we have no theory of mass terms like "fire", "water", "snow", nor for sentences about belief, perception, and intention, nor for verbs of action that imply purpose. And finally, there are all the sentences that seem not to have truth-values at all: the imperatives, optatives, interrogatives, and a host more. A comprehensive theory of meaning for a natural language must cope successfully with each of these problems.[36]

Since the publication of "Truth and Meaning", philosophers of language – including Davidson himself – have expended much effort in attempting to show how the various locutions he mentions in this passage can be brought within the compass of a systematic theory of meaning. I have not had space to look at any of the details of these attempts in this chapter, but I hope that I have given the reader some sense of what it is that these philosophers of language have been aiming at.

Further reading

Davidson's main papers on the philosophy of language are collected in his *Inquiries into truth and interpretation*. The best overall introduction to his philosophy is S. Evnine, *Donald Davidson*: this is especially good on situating Davidson's philosophy of language in the more general context that includes his philosophy of mind and metaphysics. See also B. Ramberg, *Donald Davidson's philosophy of language*, M. Platts, *Ways of meaning*, S. Blackburn, *Spreading the word*, Chapter 8, and C. Hookway, *Quine*, Chapter 10. For a useful collection of papers, see E. Lepore (ed.), *Truth and interpretation: perspectives on the philosophy of Donald Davidson*. Davidson's philosophy of language cannot be studied adequately without a knowledge of his philosophy of mind: for this, see Davidson's collected papers, *Essays on actions and events*, and the collections, E. Lepore and B. McGlaughlin (eds), *Actions and events: perspectives on the philosophy of Donald Davidson*, and M. Hintikka and B. Vermazen (eds) *Essays on Davidson: actions and events*. Tarski's results on truth are set out in his "The concept of truth in formalized languages", in his *Logic, semantics, metamathematics*. This is a difficult and highly technical paper, and Tarski's work is probably best approached via the more informal "The semantic conception of truth", *Philosophy and Phenomenological Research* (1949), and "Truth and proof", *Scientific American* (1967). There is a good – but terse – presentation of Tarski's theory of truth in Platts, *Ways of meaning*, Chapter 1; see also the presentations in W. V. O Quine, *Philosophy of logic*, and S. Haack, *Philosophy of logics*. For a comprehensive discussion of interpretations of Tarski, see P. Milne, "Tarski on truth and its definition", in T. Childers, P. Kolar, and V. Svobada (eds) *Logica '96*.

Chapter 9

Sense, objectivity and metaphysics

In this chapter, we return to an issue which loomed large in Chapter 3: the relationship between the philosophy of language and metaphysics. Philosophers no longer believe the positivist idea that philosophy of language can enable us to dispense with metaphysical debate: instead, the philosophy of language has come to be viewed as a *tool* we might use in attempting to get clearer on what metaphysical questions are and on how they might be answered. In particular, philosophy of language has come to be regarded as central in the metaphysical debates between *realists* and their opponents. The literature on this topic is vast and complex: in this chapter our aim is simply to provide a rough map of some of the main territory.

9.1 Realism

What is it to be a realist about the subject matter of a particular discourse or area of enquiry? Take discourse about ordinary, macroscopic objects, such as tables, chairs, sticks and stones; or discourse about what is morally right and wrong, about ethical value. *To be a realist about the subject matters of these discourses is to think that our thought about them aspires to reflect an objective reality, and sometimes succeeds in this aim.* Thus, when I judge that there are three chairs in the room, I express a *belief* that aims to reflect an objective fact; and beliefs such as this often do *succeed* in reflecting the objective facts of the matter, so that the judgement in question is *true*. Likewise in the case of moral discourse: when I judge that killing is wrong, I am expressing a belief that aims to reflect an objective fact and is successful in this aim.

But can we say something more specific about what it is for our thought "to aspire to reflect an objective reality"? One way to start on this would be as follows: to be a realist about the subject matter of, for example, discourse about ordinary, macroscopic objects is to think that the sentences of this discourse *possess objective truth-conditions*. Likewise, to be a realist about morals is to think that the sentences of moral discourse possess objective truth-conditions. And to think that we sometimes succeed in this aim of getting our thought to reflect an objective reality is to think that these objective truth-conditions are sometimes satisfied.

Now we have the task of spelling out what is meant by the term "objective" in this characterization of realism: what does it mean to say that the sentences of a discourse have objective – as opposed to, say, subjective – truth-conditions? This task will occupy us, in one way or another, in the rest of this chapter. We'll work towards answering it by first considering some ways of *rejecting* realism about particular areas of enquiry.[1]

9.2 Noncognitivism and the Frege–Geach problem

One way of denying that the sentences of a given discourse have objective truth-conditions would be to deny that they have truth-conditions *at all*. Say that if a sentence has truth-conditions then it is *truth-apt*: apt to be true or false, or apt to be assessed in terms of truth and falsity. One way of denying that a given set of sentences have objective truth-conditions would be to deny that they are truth-apt. In fact, we have already seen an example of this sort of view in section 3.6, when we looked at the logical positivist account of ethical language. According to Ayer, a sentence like "Stealing is wrong" is not the sort of sentence that can be assessed in terms of truth and falsity: in uttering it we are not even purporting to represent some fact about the world, some condition in the world whose obtaining would render the utterance true. The function of "Stealing is wrong" is not to express beliefs that aim to represent the world and that can be true or false, but rather to express feelings, emotions or, generally, *noncognitive sentiments* that are incapable of being true or false.

One way of opposing realism about morals, therefore, would be to deny that moral sentences are truth-apt: they do not express beliefs, which can be true or false, but rather noncognitive sentiments that can neither be true nor false. This way of opposing realism is known as *noncognitivism.*

If noncognitivism were plausible, it would solve many worries philosophers have had about the metaphysics of morality. Since the *purpose* of moral discourse is not to state facts, we do not have to include moral facts in our inventory of the sorts of fact the world contains in order to legitimize our moral practices.[2] Given that many philosophers find moral facts hard to countenance – "queer metaphysical entities" – they would say that this is just as well.

Unfortunately, however, noncognitivism faces very serious difficulties. The main problem faced by noncognitivism is known as the "Frege–Geach Problem". According to noncognitivism, when I judge that murder is wrong, I am not expressing a belief, but rather expressing some noncognitive attitude, incapable of being true or false. This is an account of the semantic function of "Murder is wrong" in a context in which it is apparently being asserted that murder is wrong. But the sentence can occur in many, many contexts in which it is clearly *not being asserted*: for example, if I say that *if murder is wrong, then getting your little brother to murder people is wrong*, I am not necessarily expressing disapproval of murder. (If I assert a conditional generally, I need not commit myself to accepting its antecedent: for example, if I say that if it is raining, the streets will be wet, I am not thereby accepting that it is actually raining.) The question for the noncognitivist is therefore this: what is the semantic function of the occurrence of "Murder is wrong" in the antecedent of the above conditional?

Since I am not there expressing disapproval of murder, the account of its semantic function must be different from that given for the straightforward assertion that murder is wrong. But now we are going to have a problem in accounting for the following apparently valid inference:

(1) Murder is wrong.
(2) If Murder is wrong, then getting your little brother to murder people is wrong.

Therefore:

(3) Getting your little brother to murder people is wrong.

If the semantic function of "Murder is wrong" as it appears in (1) is different from its semantic function as it appears in (2), isn't someone arguing in this way simply guilty of *equivocation*? In order for the argument to be valid, the occurrence of "murder is wrong" in (1) has to *mean the same thing as* the occurrence of "murder is wrong" in (2). But if "murder is wrong" has a different semantic function in (1) and (2), then it certainly doesn't mean the same thing in (1) and (2). So the above argument is apparently no more valid than:

(1*) My beer has a head on it.
(2*) If something has a head on it, then it must have eyes and ears.

Therefore:

(3*) My beer must have eyes and ears.

This argument is obviously invalid, because it relies on an equivocation on two senses of "head", in (1*) and (2*) respectively.[3]

Another way of putting essentially the same point: in elementary logic, how would we try to figure out how a given argument is valid? One way would be to construct a truth-table, and check whether there are any cases in which all of the premises are true and yet the conclusion is false. If there are, the argument is invalid; if there are not, the argument is valid. But how can this procedure even make sense when some of the premises (e.g (1)) in the argument are not even assessable in terms of truth and falsity?

The Frege–Geach challenge to the noncognitivist is thus to answer the following question: How can you give a noncognitivist account of the occurrence of moral sentences in "unasserted contexts" – such as the antecedents of conditionals – without jeopardizing the intuitively valid patterns of inference in which those judgements figure?

Simple as this problem seems, noncognitivists have found it extremely difficult to answer.[4] This suggests that opposition to realism about a particular declarative discourse cannot take the form of a simple denial that the sentences of that discourse are truth-apt or possess truth-conditions.

9.3 Realism and verification-transcendent truth

Denying that sentences have truth-conditions does not therefore give us a plausible way of denying realism, the claim that they have objective truth-conditions. This takes us back to the question about objectivity that we raised at the end of section 9.1. Maybe opposition to realism can be framed as the claim that sentences have truth-conditions (so that the Frege–Geach problem is avoided), but that these truth-conditions are not objective. But what does this mean? What does it mean to say that the truth-conditions of a range of sentences *are* "objective"? One way of fleshing this out has been suggested in a series of influential works by Michael Dummett: to say that a range of sentences have objective truth-conditions is to say that those truth-conditions are potentially *verification-transcendent*. To say that a truth-condition is potentially verification-transcendent is to say that we may be incapable, even in principle, of determining whether or not it obtains. Thus, consider discourse about the past: intuitively, the sentence "James II[5] suffered a migraine in 1665, on the afternoon of his 32nd birthday" has a truth-condition – James's suffering a migraine on the afternoon in question – and we can say that this condition either obtained or it did not, even though we may have no way, even in principle (because all the evidence appears to have vanished and time travel is impossible) of determining which of these was the case. Thus, "James II had a migraine on the afternoon of his 32nd birthday" has a truth-condition, and we may be incapable of determining, even in principle, whether that condition obtained or not: it is potentially verificationtranscendent. Likewise, consider arithmetical discourse. Goldbach's conjecture, that every even number greater than two is the sum of two primes, has a potentially verification-transcendent truth-condition: it has a determinate truth-value even though we are incapable of determining what this truth-value is, since we cannot as yet provide either a proof of the conjecture or a counterexample to it.

Thus, sentences about the past and about arithmetic have potentially verification-transcendent truth-conditions: in this sense their truth-conditions are objective. Now, why is the claim that the sentences of a discourse are potentially verification-transcendent a way of cashing out realism about the subject-matter of that discourse? In other words, why is it a way of cashing out the idea that our thought about that subject matter aspires to reflect an objective reality? In order to see this we have to recall that the sense of a sentence is given by its truth-conditions, and that understanding a sentence consists in grasping its sense. Thus, understanding a sentence consists in grasping its truth-conditions. Any thesis about the truth-conditions of a set of sentences is *inter alia* a thesis about what our understanding of those sentences consists in. In a slogan, a *theory of meaning is also a theory of understanding.* Thus, someone who accepts that the truth-conditions of a region of discourse are potentially verification-transcendent also accepts that our understanding of the sentences of that discourse consists in our grasp of potentially verification-transcendent truth-conditions. And now the connection with realism about that discourse is relatively easy to see. As Crispin Wright puts it:

> To conceive that our understanding of statements in a certain discourse is fixed ... by assigning them conditions of potentially [verification]-transcendent truth is to grant that, if the world co-operates, the truth or falsity of any such statement may be settled beyond our ken. So we are forced to recognise a distinction between the kind of state of affairs which makes

such a statement acceptable, in the light of whatever standards inform our practice of the discourse to which it belongs, and what makes it actually true. The truth of such a statement is bestowed on it independently of any standard we do or can apply; acceptability by our standards is, for such statements, at best merely congruent with truth. Realism in Dummett's sense is thus one way of laying the essential semantic groundwork for the idea that our thought aspires to reflect a reality whose character is entirely independent of us and our cognitive operations.[6]

We can thus conceive of the metaphysical debate between realists and their opponents – antirealists – in a particular region of discourse D as concerning whether the sentences of D can plausibly be viewed as possessing potentially verification-transcendent truth-conditions.

REALISM: *the sentences of D have truth-conditions (are truth-apt) and these truth-conditions are potentially verification-transcendent.*

ANTIREALISM: *the sentences of D have truth-conditions (are truth-apt) but those truth-conditions are not potentially verification-transcendent.*[7]

Realism, as thus conceived, appears highly intuitive, and is apparently hinted at by some of the most influential philosophers of language that we have considered in this book. Davidson, for example, writes: "We can be realists in all departments. We can accept objective truth-conditions as the key to meaning, and we can insist that knowledge is of an objective world independent of our thought and language."[8] And Frege writes: "A thinker does not create [thoughts] but must take them as they are. They can be true without being grasped by a thinker."[9] If a thought – the sense of a sentence – can be determinately true or false even though that thought is not even grasped by a thinker, then the sentence in question can be true or false even though thinkers are incapable, even in principle, of determining its truth-value.

How, then, can we resolve the metaphysical debate between realism and antirealism about a particular region of discourse? In the next section we look at some of the main arguments against realism.

9.4 Acquisition, manifestation and rule-following: the arguments against verification-transcendent truth

The debate between realism and anti-realism about a region of discourse is a debate about the nature of the truth-conditions possessed by the sentences of that discourse. Any account of the truth-conditions of a range of sentences will be unacceptable if it cannot cohere with a plausible account of what our *understanding* of those sentences consists in. Dummett's strategy is thus to argue that the account of linguistic understanding that realism leads to is completely implausible, so that realism must be rejected. The metaphysical debate concerning the plausibility of realism thus boils down to a debate within the philosophy of language.

Why, then, does the antirealist think that we cannot plausibly construe linguistic understanding as grasp of potentially verification-transcendent truth-conditions? There are three main arguments.

9.4.1 The acquisition challenge
Suppose that we are considering some region of discourse D, the sentences of which we intuitively understand. Suppose, for *reductio*, that the sentences of D have potentially verification-transcendent truth-conditions. Thus,

(a) We understand the sentences of D.
(b) The sentences of D have verification-transcendent truth-conditions.

Now, from (a) together with thesis 10 (Ch. 2) we have

(c) We grasp the senses of the sentences of D: that is, we know their truth-conditions.

We now add the apparently reasonable constraint on ascriptions of knowledge:

(d) If a piece of knowledge is ascribed to a speaker, then it must be at least in principle possible for that speaker to have *acquired* that knowledge.

So

(e) It must be at least in principle possible for us to have acquired knowledge of the verification-transcendent truth-conditions of D.

But

(f) There is no plausible story to be told about how we could have acquired knowledge of verification-transcendent truth-conditions.

So, by *reductio*, we reject (b) to get:

(g) The sentences of D do not have verification-transcendent truth-conditions, so realism about the subject matter of D must be rejected.

The crucial premise here is obviously (f). Wright puts the point as follows:

> How are we supposed to be able to *form* any understanding of what it is for a particular statement to be true if the kind of state of affairs which it would take to make it true is conceived, *ex hypothesi*, as something beyond our experience, something which we cannot confirm and which is insulated from any distinctive impact on our consciousness?[10]

However, as Wright notes, this argument is at best inconclusive. It really only presents the realist with a challenge:

> In order to be more than a challenge, [it] would need the backing of a proven theory of concept-formation of a broadly empiricist sort. [And] the traditional theories of that sort have long been recognized to be inadequate.[11]

The challenge to the realist is thus: give some plausible account of how the knowledge of verification-transcendent truth-conditions that you impute to speakers could have been acquired. Whether or not this challenge can be met by the realist is very much an open question, in the absence of a proven theory of concept acquisition.

9.4.2 The manifestation argument

Suppose that we are considering region of discourse D as before. Then this argument can be set out as follows:

(a) We understand the sentences of D.

Suppose, for *reductio*, that

(b) The sentences of D have verification-transcendent truth-conditions.

From (a) and thesis 10 we have:

(c) We grasp the senses of the sentences of D: that is, we know their truth-conditions.

We then add the following premise, which stems from the Wittgensteinian insight that understanding does not consist in the possession of an inner state, but rather in the possession of some practical ability (see section 5.1):

(d) If speakers possess a piece of knowledge that is constitutive of linguistic understanding, then that knowledge should be *manifested* in speakers' use of the language, that is, in their exercise of the practical abilities which constitute linguistic understanding.

It now follows from (a), (b) and (c) that:

(e) Our knowledge of the verification-transcendent truth-conditions of the sentences of D should be manifested in our use of those sentences, that is, in our exercise of the practical abilities that constitute our understanding of D.

Since

(f) Such knowledge is never manifested in the exercise of the practical abilities which constitute our understanding of D,

it follows that

(g) We do not possess knowledge of the truth-conditions of D.

(g) and (c) together give us a contradiction, whence, by *reductio*, we reject (b) to obtain:

(h) The sentences of D do not have verification-transcendent truth-conditions, so realism about the subject matter of D must be rejected.

The basic point is that, so far as an account of speaker's understanding goes, the ascription of knowledge of verification-transcendent truth-conditions is simply *redundant*: there is no good reason for ascribing it. Consider one of the sentences we considered earlier as candidates for possessing verification-transcendent truth-conditions, "James II had a migraine on the afternoon of his 32nd birthday" or "Every even number greater than two is the sum of two primes". The realist account views our understanding of these sentences as consisting in our knowledge of a potentially verification-transcendent truth-condition. But

How can that account be viewed as a description of any *practical* ability of use? No doubt someone who understands such a statement can be expected to have many relevant practical abilities. He will be able to appraise evidence for or against it, should any be available, or to recognize that no information in his possession bears on it. He will be able to recognize at least some of its logical consequences, and to identify beliefs from which commitment to it would follow. And he will, presumably, show himself sensitive to conditions under which it is appropriate to ascribe propositional attitudes embedding the statement to himself and to others, and sensitive to the explanatory significance of such ascriptions. In short: in these

289

and perhaps other important respects, he will show himself competent to use the sentence. But the headings under which his practical abilities fall so far involve no mention of evidence-transcendent truth-conditions.[12]

This establishes (f), and the conclusion follows swiftly. A detailed assessment of the plausibility of this argument is impossible here: but we should note that premise (d) depends upon an interpretation of Wittgenstein's rule-following considerations, and that this (see Chs 5 and 6) is an extremely controversial matter. In particular, one issue that needs to be addressed is whether the interpretation of premise (d) required for the antirealist argument is left intact by McDowell's interpretation (section 6.7) according to which understanding can harmlessly be construed as a state of mind.

9.4.3 The argument from rule-following

The third antirealist argument involves a more direct use of Wittgenstein's rule-following considerations. In expounding this argument Wright introduces a number of different species of objectivity. First of all, there is the sort of objectivity that is possessed by regions of discourse whose sentences have potentially verification-transcendent truth-conditions. Wright calls this the *objectivity of truth*:

> To hold that a class of statements may be fully intelligible to us although resolving their truth-values may defeat our cognitive powers (even when idealized) may naturally be described as believing in the *objectivity of truth*.[13]

In addition, there is a distinct notion of objectivity, which Wright calls the *objectivity of meaning*: this is the notion that

> The meaning of a statement is a real constraint, to which we are bound, as it were, by contract, and to which verdicts about its truth-value may objectively conform, quite independently of our considered opinion on the matter.[14]

Now, Wright argues that if a discourse exhibits objectivity of truth then it follows that it must also exhibit the objectivity of meaning:

> The objectivity of meaning is a manifest implication of the objectivity of truth. If statements of certain sorts can be undetectably true, then we have no alternative but to think of their meanings as, so to speak, reaching into regions where we cannot follow: there is *already* a verdict about the truth-value of such a statement which – if it is intelligible to suppose that our cognitive powers could be appropriately extended – our present understanding of its constituents and syntax would oblige us to give once we had investigated matters properly.[15]

Since objectivity of truth entails objectivity of meaning, we can attack the idea that a discourse exhibits objectivity of truth – has sentences with verification-transcendent truth-conditions – by attacking the idea that it exhibits objectivity of meaning. For a given discourse D, the shape of the argument is therefore:

(a) If D exhibits objectivity of truth then it exhibits objectivity of meaning.
(b) D does not exhibit objectivity of meaning.

Therefore:

(c) D does not exhibit objectivity of truth, that is, the sentences of D do not have potentially verification-transcendent truth-conditions, so that realism about D must be rejected.

This argument is certainly valid, and premise (a) seems plausible enough. But what is the argument for premise (b)? Recall that in section 6.6 we looked at Wright's "judgement-dependent" conception of meaning. Wright argues that we must view meaning as judgement-dependent if we are to avoid the sceptical paradox about meaning, which Kripke reads into Wittgenstein's rule-following considerations. The proper upshot of the rule-following considerations, Wright thinks, is thus that meaning is judgement-dependent. *But if meaning is judgement-dependent, we have to give up the objectivity of meaning.* If the meaning we attach to a statement S is determined by our best judgements, then it is certainly not the case that the meaning of S "is a constraint ... to which verdicts about its truth-value may objectively conform, or fail to conform, *quite independently of our considered opinion on the matter*" (emphasis added).

The plausibility of the argument from rule-following against verification-transcendent truth thus depends on the plausibility of Wright's judgement-dependent conception of meaning. This is a highly controversial matter. Recall from section 6.7 that McDowell opposes Wright's interpretation of Wittgenstein, and he argues that, if we give up the judgement-independent conception of meaning, we will not be able to find room for the idea that meaning is genuinely normative. In effect, McDowell thinks we have to accept the objectivity of meaning on pain of losing the notion of meaning altogether. And given that we have to accept the objectivity of meaning, there is no threat to the idea that our sentences can have potentially verification-transcendent truth-conditions: "There is no standpoint from which we can give a sense-making characterization of linguistic practice other than that of immersion in the practice: and from that standpoint our possibly verification-transcendent world is certainly in the picture."[16] Evaluating the antirealist argument from rule-following, then, depends upon attaining a plausible perspective on the correct interpretation and implications of Wittgenstein's rule-following considerations. This provides us with additional impetus for tackling the issues raised in Chapter 6 of the present book.

Those, then, are the three main antirealist arguments developed by Dummett and his followers. Evaluation of these arguments is far outwith the scope of this book. In the remainder of this section, we simply note some features of the antirealist position which they attempt to establish.

Note 1: A sentence is said to be *effectively decidable* if there is some procedure that a speaker can in principle apply in order to determine whether or not the sentence is true. Thus, "2 + 2 = 4" and "John Major had cornflakes for breakfast yesterday" are both effectively decidable: we can carry out an elementary arithmetical calculation in the first case, and we can gather the obvious sorts of evidence in the second case, in order to determine the truth-values of the respective sentences. But "James II had a migraine on the afternoon of his 32nd birthday" and "Every even number greater than two is the sum of two primes" are *not known to be decidable*: in neither case do we know a procedure that we can apply to determine whether or not they are true. Now intuitively, we think that even though these sentences are not known to be decidable, we can nevertheless still assert that they are either true or false: "Every even number greater than two is the sum of two primes" has a determinate truth-value, it's just that we cannot work out what this truth-value is. In other words, even though the sentence is not known to be decidable, we still think that the *principle of bivalence*, that every (nonvague) sentence is determinately either true or false, applies to it. Now this is an idea that is put under pressure by the conclusion of the antirealist arguments we have been considering. If truth is not verification-transcendent, it is *epistemically constrained.* One way to spell out what it means to say that truth is epistemically constrained is to say that it must be construed in terms of some notion like *correct* or *warranted assertability*: to say that a sentence is true is to say that there is a warrant to assert it, or that it possesses some other property that is constructed out of warranted assertability.[17] Now given that truth is thus epistemically constrained, what can we say about "Every even number greater than two is the sum of two primes"? We do not have a warrant to assert this – since no one has yet been able to construct a mathematical proof of it – nor do we have a warrant to assert its negation – since no one has yet produced a counterexample to it, or established that such a counterexample must exist. Given this, and given that truth is to be construed in terms of warranted assertability, we cannot assert that the sentence "Every even number is the sum of two primes" is either true or false. That is to say, *we cannot assert* a priori *the principle of bivalence for sentences that are not known to be decidable*: we cannot assert, *a priori*, that they are either true or false.

Note 2: The antirealist thus claims that we cannot assert *a priori* the principle of bivalence, at least as applied to sentences that are not known to be decidable. Now the principle of bivalence – that every (nonvague) sentence is determinately either true or false is closely associated with the theorem of classical logic known as the *law of excluded middle*:

$$\vdash P \vee -P.$$

Refusing to assert *a priori* the principle of bivalence, as the antirealist proposes, thus appears to threaten the law of excluded middle, and the classical system of logic which is founded upon it. There is much debate among antirealists as to whether antirealism implies *revisionism* about classical logic: Dummett has argued that antirealism implies that classical logic must be given up in favour of some form of *intuitionistic* logic that does not have the law of excluded middle as a theorem.[18]

Note 3: It is important to be clear that although the antirealist claims that we cannot assert that sentences not known to be decidable are either true or false, he is *not* claiming that we *can* assert that they are *neither* true nor false. Dummett is explicit that, although the antirealist does not wish to assert *a priori* the principle of bivalence, he does not reject the principle of *tertium non datur*, that there is no third truth-value ("neither true nor false") standing between truth and falsity.[19]

Note 4: Note that the antirealist attitude to sentences that are not known to be decidable is completely different from the logical positivist attitude to sentences that are not in principle verifiable. Whereas the logical positivist claims that such sentences – because they are in principle unverifiable – are literally meaningless (see Ch. 3), the antirealist claims that sentences that are not known to be decidable *are* meaningful but that their meanings have to be construed in terms of an epistemically constrained notion of truth.

Note 5: The approach to metaphysical questions exhibited here is indicative of Dummett's view that the philosophy of language – the theory of meaning – has a *foundational* role to play within philosophy. Dummett believes that one of the reasons why philosophical speculation about metaphysical issues has made little progress over the centuries is that the opposing positions in various metaphysical disputes have only been explained in pictorial, or metaphorical terms:

Even to attempt to evaluate the direct metaphysical arguments, we have to treat the opposing theses as though their content were quite clear and it were solely a matter of deciding which is true; whereas ... the principal difficulty is that, while one or another of the competing pictures may appear compelling, we have no way to explain in non-pictorial terms what accepting it amounts to.[20]

Dummett's approach is intended to remedy this: the metaphysical disputes are recast as disputes about "the correct model of meaning for statements of the disputed class", thus giving the debates some nonmetaphorical content, and enabling the disputes to be resolved within the theory of meaning.[21]

Note 6: Dummett's view that the philosophy of language has a foundational role to play within philosophy is mirrored by his stance on the linguistic meaning/mental content priority issue (see section 6.1):

It has until recently been a basic tenet of analytical philosophy ... that the philosophy of thought can be approached only through the philosophy of language. That is to say, there can be no account of what thought is, independently of its means of expression; but the purpose of the philosophy of thought can be achieved by an explanation of what it is for words and sentences to have the meanings that they bear, an explanation making no appeal to an antecedent conception of the thoughts those sentences express.[22]

9.5 Grades of objectivity: Wright on antirealism

To be a realist about a certain area of discourse is to view the sentences of that discourse as possessing objective truth-conditions. In the previous section, we looked at Dummett's way of cashing out the notion of an objective truth-condition: a truth-condition is objective if it is potentially verification-transcendent. Thus, one way to oppose realism, to espouse antirealism, is to deny that truth is potentially verification-transcendent and to argue that truth must be viewed as epistemically constrained. But is this the best way of cashing out the metaphysical debates between realists and their opponents? Although Dummett's way of characterizing the metaphysical debate seems to be appropriate in some cases – for example, mathematics, statements about the past, statements about the external world – there are other cases where it simply seems besides the point. Consider discourse about, for example, morals or comedy. It seems that in these cases a moral realist would not have to claim that the truth-conditions of the relevant sentences are potentially verification-transcendent and that both the moral realist and the moral antirealist can *agree* that statements about comedy or moral value do not have verification-transcendent truth-conditions:

> There are, no doubt, kinds of moral realism [or realism about comedy] which do have the consequence that moral [or comic] reality may transcend all possibility of detection. But it is surely not essential to any view worth regarding as realist about morals [or comedy] that it incorporate a commitment to that idea.[23]

Intuitively, a sensible version of realism about "That remark was funny" or "That deed was wrong" does not have to view facts about funniness or wrongness as potentially verification-transcendent. So, although construing objective truth-conditions as verification-transcendent truth-conditions may be useful for characterizing realism about some areas of discourse, there are other areas for which this is not a useful characterization. The upshot of this is that we need other ways of fleshing out the notion of an objective truth-condition, other ways of construing objectivity. The most important recent work in the area of overlap between the philosophy of language and metaphysics has consisted of attempts to do just this. In this section, we'll briefly sketch one such attempt in very broad outline, that developed by Crispin Wright.

Wright argues that noncognitivism – the denial that the sentences of a discourse are truth-apt or even possess truth-conditions – does not provide a useful way of formulating opposition to realism. The debate between realism and antirealism about a discourse takes place only *after* it has been granted that the sentences of that discourse are truth-apt. There are two main parts to Wright's sketch of the shape of the debates. First, he develops a version of *minimalism about truth-aptness*, according to which all of the discourses – including morals, comedy, the external world, mathematics, the past, and so on – do turn out to be truth-apt. Secondly, he develops a *number* of ways of characterizing realism and antirealism about discourses whose truth-aptness has already been granted – that is, a number of different ways in which truth-conditions can be objective. It turns out that viewing the sentences of a discourse as having potentially verification-transcendent truth-conditions is only *one* of a *number* of ways of characterizing realism and the notion of objective truth-conditions. We'll look at these two parts of Wright's sketch in turn.

9.5.1 Minimalism about truth-aptness

According to minimalism about truth-aptness, a class of sentences is truth-apt if the following two conditions are satisfied:

(a) *Discipline*: The sentences figure in an area of discourse that is disciplined. There must be standards operative with respect to which uses of those sentence are judged to be appropriate or inappropriate. There must be acknowledged standards for the proper and improper use of those sentences.

(b) *Syntax*: The sentences must possess the right sort of syntactic features. In particular, they must be capable of conditionalization, negation, embedding in propositional attitudes, and so on.

If these conditions are met, then on the minimalist theory of truth-aptness there is simply no option but to concede that the sentences are truth-apt, and apt to be evaluated in terms of truth and falsity. And these conditions are met in all of the discourses that have been the focus of metaphysical debate. Take a moral claim like "It is morally right to give to charity." Moral discourse is certainly disciplined: there are acknowledged standards governing the use of moral sentences. There are circumstances under which the utterance of "It is right to give to charity" would be deemed appropriate, and circumstances under which it would be deemed inappropriate. And there seems to be no problem in satisfying the condition concerning syntax: we can perfectly well say things like "If giving to charity is right then I will donate to charity the next time I am asked to do so by a reputable charity", "It is not right to give to charity", "I believe that it is right to give to charity". All of these are syntactically kosher. So, both of the conditions that minimalism imposes on truth-aptitude are satisfied by "It is right to give to charity" (and by other declarative sentences of moral discourse). The sentence is therefore truth-apt.[24] The same goes for "That joke was hilarious", "Every even number greater than two is the sum of two primes", "James II had a migraine on the afternoon of his 32nd birthday".

9.5.2 The marks of realism

Given that the sentences of a region of discourse are, courtesy of minimalism, truth-apt, how can we characterize realism about that discourse? One way is given by Dummett's characterization of realism:

Mark 1: verification-transcendence. The sentences of the region have truth-conditions that are potentially verification-transcendent.

But as we saw, this mark doesn't give us a good way of getting a handle on the realist/antirealist debates about morals and comedy, because the realist and antirealist can agree in those cases that discourse about morals and discourse about humour do not satisfy this mark. In order to deal with this, and to widen the range of realist/antirealist disputes that we can capture, Wright develops a number of other "marks of realism":

Mark 2: cognitive command. It is a priori that, if two practitioners of the discourse differ in their judgements, then given that the divergence of opinion is not due to vagueness, at least one of them is making some cognitive error.

Discourse about comedy, for example, might appear to fail cognitive command: if Jones thinks Benny Hill is funnier than

Billy Connolly, and Smith thinks Billy Connolly is funnier than Benny Hill, then even if this divergence in opinion is not attributable to vagueness, it is not *a priori* that either Smith or Jones is prey to some sort of cognitive malfunction. It may just be that they have different noncognitive senses of humour. This contrasts with beliefs about the shape of middle-sized physical objects: if Smith says the object is square and Jones says it is round, then it is *a priori* that unless the disagreement is explicable on the grounds of vagueness, at least one of Smith and Jones will be prey to some sort of cognitive shortcoming.

Mark 3: width of cosmological role. The truth-conditions of the sentences of the discourse feature in the explanation of facts other than the holding of speakers' beliefs, and do so other than via their role in the explanation of the holding of those beliefs.

Moral discourse appears to fail this condition: moral facts only seem to have an impact on reality via the contribution they make to explanations of our moral beliefs (for example, the injustice of a given social system, such as slavery, certainly can have effects on the world [for example, it can lead to the eventual downfall of that system], but only via human *attitudes* to slavery). This contrasts with discourse about middle-sized physical objects, which appears to satisfy the condition: facts about middle-sized physical objects can figure in explanations of other sorts of facts and other than via the role they play in explaining why we have beliefs about them (for example, the fact that the snowman melted explains why the ground is wet).

Mark 4: judgement-independence. The central predicates of the region of discourse are *judgement-independent* (in the sense of section 6.6).

As we saw in section 6.6, Wright argues that discourse about meaning and discourse about intention both fail this condition (and he argues that it is satisfied by discourse about the *shape* of medium-sized physical objects).

These four marks require substantial elaboration and development which we cannot attempt here. What is important is the shape they allow us to impose on realist/antirealist debates. One way in which the sentences of a discourse can have objective truth-conditions is for that discourse to satisfy Mark 1: but other ways are provided by the satisfaction of some of the other marks. And there is no reason why a discourse cannot satisfy some of the marks, but not all of them: for example, discourse about colour may satisfy Mark 3, but not marks 1, 2 and 4. What this means is that the shape of the debate between realism and antirealism is far more messy than Dummett conceived. At the realist end of the spectrum, there will be discourses whose sentences have objective truth-conditions, in the senses of "objective" given by each of marks 1–4. And at the antirealist end of the spectrum there will be discourses that fail to satisfy any of the various marks of realism, which have truth-conditions that are not objective in any of the senses defined by these marks. But in between there will be many discourses that satisfy some of the marks, but not all, which may possess objective truth-conditions in some of the senses defined by the marks, but not all.[25]

On Wright's conception of the realist/antirealist debate, then, the debate has to proceed in a much more *piecemeal* fashion than that envisaged by Dummett.[26]

9.6 Two threats of quietism

That, then, is an outline of Wright's conception of the general shape of the realist/antirealist debate. This conception of the shape of metaphysical debate is threatened by *quietism*, which is the view that "significant metaphysical debate is impossible". Quietism threatens to close down metaphysical debate in two ways, one direct, one indirect.

The *direct* route to quietism proceeds via Wittgenstein's rule-following considerations. As we saw above, Wright believes that the rule-following considerations endanger the objectivity of meaning, the view that "the meaning of a statement is a real constraint, to which we are bound ... by contract, and to which verdicts about its truth-value may objectively conform, quite independently of our considered opinion on the matter". The meaning of a statement imposes requirements on what counts as correct use of the statement, which, once they are in place, determine which uses are correct and incorrect independently of any opinions we may subsequently form. The problem is that if the rule-following considerations destroy the idea that meanings are objective in this sense, they thereby threaten the various ways in which antirealists attempt to draw comparisons concerning objectivity. For example, we saw in section 9.4 that objectivity of truth implies objectivity of meaning. If a global rejection of objectivity of meaning is forced by the rule-following considerations, then so will a global rejection of objectivity of truth. And if no discourses possess objectivity of truth, appealing to failure of objectivity of truth will be useless for drawing metaphysical comparisons between discourses. Likewise, since the truth of any statement is a function of its meaning together with facts about the world (see section 5.3), rejection of objectivity of meaning may entail that *all* predicates are judgement-dependent. The possibility of appealing to the judgement-independent/judgement-dependent distinction in order to draw a metaphysical contrast between discourses will be endangered. In short, the rule-following considerations seem to threaten us with quietism about objectivity: the view that no principled, metaphysically interesting contrasts between grades of objectivity can be drawn.

Antirealists try to find ways of avoiding quietism, while retaining their interpretation of the rule-following considerations.[27] But we should note that some philosophers, such as McDowell, think that there is a different, *indirect*, way in which quietism can close down metaphysical debate. As we saw above, McDowell does not view the rule-following considerations as threatening the objectivity of meaning. So the metaphysical relevance of the various marks of truth, such as verification-transcendence and judgement-independence, is not threatened in the direct manner envisaged in the previous paragraph. The distinctions the antirealist wishes to draw can still be drawn: instead, the rule-following considerations are taken to threaten the idea that there is any interesting metaphysical *point* to be made by appealing to the distinctions in the first place. For example, it might be argued that the metaphysical relevance of Wright's judgement-independent/judgement-dependent distinction depends upon a conception of detecting or tracking facts

301

that the rule-following considerations actually display to be untenable. The idea would be that the distinction depends upon a notion of detection or tracking reminiscent of the "master-thesis" discussed in section 6.7: we can only think of ourselves as detecting or tracking facts of states of affairs that just "stand there", which are normatively inert. Wright would be interpreted as arguing that since facts about meanings are not normatively inert (they sustain substantial, *a priori* relations to facts about correct use), we cannot think of ourselves as detecting or tracking them, and must instead view them as judgement-dependent. McDowell would argue that once this notion of detection or tracking has been rejected, as it must be if we are to avoid losing our grip on the notion of normativity of meaning altogether, the judgement-independent/judgement-dependent distinction loses its metaphysical bite, since it was a distinction between discourses in which our best judgements play a tracking or detecting role and discourses in which such judgements play a constitutive role.

The issue of whether antirealists can block these two threats of quietism about metaphysics and objectivity is complex and difficult. For one thing, it depends on getting clear about the proper implications of Wittgenstein's reaction to KW's sceptical paradox about rule-following (section 6.7). It also depends on getting clearer about the precise formulation of the "marks of realism" discussed in section 9.5. But it is very much a *live* issue, and represents perhaps the most interesting question concerning the relationship between meaning and metaphysics facing philosophers of language as the twentieth century draws to a close.

Further reading

For recent attempts to defend noncognitivism against the Frege–Geach problem, see S. Blackburn, *Spreading the word*, Chapters 5 and 6, and A. Gibbard, *Wise choices, apt feelings*, Chapter 5. For an overview of the difficulties faced by noncognitivism, see B. Hale, "Can there be a logic of attitudes?", in J. Haldane and C. Wright (eds), *Reality, representation, and projection*.

Dummett's writings are extensive and difficult. A clear account of the general project can be found in the introduction to *The logical basis of metaphysics* (though the rest of this book is extremely tough). Relevant papers are "Truth", "Realism", "The philosophical basis of intuitionistic logic", and "The reality of the past", all reprinted in Dummett's *Truth and other enigmas*, and "What is a theory of meaning?(II)", reprinted in his *The seas of language*. Important articles critical of Dummett include John McDowell's "On the reality of the past", in C. Hookway and P. Pettit (eds), *Action and interpretation*, and "Anti-realism and the epistemology of understanding", in J. Parret and H. Bouveresse (eds), *Meaning and understanding*. Perhaps the best place to start on Dummett, and on antirealism generally, is the introduction to Wright's collected papers, *Realism, meaning, and truth* (in which he also responds to some of McDowell's criticisms). Wright's own conception of the shape of the realist/ antirealist debate is developed in his *Truth and objectivity*: the first five chapters of this are devoted to developing the "marks of realism" discussed in section 9.5, and the sixth chapter contains an extensive discussion of the threats of quietism discussed in section 9.6.

Notes

Chapter 1. Frege: Semantic value and reference

1. Note that in this chapter and the next I have concentrated on presenting the core of Frege's philosophy of language in a simple and straightforward manner. Frege's system is enormously complicated, and no short presentation can do justice to the complexities that detailed exegesis would involve. Forced between presenting Frege's views in a short and accessible manner and respecting the texts down to the last letter, I have opted for the former. Those wishing to follow up exegetical questions should consult the works listed under further reading for Chapter 2.

2. Although other philosophers and logicians – such as Boole – contributed to the invention of modern logic, Frege is usually viewed as its most important founding father. Note that Frege's logical *notation* is much more cumbersome than the standard notation taught nowadays and used in this book (though nothing turns on this difference for our purposes).

3. Note, though, that Frege himself would not have appealed to modal notions – such as necessity and possibility – in explaining validity. This is because of views he held about the nature of logic, which we needn't concern ourselves with here.

4. The great advantage of Frege's logic is its capacity to deal with relational predicates, as well as one-place predicates. This is displayed in the Fregean formalization of (13). See E. J. Lemmon, *Beginning logic*, Chapters 3 and 4.

5. We would actually have to complicate matters just a little more by including brackets in the vocabulary and rules governing them among the syntactical rules. But we can afford to ignore these complications for present purposes.

6. This is often translated as "reference" or "meaning". I have chosen the technical term "semantic value" in place of these, since Frege's notion has a precise definition that applies to types of expression (e.g. predicates) we would not normally take as referring to anything in the ordinary sense of reference. I have altered passages from Frege quoted in the text accordingly, and have signalled this by the use of square brackets.

7. For ease of reference, all of Frege's theses are listed in an appendix at the end of Chapter 2.

8. This probably explains in part why Frege's term *Bedeutung* is often translated as "reference". But, as noted above, this is best avoided, since it makes the idea that the notion of *Bedeutung* can be applied to predicates, for example, seem quite odd, when in fact it is no odder than its application to names.

9. G. Frege, "On sense and meaning", p. 63.

10. We need to distinguish between the notion of an ordered pair and the notion of a *set*, represented by the use of curly brackets { , }. Roughly, a set is a collection of objects, where the order of the objects is irrelevant to the identity of the set. Thus, {1, 2} is the *same* set as {2, 1}. In the case of an ordered pair (represented by normal brackets), the order does matter. So, for example, (1, 2) is a different ordered pair from (2, 1). *Mutatis mutandis* for ordered triples, etc.

11. G. Frege, "Function and concept", p. 24.

12. Note that we have distinguished between *functional expressions*, which are linguistic items (such as predicates), and *functions*, which, according to Frege, are extra-linguistic, abstract entities. Thus, the semantic value of a functional expression is a function. See the section which follows.

13. Rather than long-windedly speaking of the extension of the function that a functional expression stands for, in the text I have simply spoken of the extension of a functional expression. Two functional expressions have the same extension, if the functions they stand for have the same extension.

14. Note that Frege himself – for reasons that needn't concern us

here – would have demurred from this: see M. Dummett, *Frege: philosophy of language*, p.209. I gloss over this here in order to keep things simple (see *n*. 1).

15. This displays how Frege gives a systematic account of meaning in both of the senses distinguished in the Preface: theses 1–7 provide part of a systematic theory of meaning in the "informal" sense, and we now see how they can be used as a basis for a systematic theory of meaning in the "formal" sense.

16. Note that thesis 6 allows us to simplify things: we can specify the semantic values of incomplete expressions by specifying their extensions (that is, the extensions of the functions that they stand for). Note also that we don't need a separate axiom giving the extension of the universal quantifier, since this is taken care of by the second half of compositional axiom 3.

17. As an exercise, the reader should attempt to derive statements of the truth-conditions of the other two sentences we looked at.

Chapter 2. Frege and Russell: sense and definite descriptions

1. Without giving up these theses, that is, as applied to cases where belief contexts and the like are not involved. To anticipate, Frege introduces the notion of sense, and then formulates thesis 15 to deal with the special case of sentences involving belief contexts.

2. Contexts, such as "believes that ...", that appear to threaten thesis 3, are known as intensional contexts. Other examples of intensional contexts are "wishes that ..." and "It is necessarily the case that ...".

3. Note that there is a hidden premise here: if S knows the reference of "a" and the reference of "b", and if the reference of "a" is in fact identical to the reference of "b", then S knows that the reference of "a" is identical to the reference of "b". Is this plausible? Can you think of a possible situation in which the antecedent is true and the consequent is false? Also, the argument in the text is for the specific case of proper names, but it should be clear enough how it generalizes to the cases of sentences and predicates.

4. G. Frege, "On sense and meaning", p.58.

5. There are some problems here, which we cannot pause to discuss. For example, all logically true sentences have the same truth-condition, so it would follow that they have the same sense.

6. M. Dummett, *Frege: philosophy of language*, p.91.

7. *Ibid*., p.93.

8. *Ibid*.

9. G. Frege, *The foundations of arithmetic*, p.x.
10. Frege, "On sense and meaning", pp.60–61.
11. J. Locke, *An essay concerning human understanding*, III, ii, 2.
12. Some Locke scholars have denied that ideas are mental images for Locke, but the case against them seems to me to be pretty conclusive. See G. McCulloch, *The mind and its world*, Chapter II. For the opposing point of view, see J. Yolton, *Perceptual acquaintance from Descartes to Reid*.
13. J. Locke, *Essay*, II, x, 5.
14. The argument is cryptically stated in section 26 of Frege, *The foundations of arithmetic*. It is developed by G. McCulloch in Chapter III of *The mind and its world*, and I follow McCulloch's excellent exposition in what follows. I should point out, however, that I try to squeeze a stronger conclusion out of the argument than McCulloch. McCulloch uses the argument to discredit Locke's theory of communication, but he thinks that it leaves open the possibility of a view which "takes over the bulk of Frege's theories of sense and reference, [which uses the theory of reference to explain communication], but which uses Lockean ideas to do the jobs earmarked for sense" (pp.74–5). McCulloch goes on to develop arguments along Wittgensteinian lines against this sort of position. The argument I now give in the text suggests that the original Fregean argument actually provides us with the resources to mount an attack on Locke's view, construed as an account of sense, and so can be used to supplement the Wittgensteinian arguments that McCulloch goes on to develop.
15. Frege, "On sense and meaning", p.59.
16. Locke, *Essay*, II, xxxii, 15.
17. Note that we would have to widen the initial inversion hypothesis to take care of things like "Yellow is more like white than is blue", and so on. But there seems to be no good reason why such a widening cannot in principle be carried out.
18. Locke, *Essay*, II, xxx, 15.
19. For further attacks on the Lockean account of sense, see section 5.1.
20. The issues about objectivity and normativity are not independent. Both are essential facets of Frege's opposition to *psychologism*, the doctrine that logic is a branch of empirical psychology. Viewing sense as a matter of the possession of mental images is obviously a slide in the direction of psychologism, since sense determines semantic value, which in turn determines whether or not logical inferences are valid. Frege's point is that this sort of view of sense, in addition to failing to accommodate its objectivity, would also fail

to accommodate its essential normativity: the laws of logic would become laws of a descriptive science, psychology, rather than normative laws of thought.

21. Frege, "On sense and meaning", p.60.
22. *Ibid.*, p.58.
23. *Ibid.*
24. For example, Russell's theory of definite descriptions (see section 2.7), a paradigm example of analytic philosophy, would not have been possible if Frege's symbolic logic had not been invented.
25. It is especially ironic that this should be an apparent consequence of views held by someone dubbed "the founder of analytic philosophy"!
26. The issues concerning sense and analysis are obviously considerably more complicated than I imply here. For a full discussion see M. Beaney, *Frege: making sense*.
27. Frege, *The foundations of arithmetic*, p.x.
28. Dummett, *Frege: philosophy of language*, p.268.
29. G. Evans, *The varieties of reference*, p.24.
30. *Ibid.*, p.23.
31. In fact, Evans argues for an interpretation of Frege on which he is not literally advancing thesis 13. See especially section 1.6 of *The varieties of reference*. The issues here are complicated and, needless to say, extremely controversial. Note that Frege may try to get round this problem by assigning bearerless names an arbitrary object – the number zero, say – as their semantic value. But this is highly problematic. As G. McCulloch puts it "from the point of view of the meaning-theorist's enterprise, there is an evident problem in reaching for the logician's technical solution of supplying some arbitrary object as semantic value. For a semantic representation which has it that 'The present King of France' is not about a man, or someone who rules France, but instead concerns some arbitrary object like zero, has surely lost all contact with linguistic reality" (*The game of the name*, p.46).
32. This contrasts with Frege himself, who held that arithmetic is analytic.
33. Some philosophers have tried to avoid this problem by widening the sense-giving description, so that it becomes a large disjunction of all of the properties commonly attributed to the putative bearer. See J. Searle "Proper names". Kripke responds that this suggestion falls to essentially the same objection: it will still be at best a contingent truth that the bearer has any of the properties mentioned in the disjunction. See *Naming and necessity*, p.62. For Searle's reply, see his *Intentionality*, pp.242–61.

34. Dummett, *Frege: philosophy of language*, pp. 98–9; see also Evans, *The varieties of reference*, p.18.

35. It should be noted that, in addition to the problems outlined, Frege faces further problems stemming from the fact that he sees senses as abstract objects: they are neither physical, nor mental, and subsist in what he calls "the third realm". Given that senses are abstract, there is no possibility of our coming into causal contact with them, so how can we ever know anything about them?

36. Evans, *The varieties of reference*, pp. 25–6.

37. Does not this show that a systematic theory of sense – of truth-conditions – does not require us to ascribe senses to the subsentential expressions of the language with which it deals, since the senses of sentences are generated purely on the basis of axioms spelling out the *semantic values* of the subsentential expressions? This would be a mistake. The axioms specify the semantic values of the subsentential expressions, but they must specify them in a way that reflects how they are determined by the senses the competent speakers of the language associate with them. The idea is that the axioms of the semantic theory display the senses of the subsentential expressions, even though they do not explicitly state them. Dummett puts the point as follows: "In the case in which we are concerned to convey, or stipulate, the sense of an expression, we shall choose the means of stating what the referent [semantic value] is which displays the sense; we might here borrow a famous pair of terms from the *Tractatus*, and say that, for Frege, we say what the referent [semantic value] of a word is, and thereby show what its sense is" (*Frege: philosophy of language*, p.227). See also Evans, *The varieties of reference*, pp. 25–7.

38. Dummett, *Frege: philosophy of language*, p.84.

39. So, the following all give correct accounts of the truth-conditions of the sentences quoted:
"Fido is a dog" is true iff Fido is a dog
"Fido is a dog" is true iff Fido is a cur
"Fido is a cur" is true iff Fido is a dog
"Fido is a cur" is true iff Fido is a cur.

40. This shows how (17), (18), and (19) are connected: it tells us why, for example, (17) might be the answer to (18), or a report that (19) has been obeyed.

41. See, for example, Dummett, *Frege: philosophy of language*, p.95, where he explicitly speaks of force as an ingredient in meaning, alongside sense and tone. For criticism of Dummett's conception of the role of force, see C. McGinn, "Semantics for non-indicative sentences".

42. Note, though, that when I utter (17) in the example just outlined, I also perform the speech-act of asserting that Jones is an efficient administrator, because of the sentence-meaning of (17). This shows that it is possible to perform more than one speech-act (and even more than one type of speech-act) by means of a single utterance.

43. Note the direction of explanation here: an account of sentence-meaning is given, and this is then used as input in an explanation of speaker's-meaning. Many philosophers think that the order of explanation should actually be the reverse of this: the notion of speaker's-meaning should be elucidated first, and the notion of sentence-meaning then elucidated in terms of it. This issue will be discussed in Chapter 7.

44. Note that it is important that we take the predicate to be " ... is *a* king of France". If we took it as " ... is *the* King of France" we would be using the very notion we are attempting to analyze.

45. Note that Russell is therefore misdescribing the conclusion of his theory of descriptions when he claims that it entails that a description does not possess "any significance on its own account". On Russell's theory, descriptions do possess significance on their own account, by having second-level functions, rather than objects, as their semantic values. See McCulloch, *The game of the name*, p.65, fn. 8. This will be important in what follows.

46. B. Russell, *Introduction to mathematical philosophy*, p.178.

47. B. Russell, "The philosophy of logical atomism", p.201.

48. B. Russell, "On denoting", p.48.

49. Note that Russell uses slightly different terminology. The case where the description has wide scope with respect to the negation operator described by Russell is one in which the description has a "primary occurrence"; the case in which the description has narrow scope with respect to the negation operator is one in which it has a "secondary occurrence".

50. Russell, "On denoting", p.53.

51. Russell, "On denoting", p.50. Note that he uses "meaning" for "sense" and "denotation" for "semantic value".

52. Note that scope issues, of the sort discussed in section 2.8, also arise when definite descriptions appear in sentences that contain propositional attitude operators, such as "believes that ...". For example, the following would be a case in which the definite description has narrow scope with respect to "believes that ...":

(∗) One and only one man wrote *Fidelio* and Smith believes that that man had cirrhosis of the liver.

Clearly, in this sort of case, the substitution of the definite description by another which in fact picks out the same individual will not result in a change in truth-value. If (∗) is true, so is

(∗∗) One and only one man wrote the Moonlight Sonata and Smith believes that that man had cirrhosis of the liver.

So substitutions of descriptions which pick out the same individual are fine, so long as the descriptions have wide scope (or primary occurrences) in the relevant sentences. Russell describes this by saying that his theory does not interfere with "verbal substitutions" of one description for another. Matters are different when a description has narrow scope, as in

(∗∗∗) Smith believes that one and only one man wrote *Fidelio* and that that man had cirrhosis of the liver.

See the discussion on p. 52 of Russell, "On denoting".

53. Perhaps the way forward here is to follow Frege in retaining a notion of sense – thereby allowing us to deal with the problems of substitution into belief contexts and informativeness – but to neutralize the problem of bearerless names by rejecting Frege's thesis 13 (an expression can have a sense even if it lacks a semantic value). See Evans, *The varieties of reference* for a similar strategy.

54. B. Russell, *The problems of philosophy*, pp.29–30.

55. *Ibid.*, p.30.

56. M. Sainsbury, "Philosophical logic", p.71.

57. M. Sainsbury, "Frege and Russell", p.670.

58. Recall that Frege appeared to get into trouble in his sense-based account of communication because he was willing to view the senses of proper names as given by descriptions. Given that taking senses as descriptions fails to deliver an adequate account of communication, and that Russell's attempt to account for communication without invoking sense at all also fails, this provides further impetus for the suggestion that we ought to retain the notion of sense for proper names and explain it otherwise than in terms of associated descriptions.

59. Note that in these two chapters our strategy has been as follows. We take a stretch of natural language, and our aim is to apply Frege's theory of semantic value to it. But in order to do this, we have to be able to translate it into the language of Frege's logical symbolism. But even though simple arguments can be translated into the formal language, what assurance do we have that all of the parts of language that we would intuitively take to be

significant can be so formulated? It should be pointed out that Frege thought this an impossible task in the case of natural language: his main interest was in the language of science and mathematics. But other philosophers have not shared Frege's pessimism over the prospects of applying his ideas to natural language: this is a point we'll return to (see Ch. 8).

Chapter 3. Sense and verificationism: logical positivism

1. A.J. Ayer, *Logical positivism*, p.11.
2. H. Hahn, "Logic, mathematics, and knowledge of nature", p.159.
3. For ease of exposition, I'll sometimes just speak of statements, rather than sentences expressing thoughts. So, for example, rather than speaking of "sentences which are literally meaningful in virtue of expressing empirically verifiable thoughts", I'll speak of "statements which are literally meaningful in virtue of being empirically verifiable".
4. A.J. Ayer, *Language, truth, and logic*, p.35. A "pseudo-proposition" is something which appears to express a genuine thought, but in fact expresses no thought.
5. *Ibid.*, p.35.
6. Someone might respond that these generalizations of the verification principle to commands, expressions of intention, expressions of desire, and so on, are too weak, since they seem to be satisfied by commands and expressions of intention concerning the absolute. For example, what about "Utter a sentence about the absolute!", "I, a metaphysician, intend to write a treatise on the Absolute"? If I say "The absolute is expanding at an ever increasing rate", or write a treatise called *The nature of the absolute*, haven't I observably obeyed the command, or implemented the intention, and doesn't this show that these sentences actually satisfy the generalized version of the verification principle? The answer is that it does not: the logical positivist can respond that you have not succeeded in obeying the command, or implementing the intention. Rather, you have only succeeded in uttering a sentence, or writing a treatise, *containing the word* "Absolute".
7. This generalized version of the verification principle arguably features in many philosophical arguments from the second half of the twentieth century: Wittgensteinian arguments against the possibility of private language, and antirealist arguments, in the style of Dummett, to mention but two. Perhaps this helps explain

Ayer's rather caustic remark in his autobiography that "the verification principle is seldom mentioned and when it is mentioned it is usually scorned; it continues, however, to be put to work. The attitude of many philosophers towards it reminds me of the relation between Pip and Magwitch in Dickens's *Great expectations*. They have lived on the money, but are ashamed to acknowledge its source."(*Part of my life*, p.156.)

8. Ayer, *Language, truth, and logic*, pp.38–9.

9. *Ibid.*, p.39.

10. Of course, for this implication, we need the assumption that mere facts about meaning cannot provide an adequate basis for answering the question one way rather than another. This is the analogue of the assumption, in the immediately preceding case, that the statement in question is not analytically true.

11. Ayer, *Language, truth, and logic*, p.13.

12. *Ibid.*

13. A. Church, Review of *Language, truth, and logic*, *Journal of Symbolic Logic* (1949).

14. The material in this section is more demanding than that of the rest of the chapter. Readers completely new to the philosophy of language may wish to skip the section, move directly to section 3.4, and return to the present chapter after reading Chapters 4 and 5.

15. J. Foster, *Ayer*, p.16.

16. *Ibid.*, p.17.

17. *Ibid.*, p.22.

18. *Ibid.*

19. *Ibid.*, p.27.

20. *Ibid.*, pp.29–30.

21. *Ibid.*, pp.28–9.

22. *Ibid.*, p.29.

23. *Ibid.*

24. For more on the distinction between constitutive and epistemological scepticism, see Chapters 4 and 5.

25. Ayer, *Language, truth, and logic*, p.78.

26. *Ibid.*, p.16.

27. *Ibid.*, p.72, emphasis added.

28. H. Hahn, "Logic, mathematics, and knowledge of nature", p.148.

29. Ayer, *Language, truth, and logic*, p.75.

30. *Ibid.*, pp.75–6.

31. *Ibid.*, p.82.

32. *Ibid.*, p.84.

33. *Ibid.*

34. *Ibid.*, p.85.
35. Hahn, "Logic, mathematics, and knowledge of nature", p.152.
36. *Ibid.*, p.153.
37. Ayer, *Language, truth, and logic*, p.86.
38. Hahn, "Logic, mathematics, and knowledge of nature", p.157.
39. Ayer, *Language, truth, and logic*, p.80.
40. B. Russell, "Logical positivism", p.367.
41. R. Carnap, "The old and the new logic", p.145.
42. W.V.O. Quine, "Truth by convention", p.351.
43. *Ibid.*, p.352.
44. Note that insofar as Quine's objection is levelled specifically against conventionalism about logic, it may leave scope for a conventionalist account of mathematics. We will have to use logic in deriving individual mathematical truths from the relevant general conventions, but this will not be circular as in the logical case.
45. R. Carnap, "Empiricism, semantics, and ontology", p.242.
46. *Ibid.*, p.245.
47. *Ibid.*, pp.250, 256.
48. C. Hookway, *Quine*, p.33.
49. Hookway writes as if he is unaware of Carnap's distinction between logical and factual frameworks, and as though once a framework has been chosen, all of the internal questions that can be raised within it are synthetic. Introducing the notion of a linguistic framework, he writes: "Each embodied a system of logical principles, and the terms employed in each were given meaning by analytic principles or 'meaning postulates' *linking claims employing them, directly or indirectly, to observational claims*" (*ibid.*, p.31, emphasis added). This suggests that he takes all frameworks to be factual: all internal questions are factual, and the analytic truths are themselves part of the framework. Again, this is a misinterpretation of Carnap: according to Carnap, the conventions composing the frameworks are neither analytic nor synthetic, the distinction between analytic and synthetic truths being drawn *within* the framework concerned.
50. Ayer, *Language, truth, and logic*, p.107, emphasis added.
51. *Ibid.*
52. *Ibid*, p.15.
53. *Ibid.*, p.107.
54. *Ibid.*, p.108.
55. Assuming, of course, that Ayer can provide a convincing response on behalf of logical positivism to the general problem of other minds. This is no easy task, obviously, but we can grant Ayer his

solution to the other minds problem at this point without jeopardizing the objection developed in the text.

56. Could Ayer respond here by claiming that ethical sentences serve to express natural (i.e. not specifically moral) forms of emotion? All Ayer would require in order to save the claim that ethical sentences possess genuine emotive significance would be a solution to the problem of other minds, which he is going to have to solve anyway. Assessing this suggestion would take us too far afield at this point, but it seems unlikely that it would be acceptable to Ayer. In Chapter VI of *Language, truth, and logic*, Ayer is content to use Moore's "open-question" argument against theories that attempt to define ethical symbols in naturalistic terms. It is plausible that the arguments Ayer uses against naturalistic cognitivism would carry over to apply to noncognitivist theories which attempt to view ethical sentences as expressing only natural (i.e. non-moral) sentiments.

57. Ayer, *Language, truth, and logic*, p.94.
58. *Ibid.*, p.95.
59. *Ibid.*
60. *Ibid.*

Chapter 4. Scepticism about sense (I): Quine on analyticity and translation

1. W.V.O. Quine, "Two dogmas of empiricism", pp.20–21.
2. *Ibid.*, p.20.
3. See Chapter 1, where we note that in Frege's logical language, the semantic value of a predicate is its extension, and expressions with the same semantic value can be intersubstituted *salva veritate*.
4. Quine, "Two dogmas of empiricism", p.30.
5. P. Grice & P. Strawson, "In defense of a dogma", p.146.
6. So called because it underlies the strategy adopted by Socrates in Plato's dialogues. For example, in *The republic* Socrates asks for explicit noncircular definitions of "good" and "justice".
7. Quine, "Two dogmas of empiricism", p.32.
8. Grice & Strawson, "In defense of a dogma", p.153.
9. Quine, "Two dogmas of empiricism", p.41.
10. *Ibid.*, p.42.
11. *Ibid.*, p.43.
12. Note that insofar as the distinction between linguistic and factual

components of a sentence corresponds to Frege's distinction between sense and semantic value, Frege's distinction is also endangered by Quine's argument here.

13. C. Wright, "Inventing logical necessity", p.192.
14. W. V. O. Quine, *Word and object*, p.27.
15. *Ibid.*, pp.29–30.
16. G. Evans, "Identity and predication", pp.27–8.
17. *Ibid.*, p.27.
18. *Ibid.*, p.25.
19. Quine, *Word and object*, p.68.
20. Note that to say that x satisfies "gavagai" is just to say that x is in the extension of "gavagai" (or that x is paired with the truth-value T in the extension of "gavagai").
21. I'm simplifying here somewhat. Technically, we ought to have an axiom spelling out the reference of the name "**a**", and a compositional axiom governing the coupling of names with predicates. But it should be obvious how the semantic theory described in the text can be extended to include these. I leave this as an exercise for the reader.
22. For a development of this idea see G. Evans's "Semantic theory and tacit knowledge". Note that when we speak of an object possessing a *disposition*, we could mean either (a) a *behavioural regularity* which that object exhibits, or (b) an *underlying state* of the object that *causally explains* the behavioural regularity in question. When we say that, for example, sugar is disposed to dissolve in water we could be referring either to the behavioural *regularity* (dissolving in water in standard conditions of temperature and pressure) that sugar displays; or we could be referring to some *underlying state* that sugar possesses and that explains *why* sugar exhibits the behavioural regularity in question. Evans makes it clear that he is working with the second, "full-blooded", notion of a disposition. The notion of a disposition is a very important and controversial one in many areas of contemporary philosophy, including philosophy of mind, philosophy of science, and metaphysics. For a comprehensive treatment, see Stephen Mumford, *Dispositions*.
23. For further discussion, see C. Hookway, *Quine*, esp. pp.155–62. There may be a case for thinking that Hookway has not described Evans's response as well as he might have. As noted in the text, Hookway says that according to Evans, acceptance of a theory of meaning containing (8) will involve the attribution to speakers of two dispositional states underlying their uses of "blap". We can then check empirically to see whether they actually have two such

dispositions, and see thereby whether the acceptance of the relevant theory of meaning is empirically justified. But maybe this is not the best way to frame Evans's response. In "Semantic theory and tacit knowledge" Evans's requirement is that *there be a disposition corresponding to each expression for which the theory provides a distinct axiom*. Now in the theory of meaning containing axiom (8) there is only one disposition corresponding to "blap" attributed to speakers: the disposition to assent to "Yo, blap gavagai" in the presence of undetached rabbit parts which are parts of white animals, and "Yo, blap x" for "x" other than "gavagai" when x is white. So on Evans's account, the acceptance of the theory containing (8) requires the attribution of only one disposition, the disposition described above, and not two dispositions as claimed by Hookway. But now the real problem with the acceptance of the theory containing (8) becomes apparent. As noted in the previous footnote, Evans is explicitly working with a full-blooded notion of a disposition, as an underlying state that causally explains the obtaining of a behavioural regularity. But what sort of unitary underlying state of a subject could underlie a "bifurcated" regularity like the regularity that corresponds to (8)? This is a difficult question to answer, but the onus is surely on Evans's opponent to spell out what sort of state could underly a disposition like that which corresponds to (8).

24. W. V. O. Quine, "On the reasons for the indeterminacy of translation", p.178.
25. *Ibid.*, p.179.
26. *Ibid.*
27. *Ibid.*, p.181.
28. Quine, "On the reasons for the indeterminacy of translation", p.180.
29. See Hookway, *Quine*, p.203, and passim for much useful discussion of Quine's realism about physics.
30. N. Chomsky, "Quine's empirical assumptions", p.67.
31. R. Kirk, *Translation determined*, p.136.
32. Hookway, *Quine*, p.137.
33. Kirk, *Translation determined*, p.143.
34. *Ibid.*
35. *Ibid.*, p.145.
36. *Ibid.*, p.146. Of course, Quine cannot appeal at this point to the claim that translation of the lower-level theoretical sentences is indeterminate: Fred does not accept that the lower-level sentences are undetermined by possible observations, so the argument from above has to grant him the idea that they have determinate translations.

37. S. Kripke, *Wittgenstein on rules and private language*, p.56.
38. This is especially important, given the manifest inadequacies of behaviourist philosophies of mind and psychology. For an account of the standard objections to behaviourism, see P. Carruthers, *Introducing persons*.
39. Note that I have concentrated here on Quine's views, as presented in only three works: "Two dogmas of empiricism", *Word and object* and "On the reasons for the indeterminacy of translation". Readers should note, though, that this is really only a snapshot of three very important time slices of Quine's work. For Quine's latest views, see his *The pursuit of truth*.

Chapter 5. Scepticism about sense (II): Kripke's Wittgenstein's sceptical paradox

1. Kripke is careful not to present this as straightforward exegesis of Wittgenstein. He writes that "the present [work] should be thought of as expounding neither 'Wittgenstein's' argument nor 'Kripke's': rather Wittgenstein's argument as it struck Kripke, as it presented a problem for him"(*Wittgenstein on rules and private language*, p.5). In what follows I'll just speak of "Kripke's Wittgenstein", and abbreviate this by "KW". For an alternative interpretation of Wittgenstein, see section 6.7.
2. Note that KW, like Quine, is arguing for a constitutive scepticism via an epistemological route. See section 4.7.
3. Kripke says that the problem is set up in this way, with respect to past meanings, in order to enable the sceptic intelligibly to formulate his argument at all – the sceptic at this point does not call our present meanings into question, so that he can present his sceptical argument to us: "Before we pull the rug out from under our own feet, we begin by speaking as if the notion that at present we mean a certain function ... is unquestioned and un-questionable. Only past usages are to be questioned. Otherwise, we will be unable to formulate our problem"(*Wittgenstein on rules and private language*, pp.13–14). Of course, once the sceptical conclusion has been established with respect to past meanings, it can be generalized to encompass present meanings too, for we can always imagine ourselves running the sceptical argument tomorrow about what we presently mean by the "+" sign.
4. S. Kripke, *Wittgenstein on rules and private language*, pp.8–9.
5. Note that although KW's argument has obvious affinities with Quine's argument from below for the indeterminacy of translation,

it is much stronger than Quine's argument, insofar as it allows us access to a wider range of facts in our search for the facts that constitute meaning. Quine rules out an appeal to facts of the sort mentioned in (b) from the start, whereas KW's argument is that even if we suppose ourselves to have idealized epistemic access to these sorts of fact, we will still be unable to find a fact that can constitute our meaning one thing rather than another.

6. Kripke, *Wittgenstein on rules and private language*, p.15.
7. *Ibid.*, p.16.
8. L. Wittgenstein, *Philosophical investigations*, section 198.
9. Here I am merely summarizing the rich battery of arguments that Colin McGinn, drawing extensively on Wittgenstein's texts, develops against the suggestion that understanding might be constituted by the occurrence of mental images, etc. See McGinn's *Wittgenstein on meaning*, pp.1–7, for some excellent exposition. See also the Fregean argument that is developed against Locke's imagist theory of meaning in section 2.3 of the present work.
10. Kripke, *Wittgenstein on rules and private language*, p.51.
11. *Ibid.*, p.37.
12. The passages from Wittgenstein that inspired KW's conclusion to this effect are known as "the rule-following considerations". The notion of intending to follow a rule in a certain way is analagous to meaning something by a linguistic expression. Suppose I intend to follow the rule "add 2" when writing out the following arithmetical series: 2, 4, 6, 8, 9, 10 ... Intuitively, later on in the series, certain continuations (e.g. 24, 26, 28) are determined to be correct by the rule I am following, and certain continuations are determined to be incorrect by that rule (e.g. 34, 35, 37). This is the analogue of the applications of a predicate being determined as correct or incorrect by the sense of the predicate. Just as KW will claim, of a predicate, that there are no facts of the matter as to which applications are correct and which are incorrect, he will also claim that there are no facts of the matter as to which continuations of the arithmetical series are correct or incorrect. Recall that in section 2.4 we said that generally, the sense of an expression could be thought of as a rule for determining its semantic value: this shows how KW's scepticism applies to Frege's notion of sense.
13. Kripke, *Wittgenstein on rules and private language*, p.22.
14. Talk of a "sceptical solution" is a direct reference to Hume. Kripke takes Hume to be arguing that, for example, there are no facts in virtue of which statements about causal relations are true or false, but as attempting to neutralize this conclusion by arguing that

such statements can be viewed as having some legitimate non-fact-stating role.

15. The reference is to Dummett's paper, "Wittgenstein's philosophy of mathematics".

16. Wittgenstein, *Philosophical investigations,* section 258.

17. *Ibid.,* section 202.

18. Kripke attempts to use these remarks in an exegesis of Wittgenstein's famous "private language argument". But the issues about the relationship between arguments against solitary language (a language that is in fact spoken only by a solitary individual) and arguments against private language (a language that is necessarily unintelligible to everyone except its speaker) are very complicated. See Crispin Wright, "Does PI 258–60 suggest a cogent argument against private language?", for some useful discussion.

19. For a useful survey of criticisms of the first type, see Boghossian's "The rule-following considerations", section III.

20. Boghossian's arguments can be found in "The rule-following considerations", section IV, and "The status of content".

21. The view that sentences of a certain discourse do not possess truth-conditions is called nonfactualism with respect to that discourse, since it amounts to the claim that there are no possible facts in virtue of which the sentences of that discourse might be true or false. Given the assumption that the sense of a sentence is its truth-condition, nonfactualism about meaning thus amounts to the claim that sentences ascribing meanings (truth-conditions) to other sentences do not themselves possess truth-conditions.

22. P. Boghossian, "The rule-following considerations", p.526.

23. Note that (1) is really just a reformulation of (2): to say that there is no property corresponding to the predicate "has truth-condition p" is just to say that there is no property in virtue of the instantiation (or non-instantiation) of which the sentence "S has truth-condition p" is true (or false). Which is just to say that "S has truth-condition p" – an ascription of meaning to a sentence – does not itself possess truth-conditions.

24. C. Wright, "Kripke's account of the argument against private language", p.769.

25. *Ibid.,* p.770. To say that a statement is projective is just to say that it has a non-fact-stating role.

26. Boghossian, "The rule-following considerations", p.525.

27. Kripke, *Wittgenstein on rules and private language,* p.38.

28. *Ibid.*

29. In fact, Wright, "Kripke's account of the argument against private language", p.773 *n*.5, shows that this rebuttal of the simplicity suggestion begs the question because it *assumes* nonfactualism about ascriptions of meaning, a thesis which, at the relevant stage in the dialectic, is still up for proof. But this point, of course, does not damage the application of the objection to the sceptical solution itself, for there we are *ex hypothesi* assuming the conclusion of the sceptical argument.
30. J. Zalabardo, "Rules, communities, judgements", p.36.
31. *Ibid.*, p.39.
32. Wright, "Kripke's account ...", p.770.
33. It seems to me that the only way KW can avoid the argument of the present section is to give an account of the meaning of ascriptions of meaning along *noncognitivist* lines (see section 9.2). This would interpret judgements about meaning as expressing *attitudes* (perhaps confidence that other speakers will give the same answers as oneself), in much the same way that ethical noncognitivists view moral judgements as expressing noncognitive attitudes rather than beliefs. The assertability conditions would then not be viewed as constituting the truth-conditions of ascriptions of meaning: the semantic function of such ascriptions would be viewed as that of expressing attitudes, rather than stating facts, so that the first horn of Zalabardo's dilemma would be avoided. And the second horn would be avoided because although we would not be attempting to capture the sense of ascriptions of meaning in terms of truth-conditions, we would be attempting to capture their sense by viewing them as having a different semantic function, that of expressing attitudes. There seems to be no reason why viewing KW as a noncognitivist in this sense would affect the argument against the possibility of solitary language: the claim against solitary language would be recast as the claim that in such a language there would be no distinction between the conditions under which Jones expresses confidence that he means addition by "+" and the conditions under which such confidence would be rightfully expressed. Having said that, however, viewing KW as such a noncognitivist does little to make the sceptical solution more palatable, given the long list of worries and problems faced by noncognitive theories in other areas. For a resume of such problems, see Bob Hale, "Can there be a logic of attitudes?".

Chapter 6. Saving sense: responses to the sceptical paradox

1. The term "propositional attitude" was coined by Bertrand Russell. It is relatively easy to see the reason for this term. A belief consists in taking a certain sort of attitude (the "belief-attitude") to a proposition or thought: so having the belief that Scotland will win the next World Cup consists in taking the "belief-attitude" to the proposition *that Scotland will win the next World Cup*. Likewise, having a desire to win the National Lottery consists in taking the "desire-attitude" to the proposition that you win the National Lottery, and so on. The "aboutness" of propositional attitudes is sometimes described as "intentionality". See Tim Crane, *The mechanical mind*, pp. 31–40, for a discussion.

2. Note that this only follows if the explanation in question is a *genuine* one. Obviously, if the notion of responsibility is only *apparently* explained by the notion of free will, the conclusion that the notion of responsibility is incoherent will not force the conclusion that the notion of free will is incoherent. But this is not relevant to the question at hand: we are asking what follows from KW's argument against linguistic meaning given the assumption that the Gricean explanation of the relationship between thought and language is a *genuine* one.

3. P. Boghossian, "The rule-following considerations", p.510. Colin McGinn disagrees with this claim of Boghossian's, and argues that KW's sceptical paradox cannot even be formulated at the level of mental content. It turns out that this is based on McGinn's, mistaken conception of the normativity of meaning (see section 6.5 and "The rule-following considerations", pp. 509–14).

4. P. Boghossian, "The status of content", p.171.

5. Given the conclusion of this section – that KW's arguments are of a completely general nature, applying both to linguistic items and to mental states – I won't be fastidious about distinguishing between mental content and linguistic meaning in the remainder of the chapter.

6. P. Boghossian, "The rule-following considerations", p.529.

7. *Ibid.*, p.539.

8. *Ibid.*, p.540.

9. *Ibid.*

10. *Ibid.*

11. See Lewis's paper "Radical interpretation" for this sort of story.

12. See the further reading section at the end of the chapter for references to Lewis. An extremely clear exposition of Lewis's method can be found in Chapter 2 of Michael Smith, *The moral problem*. I follow Smith's exposition in the text.

13. So, if the platitudes are "the property of redness causes us, under certain conditions, to have experiences of the property of redness" and "the property of redness is more similar to the property of orangeness than the property of blueness" and ..., T(x, y, z) will be "(x causes us, under certain conditions, to have experiences of x) & (x is more similar to y than z) & ...".

14. The right-hand side of this definition is known as the Ramsey Sentence for "red", after the British philosopher Frank Ramsey, who originated the Lewis style of reductive analysis.

15. P. Boghossian, "Naturalizing content", pp.90–91.

16. J. Fodor, *Psychosemantics*, p.97.

17. Note also that Fodor thinks that the problem should be discussed, not with respect to public language expressions, such as "horse" or "cow", but with respect to the expressions of a mental language, a language of thought, which he calls *mentalese*. In what follows, we will ignore this complication: for an account of Fodor's hypothesis that we think in mentalese, see his *The language of thought*, or for a quicker exposition, Chapter 4 of Tim Crane's *The mechanical mind*.

18. "Nomos" is the Greek word for "law", so to say that a sentence expresses a nomological truth is to say that the truth it expresses has an empirical, lawlike regularity.

19. Fodor argues convincingly against a range of suggestions as to how the optimal conditions should be cashed out: see his *A theory of content and other essays* (part I).

20. In fact, Fodor only claims to offer sufficient (rather than necessary *and* sufficient) conditions for meaning such and such in his asymmetric dependency account, but we can gloss over this for present purposes.

21. Crane, *The mechanical mind*, pp.180–81. Crane speaks of "mental representation" here, since he's discussing Fodor's views with respect to the expressions of mentalese (see *n.* 17). For our purposes, we can just read the talk of "mental representation" here as talk of "meaning".

22. Boghossian raises the worry that Fodor's asymmetric dependency account is after all just another version of the "optimal conditions" solution to KW's sceptical problem. If this is the case, the worries that we developed in sections 6.2–6.3 will apply even to Fodor's own attempted solution. See "Naturalizing content", pp.71–3.

23. For more on this aspect of Wittgenstein's views, see Chapter 1 of C. McGinn *Wittgenstein on meaning*, esp. pp.28–42.

24. L. Wittgenstein, *Philosophical investigations*, section 150.

25. *Ibid.*, section 199.

26. L. Wittgenstein, *Remarks on the foundations of mathematics*, p.344.

27. McGinn, *Wittgenstein on meaning*, p.173.

28. *Ibid.*, p.74.

29. *Ibid.*

30. S. Kripke, *Wittgenstein on rules and private language*, p.14.

31. Boghossian, "The rule-following considerations", p.513.

32. *Ibid.*

33. *Ibid.*, p.515.

34. *Ibid.*, p.516.

35. C. Wright, "Critical notice of McGinn's *Wittgenstein on meaning*", p.291.

36. *Ibid.*

37. McGinn, *Wittgenstein on meaning*, pp.169–70.

38. McGinn actually considers this rejoinder very briefly (*Wittgenstein on meaning*, p.174), and dismisses it as depending upon an "unargued reductionism" about capacities or abilities. But as we'll see in section 6.6, though the dismissal of unargued reductionism might be in order, it cannot by itself do the desired work against KW.

39. Wright, "Critical notice of McGinn", p.291. Of course, this is not to say that the Wittgensteinian point – that we should view understanding as akin to the possession of an ability – is *false*: it is just to say that even if true, it cannot *by itself* constitute an adequate response to KW's sceptical paradox. It seems to me that the objections against the capacity/ability account also apply to the "activity based model of understanding" suggested by Gregory McCulloch in *The mind and its world*, Chapter IV.

40. C. Wright, "Kripke's account of the argument against private language", p.774.

41. Kripke, *Wittgenstein on rules and private language*, p.51.

42. Of course, you may have to justify *why* you have it: but this is different from having to justify *that* you have it.

43. McGinn, *Wittgenstein on meaning*, pp.160–61.

44. Wright, "Critical Notice of McGinn", p.292. "Philosophical stone kicking", after Dr Johnson's infamous attempt to refute Berkeley's idealism by kicking a stone and saying, "I refute him thus". Wright's claim is that just as Johnson completely misses Berkeley's point, McGinn likewise misses Kripke's.

45. Wright argues that this problem is brought sharply into focus by Wittgenstein himself in some sections of the *Philosophical investigations*. See "On making up one's mind: Wittgenstein on intention" for the relevant sections.

46. The same goes for McGinn's nonreductionism about abilities and capacities (see section 6.5).

47. The exposition I give of Wright's account of judgement-dependence is necessarily concise: the reader should study carefully the papers by Wright mentioned in the section on further reading for detailed expositions and attempts to apply the conception in particular cases (such as discourse about shape, colour and morals).

48. Think about it: it would be no use taking it into a laboratory and illuminating it, or whatever, as this is more likely to *distort* the appearance of the colour it actually possesses. Conditions in which its physical microstructure is examined won't be better either. Suppose we find an object that looks red to suitable subjects in the ideal conditions specified, but with a microstructure different from that typically found in red things. What would we say: that the object isn't *really* red, or that we have discovered that there can be more than one physical basis for redness? It seems to me that we would say the latter (contrast this with a natural kind, such as gold). Note also that I'm simplifying somewhat: we need to say a bit more about what constitutes the "suitability" of a subject. See Wright, "Wittgenstein's rule-following considerations and the central project of theoretical linguistics", section III.

49. In a sense, Wright is attempting to construct a modern version of the distinction between primary and secondary qualities. Secondary qualities, like *redness*, will turn out to be judgement-dependent, while *primary* qualities, such as squareness, will turn out to be judgement-independent. So, in a way, Wright is attempting to respond to KW's sceptical paradox by viewing *means addition by "+"* as a sort of secondary quality.

50. The idea here is clear: redness is judgement-dependent, since there is a strong connection (*a priori*, nontrivial, etc.) between best opinion about redness and the facts about redness. Note that a specification of the C-conditions is trival if it formulates the conditions in such a way that they amount to the claim that the subject in question has "whatever it takes" to form the right opinion concerning, for example, redness. Plainly, the fact there is a *trivially* specified set of conditions under which best opinions covary with the facts tells us nothing interesting about redness: the covariance between best opinion and fact would be *a priori* for

any discourse, given such a trivial specification of the C-conditions. Also, the question as to whether the C-conditions are satisfied has to be logically independent of facts about redness, for the following reason. We want to claim that the facts about redness are *determined* by our best opinions about redness: but we'll lose this idea that the facts are dependent upon best opinion if the question as to whether a given opinion is best presupposes some fact or other about redness. This would make best opinion dependent upon the facts about redness, rather than vice versa.

51. As noted in Note 49, Wright argues that the conditions are satisfied in the case of colour discourse, but that they cannot be collectively satisfied in the case of discourse about shape.

52. Although Wright thinks that there are some worries about the nontriviality of the C-conditions – due to the presence of the clause ruling out self-deception – he also thinks that these can be satisfactorily dealt with. See "Wittgenstein's rule-following considerations ...", section IV.

53. J. Edwards, "Best opinion and intentional states", p.24.

54. Wright, "Wittgenstein's rule-following considerations ...", p.254.

55. For details of the other objections, see the further reading section for this chapter.

56. Boghossian, "The rule-following considerations", p.547.

57. See Wright's *Truth and objectivity*, pp.138–9.

58. Wright, "Critical notice of McGinn", p.305.

59. Wittgenstein, *Philosophical investigations*, section 124.

60. *Ibid.*, section 126.

61. *Ibid.*, section 119.

62. *Ibid.*, section 309.

63. *Ibid.*, section 254.

64. Note that Wittgenstein's conception of the role of philosophy is even more radical than that of the logical positivists (see section 3.4). According to the logical positivists, the questions of metaphysics are *pseudo-questions*; but even after these have been dispensed with, there is scope for constructive philosophical work in the form of *conceptual analysis*. According to the later Wittgenstein, philosophy doesn't even get as far as conceptual analysis: conceptual analysis only seems necessary because of our acceptance of a range of problematic assumptions, and once these assumptions have been dislodged, the need even for conceptual analysis falls away.

65. Wittgenstein, *Philosophical investigations*, section 654.

66. *Ibid.*, section 655.

67. *Ibid.*, section 217.

68. Wright, "Wittgenstein's rule-following considerations ...", p.246.
69. Wright, "Critical notice of McGinn", p.305.
70. J. McDowell, "Meaning and intention in Wittgenstein's later philosophy", p.51.
71. Wright, "Critical notice of McGinn", p.304.
72. Wittgenstein, *Philosophical investigations*, section 423.
73. Wright, quoted by McDowell in "Intentionality and interiority ...", p.163.
74. McDowell, "Meaning and intention in Wittgenstein's later philosophy", p.48.
75. *Ibid.*
76. McDowell, "Intentionality and interiority ...", pp.163–4.
77. McDowell, "Meaning and intention in Wittgenstein ...", p.41.
78. See Wittgenstein, *Philosophical investigations*, section 85.
79. McDowell, "Meaning and intention in Wittgenstein ...", p.41.
80. Wittgenstein, *Philosophical investigations*, section 201.
81. *Ibid.*
82. McDowell, "Meaning and intention in Wittgenstein ...", p.46.
83. *Ibid.*
84. *Ibid.*, p.49.
85. J. McDowell, *Mind and world*, postscript to Lecture V.
86. Needless to say, we cannot even begin to answer these extremely difficult questions here. The debate about Wittgenstein's contribution to the philosophy of meaning is one of the most hotly contested taking place in contemporary philosophy of language and mind, and we have only looked at some aspects of it in this section. See the further reading section for details.

Chapter 7. Sense, intention and speech-acts: Grice's programme

1. P.F. Strawson, "Meaning and truth", p.171.
2. *Ibid.*, p.172.
3. *Ibid.*, p.189.
4. J. Searle, "What is a speech-act?", pp.221–2.
5. P. Grice, "Meaning". p.217.
6. *Ibid.*, p.220.
7. We cannot go into the question as to the nature of convention here; but most Griceans take as their starting point the account developed in David Lewis's *Convention*.
8. P. Ziff, "On H. P. Grice's account of meaning", p.2.

9. Searle, "What is a speech-act?", pp.229–30.
10. *Ibid.*, p.230.
11. *Ibid.*, p.229.
12. *Ibid.*, pp.230–31.
13. M. Platts, *Ways of meaning*, p.91.
14. M. Davies, "Philosophy of language", p.97.
15. *Ibid.*
16. Platts, *Ways of meaning*, p.89.
17. *Ibid.*
18. *Ibid.*, p.90.
19. G. Evans, "Semantic theory and tacit knowledge", p.133.
20. C. Wright, "Theory of meaning and speaker's knowledge", pp. 227–8.
21. This difficulty would also afflict any attempt to view the states corresponding to semantic axioms as subdoxastic states, nonpropositional attitude states that nevertheless have informational content. The informational content in question would still have to be explicitly semantic. It is an interesting question whether the two difficulties we have developed can be dealt with by harnessing the Gricean account to Gareth Evans's account of the nature of the states corresponding to semantic axioms. On Evans's account, these states are neither propositional attitude states nor subdoxastic states, so that neither of our worries would apply. For a discussion of Evans's account, see A. Miller, "Tacit knowledge".
22. S. Blackburn, *Spreading the word*, p.128.
23. *Ibid*, pp.129–30.
24. E. Fricker, "Semantic structure and speaker's understanding", p.59.

Chapter 8. Sense and truth: Tarski and Davidson

1. G. Frege, *Grundgesetze*, I,32.
2. D. Davidson, *Inquiries into truth and interpretation*, p.24.
3. *Ibid.*, p.109.
4. *Ibid.*, p.20.
5. *Ibid.*, p.17.
6. See D. Davidson, *Inquiries ...*, pp.8–9, 18, 56.
7. This is the argument used against Quine in section 4.3: a theory of meaning that has an infinite number of semantic primitives, and which is therefore not finitely axiomatizable, will be in principle unlearnable. There are some worries – which we cannot go into

here – about whether Davidson really can answer (i), (ii) and (iii) by imposing the compositionality constraint on theories of meaning. For a discussion, see A. Miller, "Tacit knowledge" (i), (ii), and (iii) have also figured prominently in the work of Chomsky, which we cannot discuss in this book: see J. Lyons, *Chomsky*, for an overview.

8. In fact, there are some other, more arcane adequacy conditions that Davidson imposes, but we'll simply ignore these in what follows.

9. Davidson, *Inquiries ...*, pp.20–21.

10. M. Platts, *Ways of meaning*, p.53.

11. *Ibid.*

12. Davidson, *Inquiries ...*, pp.22–3.

13. A. Tarski, "The semantic conception of truth", p.344.

14. Tarski also imposes some conditions of "formal adequacy", designed to help avoid the semantic paradoxes. We won't consider these further conditions here. For an account of them, see the papers by Tarski listed in the section on further reading.

15. In actual fact, we would need to complicate matters a little here. As they stand, these clauses include bound variables within quotation marks: in order to avoid this, we should really use the spelling function and e.g. write $A^\wedge$"&"$^\wedge B$ instead of "A & B" (see Platts, *Ways of meaning*, Ch. 1).

16. For the generalization to the case of languages containing predicates of more than one place, see Platts, *Ways of meaning*.

17. As an exercise, the reader should attempt to show how the truth-conditions of the closed complex sentences in examples 1–3 are dependent on the semantic properties of their constituents, using instead the Fregean theory sketched in section 1.7.

18. Davidson, *Inquiries ...*, p.xiv.

19. Platts, *Ways of meaning*, pp.56–7.

20. Davidson, *Inquiries ...*, p.134.

21. *Ibid.*, p.141.

22. *Ibid.*, p.135.

23. *Ibid.*, p.142.

24. *Ibid.*, p.137.

25. Strangely, Platts writes (*Ways of meaning*, pp.58–67) as if Davidson is unaware of this problem, and suggests that Davidson will have to modify his theory along the lines suggested in J. McDowell, "Truth-conditions, bivalence, and verificationism", in order to deal with it. But as I hope I have shown, Davidson is actually acutely aware of the problem, and his solution to it takes us to the heart of his views on interpretation.

26. Davidson, *Inquiries* ..., p.xvii.
27. *Ibid.*, p.137.
28. C. Hookway, *Quine*, p.173.
29. Davidson, *Inquiries* ..., pp.153–4.
30. *Ibid.*, p.153.
31. *Ibid.*, p.125.
32. This is connected with Davidson's view that reference, as applied to subsentential expressions, has a purely instrumental role to play within the theory of meaning. See his "Reality without reference", in *Inquiries* .... See also H. Field, "Tarski's theory of truth", and J. McDowell, "Physicalism and primitive denotation", for an important exchange on this and related issues.
33. Davidson, *Inquiries* ..., p.125.
34. Hookway, *Quine*, p.174.
35. I leave it as an exercise to the reader to construct a similar story as to why theories of meaning containing (17) and (18) can be ruled out.
36. Davidson, *Inquiries* ..., p.136.

Chapter 9. Sense, objectivity and metaphysics

1. Note that in this chapter we will be concerned exclusively with issues about realism construed as issues about the objectivity of truth-conditions: we will not concern ourselves here with issues about realism construed as ontological issues about the existence of objects. Here we are concerned only with realism about, for example, mathematics construed as an issue about the objectivity of the truth-conditions of mathematical statements, not as an ontological issue about the existence of mathematical objects. For discussion of how these approaches to questions about realism are related, see the introduction to Wright's *Realism, meaning, and truth*, and his *Frege's conception of numbers as objects*.

2. Compare the strategy which the noncognitivist about morals adopts with that which is adopted in KW's sceptical solution (Ch. 5) concerning meaning.

3. Compare with the following argument:
   (a) It is raining; (b) if it is raining then the streets are wet; therefore, (c) the streets are wet.
   In this nonmoral case of *modus ponens*, why is this argument not similarly invalid in virtue of the fact that "It is raining" is asserted in (a), but not in (b)? The answer is of course that "It is raining" has the same truth-conditions as it appears in both (a) and (b): this

answer is not available to the noncognitivist in the case of examples of *modus ponens* involving moral premises.

4. For some recent noncognitivist accounts that make valiant efforts to solve the Frege–Geach problem, see S. Blackburn, *Spreading the word*, especially Chapters 5 and 6, and A. Gibbard, *Wise choices, apt feelings*. For a compelling summary of the difficulties they face, see B. Hale, "Can there be a logic of attitudes?".

5. Actually, James *VII* (of Scotland). But I refrain from correcting Wright's historical error in the text!

6. C. Wright, *Truth and objectivity*, p.4.

7. Note again that this form of opposition to realism does not involve the claim that the sentences of D are not truth-apt: so it can avoid the Frege–Geach problem that afflicts noncognitivism. Note also that there is a lot of debate about what it means to say that the truth of a sentence is not verification-transcendent. Does this mean that the sentence can be verified by us as we actually are? by someone, somewhere, as they actually are? by someone, somewhere, given some suitable idealization of their present cognitive powers? And what is permissible as a "suitable idealization"? And how can the notion of effective decidability (cf. section 9.4) be extended from the mathematical case to the empirical domain? These questions must be answered if antirealism is to have any determinate content. See Wright's *Realism, meaning, and truth*, p.32.

8. See E. Lepore (ed.), *Truth and interpretation: perspectives on the philosophy of Donald Davidson*, p.307.

9. G. Frege, "The thought ...", p.30.

10. Wright, *Realism, meaning, and truth*, p.13.

11. *Ibid.*, p.15.

12. *Ibid.*, p.17.

13. *Ibid.*, p.5.

14. *Ibid.*

15. *Ibid.*

16. J. McDowell, "Anti-realism and the epistemology of understanding", p.248.

17. This is greatly oversimplified: for more detail, see Wright's *Realism, meaning, and truth*, section v, and *Truth and objectivity*, Chapter 2, where he suggests that for certain discourses, truth may be modelled on "superassertibility". For another attempt to construe truth as essentially epistemically constrained, see H. Putnam, *Realism, truth, and history*.

18. The issues here are complex. See Wright's "Anti-realism and revisionism" and "Realism, bivalence, and classical logic", in his *Realism, meaning, and truth*.

19. See M. Dummett, *Truth and other enigmas*, p.xxx. This might seem puzzling. Suppose that the principle of bivalence corresponds to the law of excluded middle: $\vdash P \vee -P$, and that the principle of *tertium non datur* corresponds to $\vdash - - (P \vee -P)$ (is not the case that neither P nor not-P). Since it is a logically valid sequent that $- - P \vdash P$, doesn't it follow that rejecting $\vdash P \vee -P$ entails the rejection of $\vdash - - (P \vee -P)$, that is, that rejection of the principle of bivalence entails rejection of the principle of *tertium non datur*? The crucial point is that the sequent $- - P \vdash P$ that licenses this entailment is valid in classical logic *but not valid in intuitionistic logic*. Rejection of bivalence entails rejection of *tertium non datur* only given classical logic; but the Dummett-style antirealist *rejects* classical logic, and so can reject bivalence whilst holding on to *tertium non datur*.

20. M. Dummett, *The logical basis of metaphysics*, p.12.

21. Perhaps the clearest statement of Dummett's general approach to metaphysics can be found in the introduction to *The logical basis of metaphysics*. For criticism, see section 2 of S. Blackburn, "Metaphysics", in E. James and N. Bunnin (eds), *The Blackwell companion to philosophy*.

22. Dummett, *The logical basis of metaphysics*, p.3.

23. Wright, *Truth and objectivity*, p.9.

24. So minimalism about truth-aptness simply undercuts the possibility of noncognitivism, which denies that the sentences are truth-apt. There has been some debate about the relationship between noncognitivism and minimalism: for example, see the papers by Smith, Miller and Divers, and Horwich in the symposium on "Minimalism and Expressivism", in *Analysis* (January 1994).

25. So, for example, the realist and antirealist about comedy or morals can agree that discourse about comedy and discourse about morals fail to satisfy Mark 1: but they can still argue about whether these discourses are objective in any of the senses defined by marks 2–4.

26. Another way of opposing realism, which we have not considered here, is to adopt an error-theory. This admits that the sentences of the discourse are truth-apt and do have truth-conditions, but denies that such truth-conditions are ever actually satisfied. That is, it argues that the (positive, atomic) sentences of the discourse are *systematically and uniformly false*. For an example of an error-theory about moral discourse, see J. L. Mackie *Ethics: inventing right and wrong*; for an example of an error-theory about mathematical discourse, see H. Field, *Science without numbers*. For argument that error-theories do not provide a good way of

formulating opposition to realism, see Wright, *Truth and objectivity*, Chapter 1.

27. See especially Wright's *Truth and objectivity*, Chapter 6.

Bibliography

Ayer, A. J. *Language, truth, and logic* (New York: Dover Press, 1946).

Ayer, A. J. (ed.). *Logical positivism* (Glencoe, Illinois: Free Press, 1959).

Ayer, A. J. *Part of my life* (London: Collins, 1972).

Ayer. A. J. *More of my life* (London: Collins, 1983).

Beaney, M. *Frege: making sense* (London: Duckworth, 1996).

Benacerraf, P. & H. Putnam (eds). *The philosophy of mathematics* (Cambridge: Cambridge University Press, 1983).

Blackburn, S. *Spreading the word* (Oxford: Oxford University Press, 1984).

Blackburn, S. The individual strikes back. *Synthese* **58**, pp. 281–301, 1984.

Blackburn, S. Wittgenstein's irrealism. In *Wittgenstein: Eine Neubewehrung*, L. Brandl & R. Haller (eds) (Vienna: Hölder-Pickler Tempsky, 1990), pp.13–26.

Blackburn, S. Circles, finks, smells, and biconditionals. *Philosophical Perspectives* **7**, 1993.

Blackburn, S. Metaphysics. In *The Blackwell companion to philosophy*, E. James & N. Bunnin (eds) (Oxford: Basil Blackwell, 1995).

Boghossian, P. The rule-following considerations. *Mind* **98**, pp. 507–49, 1989.

Boghossian, P. Review of McGuin *Wittenstein Meaning. Philosophical Review*, 1989.

Boghossian, P. The status of content. *Philosophical Review* **99**, pp. 157–84, 1990.

Boghossian, P. The status of content revisited. *Pacific Philosophical Quarterly*, 1990.

Boghossian, P. Naturalizing content. In *Meaning in mind: essays for Jerry Fodor*, G. Rey & B. Loewer (eds) (Cambridge, Mass.: MIT Press, 1990).

Boghossian, P. Analyticity. See Hale & Wright, 1997.

Carnap, R. The elimination of metaphysics through the logical analysis of language. See Ayer, 1959, pp. 60–81.

Carnap, R. The old and the new logic. See Ayer, 1959, pp. 133–45.

Carnap, R. Empiricism, semantics, and ontology. See Benacerraf & Putnam, 1983.

Carruthers, P. *Introducing persons* (London: Croom Helm, 1986).

Chomsky, N. Quine's empirical assumptions. In *Words and objections*, D. Davidson & J. Hintikka (eds) (Dordrecht: Reidel, 1969).

Church, A. Review of Ayer (1946). *Journal of Symbolic Logic*, 1949.

Crane, T. *The mechanical mind* (London: Penguin, 1995).

Davidson, D. *Inquiries into truth and interpretation* (Oxford: Oxford University Press, 1984).

Davidson, D. *Essays on actions and events* (Oxford: Oxford University Press, 1980).

Davies, M. *Meaning, quantification, and necessity* (London: Routledge & Kegan Paul, 1981).

Davies, M. Philosophy of language. In *The Blackwell companion to philosophy*, E. James & N. Bunnin (eds) (Oxford: Basil Blackwell, 1996), pp. 90–139.

Devitt, M. Transcendentalism about content. *Pacific Philosophical Quarterly*, pp. 247–63, 1990.

Divers, J. *Possible worlds* (London: Routledge, in press).

Donnellan, K. Reference and definite descriptions. *Philosophical Review* **75**, pp. 281–304.

Dummett, M. *Frege: philosophy of language* (London: Duckworth, 1973).

Dummett, M. Wittgenstein's philosophy of mathematics. In *Truth and other enigmas* (London: Duckworth, 1978).

Dummett, M. *The interpretation of Frege's philosophy* (London: Duckworth, 1981).

Dummett, M. *The logical basis of metaphysics* (Cambridge, Mass.: Harvard University Press, 1991).

Dummett, M. *The seas of language* (Oxford: Oxford University Press, 1993).

Edwards, J. Best opinion and intentional states. *Philosophical Quarterly* **42**, pp. 21–33, 1992.

Edwards, J. Secondary qualities and the *a priori*. *Mind* **101**, pp. 263–72, 1992.

Evans, G. Semantic theory and tacit knowledge. In *Wittgenstein: to follow a rule*, S. Leich & S. Holtzmann (eds) (London: Routledge & Kegan Paul, 1981), pp. 118–37.

Evans, G. *The varieties of reference* (Oxford: Oxford University Press, 1982).

Evans, G. Identity and predication. *Journal of Philosophy* **72**, pp. 343–63.

Evnine, S. *Donald Davidson* (Palo Alto, California: Stanford University Press, 1991).

Field, H. *Science without numbers* (Oxford: Basil Blackwell, 1980).

Field, H. Tarski's theory of truth. In *Reference, truth, and reality*, M. Platts (ed.) (London: Routledge & Kegan Paul, 1980).

Fodor, J. *The language of thought* (Hassocks: Harvester Press, 1976).

Fodor, J. *Psychosemantics* (Cambridge, Mass.: MIT Press, 1987).

Fodor, J. *A theory of content and other essays* (Cambridge, Mass.: MIT Press, 1990).

Forbes, G. Scepticism and semantic knowledge. *Proceedings of the Aristotelian Society* **84**, pp. 223–37, 1984.

Foster, J. *Ayer* (London: Routledge & Kegan Paul, 1985).

Frege, G. *Grundgesetze* ('Frege Against the Formalists', *Philosophical Review* **59**).

Frege, G. *The foundations of arithmetic* (Evanston: Northwestern Illinois Press, 1953).

Frege, G. Function and concept. See Geach & Black 1960, pp. 21–41.

Frege, G. On concept and object. See Geach & Black 1960, pp. 42–55.

Frege, G. On sense and meaning. See Geach & Black 1960, pp. 56–78.

Frege, G. The thought: a logical enquiry. In *Philosophical logic*, P. Strawson (ed.) (Oxford: Oxford University Press, 1967).

Fricker, E. Semantic structure and speaker's understanding. *Proceedings of the Aristotelian Society* **83**, pp. 49–56, 1982.

Geach, P. & M. Black (eds). *Translations from the philosophical writings of Gottlob Frege* (Oxford: Oxford University Press, 1960).

Gibbard, A. *Wise choices, apt feelings* (Cambridge, Mass.: Harvard University Press, 1990).

Ginet, C. The dispositionalist solution to Wittgenstein's problem about understanding a rule. *Midwest Studies in Philosophy* **17**, pp. 53–73, 1992.

Goldfarb, W. Kripke on Wittgenstein on rules. *Journal of Philosophy* **82**, pp. 471–488, 1985.

Gower, B. (ed.). *Logical positivism in perspective* (London: Croom Helm, 1987).

Grice, P. Meaning. In *Studies in the ways of words* (Cambridge, Mass.: Harvard University Press, 1989).

Grice, P. & P. Strawson. In defense of a dogma. *Philosophical Review* **65**, pp. 141–58, 1956.

Haack, S. *Philosophy of logics* (Cambridge: Cambridge University Press, 1978).

Hahn, H. Logic, mathematics, and knowledge of nature. See Ayer, 1959, pp. 147–61.

Hahn, L. (ed.) *The Philosophy of A. J. Ayer* (Chicago: Open Court, 1992).

Hale, B. Can there be a logic of attitudes? In *Reality, representation, and projection*, J. Haldane & C. Wright (eds) (Oxford: Oxford University Press, 1993), pp. 337–63.

Hale, B. & C. Wright (eds). *The Blackwell companion to the philosophy of language* (Oxford: Basil Blackwell, 1997).

Hanfling, O. *Wittgenstein's later philosophy* (London: Macmillan, 1989).

Harman, G. Quine on meaning and existence (I). *Review of Metaphysics* **21**, pp. 124–51, 1967.

Heal, J. *Fact and meaning: Quine and Wittgenstein on the philosophy of language* (Oxford: Basil Blackwell, 1990).

Hintikka, M. & B. Vermazen (eds). *Essays on Davidson: actions and events* (Oxford: Clarendon Press, 1985).

Hodges, W. *Logic* (London: Penguin, 1991).

Holton, R. Intention-detecting. *Philosophical Quarterly* **43**, pp. 298–318, 1993.

Hookway, C. *Quine* (Oxford: Polity, 1987).

Horwich, P. The essence of expressivism. *Analysis* **54**, pp. 19–20, 1994.

Jeffrey, R. *Formal logic: its scope and limits* (New York: McGraw-Hill, 1991).

Johnston, M. Objectivity disfigured. In *Reality, representation, and projection*, J. Haldane & C. Wright (eds) (Oxford: Oxford University Press, 1993), pp. 85–130.

Kenny, A. *Frege* (London: Penguin, 1995).

Kirk, R. *Translation determined* (Oxford: Oxford University Press, 1994).

Kripke, S. *Naming and necessity* (Oxford: Oxford University Press, 1980).

Kripke, S. *Wittgenstein on rules and private language* (Oxford: Oxford University Press, 1982).

Lemmon, E. J. *Beginning logic* (London: Nelsons University Paperbacks, 1964).

Lepore, E. (ed.). *Truth and interpretation: perspectives on the philosophy of Donald Davidson* (Oxford: Basil Blackwell, 1986).

Lepore, E. & B. McGlaughlin (eds). *Actions and events: perspectives on the philosophy of Donald Davidson* (Oxford: Basil Blackwell, 1985).

Lewis, D. *Convention* (Cambridge, Mass.: Harvard University Press, 1969).

Lewis, D. How to define theoretical terms. *Journal of Philosophy* **67**, pp. 427–46, 1970.

Lewis, D. Psychophysical and theoretical identifications. *Australasian Journal of Philosophy* **50**, pp. 249–58, 1972.

Lewis, D. Statements partly about observation. *Philosophical Papers* **17**, pp. 1–31, 1988.

Lewis, D. Radical interpretation. *Synthese* **27,** pp. 331–44, date.

Locke, J. *An essay concerning human understanding* (Oxford: Oxford University Press, 1975).

Lowe, E. J. *Locke on human understanding* (London: Routledge, 1995).

Lyons, J. *Chomsky* (London: Penguin, 1970).

McCulloch, G. *The game of the name* (Oxford: Oxford University Press, 1989).

McCulloch, G. *The mind and its world* (London: Routledge, 1995).

McDowell, J. Truth-conditions, bivalence, and verificationism. In *Truth and meaning*, G. Evans & J. McDowell (eds) (Oxford: Oxford University Press, 1976), pp. 42–66.

McDowell, J. On the sense and reference of a proper name. *Mind* **86**, 1977.

McDowell, J. "On the reality of the past". In *Action and interpretation*, C. Hookway & P. Pettit (eds) 1979, pp. 127–44.

McDowell, J. Physicalism and primitive denotation. In *Reference, truth, and reality*, M. Platts (ed.) (London: Routledge & Kegan Paul, 1980).

McDowell, J. Anti-realism and the epistemology of understanding. In *Meaning and understanding*, J. Parrett & H. Bouveresse (eds) (Berlin: de Gruyter, 1981).

McDowell, J. Wittgenstein on following a rule. *Synthese* **58**, pp. 325–63, 1984.

McDowell, J. Meaning and intention in Wittgenstein's later philosophy. *Midwest Studies in Philosophy* **17**, pp. 40–52, 1992.

McDowell, J. Intentionality and interiority in Wittgenstein. In *Meaning scepticism*, K. Puhl (ed.) (Dordrecht: Reidel, 1992), pp. 148–69.

McDowell, J. *Mind and world* (Cambridge, Mass.: Harvard University Press, 1994).

McDowell, J. Reply to Crispin Wright. In *Self-knowledge and externalism*, C. McDonald, B. Smith, C. Wright (eds) (forthcoming).

McGinn, C. Semantics for non-indicative sentences. *Philosophical Studies*, **32**, pp. 301–11, 1977.

McGinn, C. *Wittgenstein on meaning* (Oxford: Basil Blackwell, 1984).

Mackie, J. L. *Ethics: inventing right and wrong* (Penguin: London, 1978).

Malcolm, N. *Nothing is hidden* (Oxford: Basil Blackwell, 1986).

Miller, A. An objection to Wright's treatment of intention. *Analysis* **49**, pp. 169–73, 1989.

Miller, A. Review article on Lowe. *The Locke Newsletter* **26**, pp. 141–55, 1995.

Miller, A. Tacit knowledge. See Hale & Wright, 1997, pp. 146–74.

Miller, A. Rule-following, response-dependence, and McDowell's debate with anti-realism. *European Review of Philosophy* (forthcoming).

Miller, A. & J. Divers. Best opinion, intention-detecting, and analytic functionalism. *Philosophical Quarterly* **44**, pp. 239–45, 1994.

Miller, A. & J. Divers. Why the expressivist about value should not love minimalism about truth. *Analysis* **54**, pp. 12–19, 1994.

Milne, P. Tarski on truth and its definition. In Logica '96, T. Childers, P. Kolar & V. Svobada (eds) (Filosofia, Prague, 1997) pp. 189–210.

Mumford, S. *Dispositions* (Oxford: Oxford University Press, in press).

Newton-Smith, W. H. *Logic* (London: Routledge & Kegan Paul, 1985).

Noonan, H. *Frege* (Oxford: Polity, in press).

Pettit, P. The Reality of Rule-Following, *Mind*.

Pettit, P. *The Common Mind: An Essay on Politics, Psychology, and Society* (Oxford: Oxford University Press, 1993).

Phillips-Griffiths, A. (ed.) *A. J. Ayer: memorial essays* (Cambridge: Cambridge University Press, 1990).

Platts, M. *Ways of meaning* (London: Routledge & Kegan Paul, 1979).

Putnam, H. The analytic and the synthetic. In *Mind, language, and reality* (Cambridge: Cambridge University Press, 1975).

Putnam, H. *Realism, truth, and history* (Cambridge: Cambridge University Press, 1981).

Quine, W. V. O. Two dogmas of empiricism. In *From a logical point of view* (Cambridge: Harvard University Press, 1953) pp. 20–46.

Quine, W. V. O. *Word and object* (Cambridge, Mass.: MIT Press, 1960).

Quine, W. V. O. On the reasons for the indeterminacy of translation. *Journal of Philosophy* **67**, pp. 178–83, 1970.

Quine, W. V. O. *Philosophy of logic* (Englewood Cliffs, New Jersey: Prentice-Hall, 1970).

Quine, W. V. O. Carnap on logical truth. See Benacerraf & Putnam, 1983, pp. 355–76.

Quine, W. V. O. Truth by convention. See Benacerraf & Putnam, 1983, pp. 329–54.

Quine, W. V. O. *The pursuit of truth* (Cambridge, Mass.: Harvard University Press, 1990).

Ramberg, B. *Donald Davidson's philosophy of language* (Oxford: Basil Blackwell, 1989).

Read, S. *Thinking about logic* (Oxford: Oxford University Press, 1994).

Russell, B. *Introduction to mathematical philosophy* (London: Allen & Unwin, 1919).

Russell, B. *Logic and knowledge.* (London: Routledge & Kegan Paul, 1956).

Russell, B. On denoting. See Russell, 1956, pp. 41–56.

Russell, B. The philosophy of logical atomism. See Russell, 1956, pp. 177–281.

Russell, B. Logical positivism. See Russell, 1956, pp. 367–82.

Russell, B. *The problems of philosophy* (Oxford: Oxford University Press, 1978).

Sainsbury, M. Philosophical logic. In *Philosophy: a guide through the subject*, A. Grayling (ed.) (Oxford: Oxford Unviersity Press, 1995), pp. 61–122.

Sainsbury, M. Frege and Russell. In *The Blackwell companion to philosophy*, E. James & N. Bunnin (eds) (Oxford: Basil Blackwell, 1996), pp. 662–77.

Schiffer, S. *Meaning* (Oxford: Clarendon Press, 1972).

Schiffer, S. *Remnants of meaning* (Cambridge, Mass.: MIT Press, 1987).

Schlick, M. Positivism and realism. See Ayer, 1959, pp. 82–107.

Schlick, M. The turning point in philosophy. See Ayer, 1959, pp. 53–9.

Searle, J. Proper names. *Mind* **67**, pp. 166–73, 1958.

Searle, J. What is a speech-act? In *Philosophy in America*, M. Black (ed.) (London: Allen & Unwin, 1965).

Searle, J. *Speech-acts* (Cambridge: Cambridge University Press, 1969).

Searle, J. *Intentionality* (Cambridge: Cambridge University Press, 1983).

Smith, M. *The moral problem* (Oxford: Basil Blackwell, 1994).

Smith, M. Why the expressivist about value should love minimalism about truth. *Analysis* **54**, pp. 1–11, 1994.

Strawson, P. F. On referring. *Mind* **59**, pp. 320–44, 1950.

Strawson, P. F. Meaning and truth. In *Logico-linguistic papers* (London 1971).

Strawson, P. F. (ed.). *Philosophical logic* (Oxford: Oxford University Press, 1985).

Sullivan, P. Problems for a construction of meaning and intention. *Mind* **103**, pp. 147–68, 1994.

Tarski, A. The semantic conception of truth. *Philosophy and Phenomelogical Research* **4**, pp. 341–76, 1949.

Tarski, A. Truth and proof. *Scientific American*, 1967.

Tarski, A. The concept of truth in formalized languages. In *Logic, semantics, metamathematics* (Indianapolis, Indiana: Hackett Publishers, 1983).

Wittgenstein, L. *Remarks on the foundations of mathematics* (Oxford: Basil Blackwell, 1956).

Wittgenstein, L. *Philosophical investigations* (Oxford: Basil Blackwell, 1974).

Wright, C. *Frege's conception of numbers as objects* (Aberdeen: Aberdeen University Press, 1983).

Wright, C. Kripke's account of the argument against private language. *Journal of Philosophy* **81**, pp. 759–77, 1984.

Wright, C. Does PI 258–60 suggest a cogent argument against private language? In *Subject, thought, and context,* P. Pettit & J. McDowell (eds) (Oxford: Oxford University Press, 1986), pp. 209–66.

Wright, C. Inventing logical necessity. In *Language, mind, and logic,* J. Butterfield (ed.) (Cambridge: Cambridge University Press, 1986).

Wright, C. *Realism, meaning, and truth* (Oxford: Basil Blackwell, 1986).

Wright, C. Scientific realism, observation, and the verification principle. In *Fact, science, and morality,* C. Wright & G. McDonald (eds) (Oxford: Basil Blackwell, 1986), pp. 247–74.

Wright, C. Theory of meaning and speakers' knowledge. See Wright, *Realism, meaning, and truth.*

Wright, C. Moral values, projection, and secondary qualities. *Proceedings of the Aristotelian Society* **62**, suppl. vol., pp. 1–26, 1988.

Wright, C. On making up one's mind: Wittgenstein on intention. In *Logic, science, and epistemology,* P. Wiengartner & G. Schutz (eds) (Vienna: Holder–Pichler–Temsky, 1988), pp. 391–404.

Wright, C. Critical notice of McGinn (1984). *Mind* **98**, pp. 289–305, 1989.

Wright, C. The verification principle: another puncture, another patch. *Mind* **98**, pp. 611–22, 1989.

Wright, C. Wittgenstein's rule-following considerations and the central project of theoretical linguistics. In *Reflections on Chomsky,* A. George (ed.) (Oxford: Basil Blackwell, 1989), pp. 233–64.

Wright, C. *Truth and objectivity* (Cambridge, Mass.: Harvard University Press, 1992).

Wright, C. Critical notice of McDowell (1994). *European Journal of Philosophy* **4**, pp. 235–54, 1996.

Wright, C. Indeterminacy of translation. See Hale & Wright, 1997.

Wright, C. Self-knowledge: the Wittgensteinian legacy. In *Self-knowledge and externalism*, C. McDonald, B. Smith, C. Wright (eds) (forthcoming).

Yolton, J. *Perceptual acquaintance from Descartes to Reid* (Oxford: Basil Blackwell, 1984).

Zalabardo, J. Rules, communities, judgements. *Critica* **63**, pp. 33–58, 1989.

Zalabardo, J. A problem for information theoretic semantics. *Synthese* **105**, pp. 1–29, 1995.

Ziff, P. On H. P. Grice's account of meaning. *Analysis* **28**, pp. 1–8, 1967.

Index